Read My Desire

OCTOBER Books

Annette Michelson, Rosalind Krauss, Yve-Alain Bois, Benjamin Buchloh, Hal Foster, Denis Hollier, and John Rajchman, editors

Broodthaers, edited by Benjamin H. D. Buchloh

AIDS: Cultural Analysis/Cultural Activism, edited by Douglas Crimp

Aberrations, by Jurgis Baltrušaitis

Against Architecture: The Writings of Georges Bataille, by Denis Hollier

Painting as Model, by Yve-Alain Bois

The Destruction of Tilted Arc: *Documents*, edited by Clara Weyergraf-Serra and Martha Buskirk

The Woman in Question, edited by Parveen Adams and Elizabeth Cowie

Techniques of the Observer: On Vision and Modernity in the Ninteenth Century, by Jonathan Crary

The Subjectivity Effect in Western Literary Tradition: Essays toward the Release of Shakespeare's Will, by Joel Fineman

Looking Awry: An Introduction to Jacques Lacan through Popular Culture, by Slavoj Žižek

Cinema, Censorship, and the State: The Writings of Nagisa Oshima, by Nagisa Oshima

The Optical Unconscious, by Rosalind E. Krauss

Gesture and Speech, by André Leroi-Gourhan

Compulsive Beauty, by Hal Foster

Continuous Project Altered Daily: The Writings of Robert Morris, by Robert Morris

Read My Desire: Lacan against the Historicists, by Joan Copjec

Read My Desire

Lacan against the Historicists

Joan Copjec

An OCTOBER Book

The MIT Press
Cambridge, Massachusetts
London, England

This book was set in Bembo by DEKR Corporation and was printed and bound in the
United States of America.

Library of Congress Cataloging-in-Publication Data

Copjec, Joan.
    Read my desire : Lacan against the historicists / Joan Copjec.
        p.   cm.
    "Many of the chapters in this book appeared in earlier versions as
    essays in various journals and books"—T.p. verso.
    "An October book."
    Includes bibliographical references and index.
    ISBN 0-262-03219-8
    1. Psychoanalysis and culture. 2. Desire. 3. Historicism. 4. Lacan, Jacques, 1901–
5. Foucault, Michel. I. Title.
BF175.4.C84C66   1994
150.19′5—dc20   94-383
                                                                   CIP

Many of the chapters in this book appeared in earlier versions as essays in various journals
and books. Chapters 2, 4, and 5 were published in *October* 49 (Summer 1989); *October* 50
(Fall 1989); and *October* 56, a special issue on "Rendering the Real," edited by Parveen
Adams (Spring 1991), respectively. Chapter 3 was published in *Between Feminism and Psy-choanalysis,* edited by Teresa Brennan (London and New York: Routledge, 1989). Chapter
6 appeared in a special issue of *New Formations* (Summer 1991), "On Democracy," edited
by Erica Carter and Renata Salecl. Chapter 7 was an essay in *Shades of Noir: A Reader*
(London and New York: Verso, 1993), which I edited.

To my mother, Ann,
and the memory of my father, John Copjec

Contents

Acknowledgments

One reason writing is so difficult is that one feels, while doing it, completely alone. Yet if this were true, writing and thinking would be impossible. The big Other aside (I don't, after all, know his or her name), it is to a number of others that I have addressed myself in writing this book and who have made it, literally, possible.

My debts were incurred in waves, two of them. The first was the period, beginning in the mid- to late-1970s, when *Screen* and *m/f* were publishing their ground-breaking texts, when *Screen* readers' meetings, the Filmmaker's Co-op in London, the Milwaukee conferences were sites of intense debates that marked me for good. I often regret that I have not seen their like since, that the rigor and excitement, the aura of urgency, commitment, and community that surrounded them, seem largely to be absent from more contemporary exchanges. I owe a great deal to the people who staged and participated in these earlier debates, and especially to a few friends whom I associate still, for various reasons, with the values they represented and the important theoretical projects they began: Parveen Adams, Homi Bhabha, Elizabeth Cowie, Mary Ann Doane, and Sandy Flitterman-Lewis.

The second wave coincided with the period when I began to define my own work not according to the object of my study, nor even as broadly theoretical, but, specifically, as Lacanian. At this moment I began to incur debts to Slavoj Žižek, who has helped me to see that the distance between abstract theory and concrete analysis can be creatively bridged, and without loss to theory; to Juliet MacCannell and Renata Salecl, who have become allies in the project of bringing Lacan and feminists to the negotiating table; to Jacques-Alain Miller, who in his seminars and in conversation opened up for me a political reading of Lacan that many other interpreters had almost entirely obscured.

To each of these lists I must add a single name, that of Joel Fineman, whose death diminished both theoretical worlds by a significant sum.

My efforts at writing were also sustained by two different professional contexts. The first was, of course, the journal *October,* where my coeditors, Douglas Crimp, Rosalind Krauss, and Annette Michelson, supplied me with ample space and encouragement to develop the arguments of the earlier chapters of this book. The second is the English and Comparative Literature departments at the University of Buffalo and my many colleagues there. I hesitate in this case to single names out for special mention for fear the list would grow too long. I do have to thank separately, however, the students in my seminars, who have, through their eagerness, intelligence, and interest, inspired me. I would also like to thank Bill Fischer for arranging for me to have leave time to put the final touches on the book. My colleagues at the Center for the Study of Psychoanalysis and Culture also deserve separate mention for giving psychoanalysis such a solid home, not only during the good times, when psychoanalysis was the "hot" discourse, but during the bad times as well. Thanks, too, to Joan Cipperman for her years of sustaining service to the Center.

I want to thank Roger Conover at the MIT Press for all his help, especially at one crucial moment when his editorial intervention proved decisive. Jenya Weinreb was a speedy, thorough, and very pleasant copyeditor of the final text; I thank her for her care.

Finally, I thank my husband, Michael Sorkin, for so much, including the fact that he would prefer that I not delay my book any longer while I try to figure out how to acknowledge him properly. Wise; because he knows that this, at least, is *not* possible.

Read My Desire

1   Introduction: Structures Don't March in the Streets

In May 1968, an angry French student scrawled across the blackboard of one of the classrooms at the Sorbonne a sentence that immediately became a slogan for student discontent: "Structures don't march in the streets." A modern equivalent of the Wordsworthian "Up, up, my friends and quit your books," the French phrase was accompanied by none of the ambivalence that surrounded its predecessor and targeted a specific, indigenous form of intellectualism—structuralism—which seemed to these students to be wholly dead and thus completely incapable of rising to the theoretical challenge posed by the urgent and chaotic events in whose midst they now found themselves. Structuralism was denounced for its universalizing program and for its adherence to empty, moribund forms, conceived at all times to be always already in place, sedimented. The dynamics of this student revolt were such that it unreflectively led to the celebration of precisely that which structuralism seemed designed to exclude: not simply the particular, but the particular in its most spontaneous and concrete form.

In the post-1968 years, celebration solidified into a number of concepts, one of which, that of the "pleb," has had a substantial influence on a certain strain of political discourse, up to and including the present, where, under the banner of "multiculturalism" or "political correctness," it sometimes returns. Proposed first by André Glucksmann, this concept named some pure instance of particularity that had the potential to undermine all the universalizing structures of power. The "pleb," as she or he was embodied in workers, students, immigrants, all those made poor, sorry, worthless, or marginal by the society in place, was conceived as endowed with "the immediacy of a knowledge (*connaissance*) which springs from the realities of suffering and resistance."[1] Following this

definition, any discourse that "originated" with the pleb was thought to
have a political value and correctness that was automatically foreclosed
to discourses "originating" with those in positions of power.

Glucksmann developed his concept of the pleb with liberal bor-
rowings from Michel Foucault, and Foucault, in turn, incorporated
Glucksmann's concept into his own thinking. But not without reserva-
tions. Interviewed by the Révoltes Logiques collective, Foucault uttered
this warning regarding the pleb, which he described as "the constant and
constantly silent target for the apparatuses of power":

> Without doubt the "pleb" must not be conceived of as the per-
> manent foundation of history . . . the never totally extinct hearth
> of every revolt. The "pleb" undoubtedly has no sociological
> reality. But there is indeed always something which in some way
> escapes the relations of power; something in the social body, in
> the classes, in the groups, in the individuals themselves which is
> not at all the more or less docile or reactive raw material, but
> which is the centrifugal movement, the inverse energy, that
> which escapes. "The" pleb, undoubtedly, does not exist; but there
> is "plebness." . . . This measure of plebness is not so much that
> which is outside relations of power as it is their limit. . . . Taking
> this point of view of the pleb . . . I do not think that [it] may be
> confused in any way with some neo-populism which substantifies
> the pleb, or some neo-liberalism which harps on the themes of
> its basic rights.[2]

One may want to quarrel with the final dismissive remark regarding the theme of rights, from which it seems clear that Foucault
accepts without argument a neopopulist definition of rights, according to
which their declaration is understood simply as the issuing of demands
by egoistic and autonomous individuals who know, and who have reason
to know better than anyone else, just what it is they want. We will simply

note for the moment that there is another way to consider the question of rights[3] and move on to a consideration of the rest of the passage. What strikes us first here is the judiciousness and intelligence with which the notion of the pleb is desubstantialized. No longer an individual or class of individuals with a special knowledge or history to which the larger social whole has little or no access, the pleb is now conceived as something totally devoid of content and thus as structurally unknowable, unthinkable, finally, of course, as nonhistoricizable. The resistance offered by the pleb does not come from some external point but is instead the very limit of the system of power, and as such not absorbable by it.

What strikes us next about Foucault's account of resistance is the dialect in which it is spoken: "'The' pleb does not exist; but there is 'plebness.'" Do your ears not detect the Lacanian inflection? Can you not hear the murmur of the famous Lacanian formulations "'The' woman does not exist [*La femme n'existe pas*]" and "There is some of One [*Il y a d'l'Un*]" behind Foucault's phrases? What's common to both the Lacanian and Foucauldian statements is a distinction between two sorts of existence, one implied by the verb *exister* and the other by the phrase *il y a*. The existence implied by the first is subject to a predicative judgment as well as to a judgment of existence; that is, it is an existence whose character or quality can be described. The existence implied by the second is subject *only* to a judgment of existence; we can say only that it does or does not exist, without being able to say what it is, to describe it in any way. If, as Foucault says, there is "plebness," we are nevertheless unable to say what it is—the truth of "plebness" will therefore always be located outside knowledge, anyone's knowledge, including that which is possessed by what we can no longer call "the" pleb him- or herself.

The thesis of this book is that, despite the insights advanced in the passage previously cited, Foucault can be charged with putting forth other arguments that run counter to, and thus exclude the possibility of, the very interpretation of "plebness" he gives here. Each of the following chapters focuses on some concept or phenomenon within the Foucauldian problematic—that is, a concept or phenomenon to which Foucault or his pupils have devoted some theoretical attention—in order to delineate more precisely what these "other arguments" are and to show how they subvert the argument articulated in the Révoltes Logiques interview. The name *Foucault,* then, does not designate in these chapters all the writings or arguments of that author, but primarily those that motivate the unfortunate turning away from the notion that subtends his argument regarding "plebness," that is, the notion of an existence without predicate, or, to put it differently, of a surplus existence that cannot be caught up in the positivity of the social. The arguments I will critique are not dispersed throughout Foucault's works but are limited to *Discipline and Punish, The History of Sexuality,* and essays and interviews of the mid to late 1970s, when Foucault reversed his position with respect to linguistic and psychoanalytic theory. Whereas he began, like many of his intellectual contemporaries, by interpreting social facts in light of semiotic structures defined by structuralism and psychical structures defined by psychoanalysis, he not only abandoned but also fiercely opposed the terms of these two disciplines in the period that concerns us. Foucault gives a summary statement of this reversal in an interview conducted during this period: "I believe that it is not to the great model of signs and language that reference should be made, but to war and battle. The history which bears and determines us is war-like, not language-like. Relations of power, not relations of sense."[4] By this he declares, in effect, a kind of solidarity with the student dissidents who also turned their backs on structuralism. Not the ivory-tower structures of linguistics, the arid formalism of a self-reflexive semiotics, but the structures of war and power, streetwise structures: structures that march in the streets; this is what Foucault appears to be advocating.

The intent is not to trivialize Foucault's rejection of linguistic or psychoanalytic models of analysis by reducing it to a mere rhetorical strategy. Rather, the point is first of all to underline the actual parallels in the discontent expressed by the students and by Foucault, known perhaps above all for his constructive dismissal of the universal intellectual in favor of the "specific" intellectual, who would define his labor as the analysis of particular institutions of power rather than of some overarching structure of domination. There is nothing wrong in this—the turn toward specificity is unquestionably sound. And if any suspicion lingers that through his emphasis on the particular he is in any way complicit in the emergence of the new populism he rightly condemns, this suspicion is easily dispersed by recalling that Foucault is concerned not with the "little people" that macrohistories overlooked, but with the microworkings of small-scale systems of power relations that produce these people. While he may always be focused on details, the minimal unit of his investigations is never simply an isolatable point, whether this be a person or a position, but always a relation.

This brings us to our second point. While the Foucauldian focus on *relations* of power and knowledge is widely hailed as a necessary corrective to more naive political theories that saw these as discrete entities, we will contend that his reduction of society to these relations is problematic. In opposition to those sociological theories that sought to explain a given social phenomenon by referring to the system of power that intervened in it, directing and distorting the phenomenon from the outside, Foucault analyzed the internal regime of power that circulated through the phenomenon itself. The various scientific texts, for example, that began in the eighteenth century to codify the myriad forms of sexual perversity and to council parents, educators, administrators, and physicians about how to protect their charges against them are read not as the edicts of a repressive power bent on putting an end to these private behaviors but as themselves part of a network of power that multiplied the points of contact or forms of relation between individuals by constructing sex as the secret core of the self. In other words, power was no longer conceived by Foucault as an external force that exerted itself *on* society, but as *immanent within* society, the "fine, differentiated, continuous" network of uneven relations that constituted the very matter of the social. Society now neatly coincided with a regime of power relations, and the former was thus conceived to structure itself by itself rather than to be structured by an external power.

Now, it is this notion of immanence, this conception of a cause that is immanent within the field of its effects, with which this book quarrels and repeatedly condemns as historicist. Since no attempt is made at a concise definition of historicism in the chapters that follow (the hope being that a more flexible definition will emerge from the various contexts provided in the discussions), it might be appropriate to hazard one here: we are calling historicist the reduction of society to its indwelling network of relations of power and knowledge.

To the extent that Foucault defined his project as the establishment of a *genealogy,* rather than a structure, of historical events, that is, to the extent that he undertook to account for the *constitution* of domains of objects and knowledges, or the *mode of the institution* of the social, and could not rest content with a mere analysis of the relations therein, he seems, in intent at least, to escape this charge of historicism. For, like the political philosopher Claude Lefort, Foucault does appear to argue that

> society cannot in itself be conceived as a system of relations, no matter how complex we imagine that system to be. On the contrary, it is its overall schema, the particular mode of its institution that makes it possible to conceptualize . . . the articulation of its dimensions, and the relations established within it between classes, groups and individuals, between practices, beliefs and representations. If we fail to grasp this primordial reference to the mode of the institution of the social, to generative principles or to an overall schema governing both the temporal and spatial configuration of society, we lapse into a positivist fiction. . . . If, for example, we grant to relations of production or the class struggle the status of reality, we forget that *social division* can only be defined . . . insofar as it represents an internal division, . . .

insofar as its terms are determined by relations, but also insofar as those relations are themselves determined by their common inscription within the same space and testify to an awareness of their inscription therein.[5]

The problem, then, is not with the way Foucault formulates his project but with the way he carries it out. For despite the fact that he realizes the necessity of conceiving the mode of a regime of power's institution, he cannot avail himself of the means of doing so and thus, by default, ends up limiting that regime to the relations that obtain within it; he becomes, despite himself, a bit of a historicist, as well as—as he himself notes—a bit of a nominalist.

What is it that prevents Foucault from accomplishing his declared task? His disallowance of any reference to a principle or a subject that "transcends" the regime of power he analyzes. He correctly and strongly believes that the principle of a regime's institution cannot be conceived as a *meta*principle, that is, as a logical observation that is simply added to all the other observations one may make about a particular regime in order to organize, embrace, or comprehend them. The principle of construction or staging cannot occupy a different, a superior, position with respect to the regime it stages. Not wishing to look for it in some exterior realm, Foucault eventually abandons, without actually acknowledging that he is doing so, his attempt to define the very principle he supposedly seeks.[6]

Yet some notion of transcendence is plainly needed if one is to avoid the reduction of social space to the relations that fill it. A rethinking of this notion is foreclosed, however, by Foucault's substitution of a battle-based model of analysis for the language-based one he inherited from structuralism and which he emphatically rejects for what he takes to be its inherent idealism. In fact the opposite is true; it is the rejection of the linguistic model, properly conceived, that leads to idealism. For the argument behind the adoption of this model—something cannot be claimed to exist unless it can first be stated, articulated in language—is no mere tautology; it is a materialist argument parallel to the rule of science which states that no object can be legitimately posited unless one can also specify the technical means of locating it. The existence of a thing materially depends on its being articulated in language, for only in this case can it be said to have an objective—that is to say, a verifiable— existence, one that can be debated by others.

A corollary of Foucault's denigration of the supposed idealism of language-based analyses is his complaint that they "flatten out" the phenomena they purport to study, that they place all phenomena on the same plane.[7] This is certainly true in one sense; a linguistically informed analysis is obliged to forgo the possibility of a metalanguage; the field of phenomena to be analyzed, therefore, cannot be stratified. No phenomenon appearing there my be taken to account for, to interpret, all the others; none stands above the others as the final interpretant, itself beyond interpretation. Yet wouldn't Foucault himself sanction such a destratification, such a demurral before the assertion of a metaprinciple? And isn't the linguistic argument against metalanguage an argument, finally, against the notion of an immanent cause, a notion that has, since Hume, been demonstrably unsupportable?

The upshot of all of this is that if Foucault is right (without meaning to be) about language's "flattening out" of phenomena in this first sense, he is wrong in a second sense. For one of the things he surely does mean is that the linguistic model completely *unfolds* the *whole* of the society it analyses, puts the whole thing on the same plane. But if we were to follow out the reasoning begun earlier, we would arrive at the opposite conclusion: an acknowledgment of metalanguage's impossibility compels us to realize that the whole of society will never reveal itself in an analytical moment; no diagram will ever be able to display it fully, once and for all. At the same time this acknowledgment does *not* compel us to imagine a society that never quite forms, where—as the deconstructionists would have it—events never quite take place, a society about which we can say nothing and do so in an endless succession of statements that forever fail to come around to the same relevant point. To say that there is no metalanguage is to say, rather, that society *never stops realizing* itself, that it *continues* to be formed over time.

For, what we do when we recognize the impossibility of meta-language is to split society between its appearance—the positive relations and facts we observe in it—and its being, that is to say, its generative principle, which cannot appear among these relations. What we do, in essence, is *install* society's generative principle, provide for it a place beyond the realm of positive appearances. Fitted out thus with a generative principle, society ceases to be conceived as a dead structure, mappable on some flat surface; society is finally by this means brought to life. And we are released from the constraints and the absurdity of a nominalist stance, which would necessitate our naming each moment of a society, each transformation of it, a different thing; it is now possible to posit the existence of a singular space, belonging to society, which various sets of relations come to fill.

Some of you will, of course, object that to refer to a split between appearance and being is to betray the basic rule of our supposedly materialist linguistic position: no existence may be posited that does not first inscribe itself in language. Yes, and the corollary is true as well: everything inscribed in language must be given a fair hearing; if its signature appears there in language, the possibility of its being must be entertained. Whenever the split between being and appearance is denied, you can bet that one particular inscription is being overlooked: that which marks the very failure of metalanguage. Language speaks voluminously in positive statements, but it also copiously speaks of its own lack of self-sufficiency, its inability to speak the whole unvarnished truth directly and without recourse to further, exegetical speech. Some elision or negation of its powers writes itself in language *as* the lack of metalanguage. This negation is no less an inscription for its not being formulated in a statement, and the being it poses presents no less a claim for our consideration.

Indeed, it is *this* writing that permits us to consider the mode of a society's institution as, strictly speaking, unspeakable, to argue that the generative principle of a society is never statable as such, the way the contents of that society are. It is only a certain quashing of its force or blockage in its functioning that allows us to suppose a regime of power to be governed by a principle that cannot be absorbed by that regime. We must not fail to notice that this says more than we have been claiming up until this point. Our position notes not only the negative fact that its principle cannot be made visible within a functioning regime but another, positive fact as well: the principle of a regime's institution always in some way *negates* the regime it institutes.

It is the absence of this type of negation from Foucault's theory that disables it, preventing it from thinking the *genealogy* of social spaces and the resistances to it. Strangely, Foucault seems to have turned inside out our point that in language is inscribed even its own negation. His belief that every form of negation or resistance may eventually feed or be absorbed by the system of power it contests depends on his taking this point to mean that every negation must be stated. Thus the prohibition "you shall not do *X*" must spell out what *X* is, must incite us to think about *X*, to scrutinize ourselves and our neighbors to determine whether or not we are guilty of *X*. The statement puts into play what it would abolish; even the disavowal becomes an avowal. What Foucault seems to overlook is that form of negation which, while written in language, is nonetheless without content. This type of negation cannot, by definition, be absorbed by the system it contests.

If all this has become a bit too abstract, I invite you to picture it another way. Let us return to May 1968 and the dissenting students, not writing their revolutionary slogans this time but watching with bemusement and an exasperation mounting to disbelief as one of their professors draws on the blackboard four cryptic diagrams that he calls "the four discourses."[8] The professor is, as you've guessed, Jacques Lacan, and many of the students gathered before him are unquestionably thinking that what they are witnessing is the very epitome of that academic structuralism against which they are now in revolt. But they are mistaken about this, and, unfortuntely, others after them will perpetuate their error. Lacan's diagrams bear no resemblance to the scientist maps drawn by the structuralists; his diagrams are offered to the audience as *anti*structuralist.

The startling claim made by Lacan is that the structures he is diagraming are *real*. This claim can only have met with the same incomprehension that it continues to elicit today. For those schooled in structuralism, which teaches us to think of *structure* as nearly synonymous with *symbolic,* the proposition presents itself as a solecism, an abuse of language. Lacan was not, naturally, ignorant of the structuralist position, which he shared at the beginning of his teaching. Later, however, his work aimed at critiquing this position, and his argument to the students and to us could at this point be formulated thus: you are right to rebel against structuralism, to complain that it diagrams only moribund relations. You are therefore right to proclaim that structures don't march in the streets—but not for the reasons you think. For the point is not, by changing your analytical model, to make structures take to the streets, to understand them as embedded or immanent in social reality. The point is rather to heed the lesson the original model had to teach: structures do not—and should not—take to the streets. They are not to be located among the relations that constitute our everyday reality; they belong, instead, to the order of the real.

This argument may be too abstract, even still. What, you may wonder, would an analysis that proceeds from this assumption look like? What difference does it make to our understanding of the actual functioning of a society? In order to answer these questions, we ask you to contemplate two examples of just such an analysis. Each is drawn from the work of Freud, and, significantly, each is associated with an inglorious history of ridicule and incomprehension. Our suggestion is that it is the proposition that underwrites them—"structures are real," or "every phenomenal field occludes its cause"—which causes them to be so radically unassimilable within, and such valuable antidotes against, everyday historicist thought.

The first example is taken from *Totem and Taboo,* where Freud provides an analysis of a society in which relations of equality and fraternity prevail among its citizens, no one is distinguished above the others, and power is shared rather than accumulated in one place. What strikes us as most remarkable about Freud's analysis is that it does not limit itself to a description of these relations, does not attempt to make this "regime of brothers"[9] coincide simply with the relations that exist among them. Instead Freud insists on going beyond these relations to posit the existence of some preposterous being, a primal father who once possessed all the power the brothers now equally share and whose murder is supposed to have issued in the present regime. No wonder so many have taken this to be one of Freud's most crackpot ideas, the wild fantasy of an incompetent ethnologist! But to call it crackpot is to miss the point that if this father of the primal horde is indeed preposterous, then he is objectively so. That is to say, he is unbelievable within the regime in which his existence *must* be unthinkable if relations of equality are to take hold.

That he is unthinkable within this regime of brothers does not gainsay the fact that the *institution* of the regime is inexplicable without him. For if we did not posit his existence, we would be incapable, without resorting to psychologism, of explaining how the brothers came together in this fashion. What Freud accounts for in *Totem and Taboo* is the structure, the real structure, of a society of equals, which is thus shown to be irreducible to the labile relations of equality that never obtain absolutely. The petty jealousies and feelings of powerlessness that threaten these relations, that block their permanent realization, betray their guilty origin, the cause that they must efface.

The second example is taken from *Beyond the Pleasure Principle,* in which Freud develops one of his other massively misunderstood notions: the death drive. The common interpretation of this text is that he develops this notion in order to counter the belief that humans are all too humanly ruled by a principle of pleasure. According to this reading, the death drive would be a second principle, co-present and at war with the pleasure principle; that is, the two principles would be seen to occupy the same space, the territory of their struggle with each other. Yet this is not what Freud says. Rather than contesting the importance of the pleasure principle, he admits its centrality in psychical life; he then seeks, by means of the death drive, to account for this centrality, to state the principle by which the principle of pleasure is installed.[10]

In other words, Freud's positing of the death drive parallels his positing of the father of the primal horde in that both are meant to answer to the necessity of accounting aetiologically for an empirical field, where the pleasure principle reigns, in one case, and where a fraternal order obtains, in the other. In each case the transcendental principle, or the principle of the principle of rule, is in conflict with the principle of rule itself, though this conflict cannot be conceived to take place on some common ground, since the first-order principle and the second-order principle are never co-present. Nor can either of these two "warring" principles ever ultimately win out over the other, since the very existence of the empirical field always presupposes the existence of its cause, and since no cause can ever exist abstractly, in the absence of that which it effects.

Earlier we said that the argument which maintains that structures are real is psychoanalysis's greatest challenge to the historicism that pervades much of the thinking of our time. But we must also acknowledge that these two powerful modern discourses—psychoanalysis and historicism, represented here by Lacan and Foucault, respectively—have in common the conviction that it is dangerous to assume that the surface is the level of the superficial.[11] Whenever we delve below this level, we are sure to come up empty. Yet the lessons each discourse draws from this conviction are strikingly divergent. Psychoanalysis, via Lacan, maintains that the exclusivity of the surface or of appearance must be interpreted to mean that appearance always routs or supplants being, that appearance and being never coincide. It is this syncopated relation that is the condition of desire. Historicism, on the other hand, wants to ground being in appearance and wants to have nothing to do with desire.

Thus, when Lacan insists that we must take desire literally, we can understand him to be instructing us about how to avoid the pitfall of historicist thinking. To say that desire must be taken literally is to say simultaneously that desire *must be articulated,* that we must refrain from imagining something that would not be registered on the single surface of speech, and that desire *is inarticulable.* For if it is desire rather than words that we are to take literally, this must mean that desire may register itself *negatively* in speech, that the relation between speech and desire, or social surface and desire, may be a negative one. As Lacan puts it, a dream of punishment may express a desire for what that punishment represses.[12] This is a truth that cannot be tolerated by historicism, which refuses to believe in repression and proudly professes to be *illiterate in desire.* The emergence of a neopopulism cannot be blamed on Foucault, but the historicism he cultivated is guilty of effacing the pockets of empty, inarticulable desire that bear the burden of proof of society's externality to itself. *Disregarding desire, one constructs a reality that is realtight,* that is no longer self-external. One paves the way for the conception of a self-enclosed society built on the repression of a named desire. This, in turn, prepares the path for the reemergence of the Glucksmanian pleb, who has only publicly to declare this desire and to claim the rights that belong to it. If this book may be said to have one intention, it is this: to urge analysts of culture to become literate in desire, to learn how to read what is inarticulable in cultural statements.

2 **The Orthopsychic Subject: Film Theory and the Reception**
— **of Lacan**

Through his appearance in *Television,* Lacan parodies the image of him-self—of his teaching—that we have, to a large extent, received and ac-cepted. Standing alone behind his desk, hands now supporting him as he leans assertively forward, now thrown upward in some emphatic gesture, Lacan stares directly out at us, as he speaks in a voice that none would call smooth of *"quelque chose, n'est-ce pas?"* This *"quelque chose"* is, of course, never made specific, never revealed, and so it comes to stand for a fact or a system of facts that is known, but not by us. This image recalls the one presented to Tabard by the principal in Vigo's *Zero for Conduct.* It is the product of the childish, paranoid notion that all our private thoughts and actions are spied on by and visible within a public world represented by parental figures. In appearing to us, then, by means of the "mass media,"[1] Lacan seems to confirm what we may call our "televisual" fear—that we are perfectly, completely visible to a gaze that observes us from afar (*tele* meaning both "distant" and [from *telos*] "complete").[2] That this proffered image is parodic, however, is almost surely to be missed, so strong are our misperceptions of Lacan. And, so, the signifi-cance of the words with which he opens his address and by which he im-mediately calls attention to his self-parody: "I always speak the truth. Not the whole truth, because there's no way to say it all. Saying the whole truth is materially impossible: words fail. Yet it's through this very impossibility that the truth holds onto the real."[3]—the significance of these words may also be missed, as they have been generally in our theories of representation, the most sophisticated example of which is film theory.

Let me first, in a kind of establishing shot, summarize what I take to be the central misconception of film theory: believing itself to be following Lacan, it conceives the screen as mirror;[4] in doing so, however, it operates in ignorance of, and at the expense of, Lacan's more radical insight, whereby the mirror is conceived as screen.

The Screen as Mirror

This misconception is at the base of film theory's formulation of two concepts—the apparatus and the gaze—and of their interrelation. One of the clearest and most succinct descriptions of this interrelation—and I must state here that it is *because* of its clarity, because of the way it responsibly and explicitly articulates assumptions endemic to film theory, that I cite this description, not to impugn it or its authors particularly— is provided by the editors of *Re-vision,* a collection of essays by feminists on film. Although its focus is the special situation of the female spectator, the description outlines the general relations among the terms *gaze, apparatus,* and *subject* as they are stated by film theory. After quoting a passage from Foucault's *Discipline and Punish* in which Bentham's architectural plan for the panopticon is laid out, the *Re-vision* editors make the following claim:

> The dissociation of the see/being seen dyad [which the panoptic arrangement of the central tower and annular arrangement ensures] and the sense of permanent visibility seem perfectly to describe the condition not only of the inmate in Bentham's prison but of the woman as well. For defined in terms of her visibility, she carries her own Panopticon with her wherever she goes, her self-image a function of her being for another. . . . The subjectivity assigned to femininity within patriarchal systems is inevitably bound up with the structure of the look and the localization of the eye as authority.[5]

The panoptic gaze defines *perfectly* the situation of the woman under patriarchy: that is, it is the very image of the structure that obliges the woman to monitor herself with a patriarchal eye. This structure thereby guarantees that even her innermost desire will always be not a transgression but rather an implantation of the law, that even the "process of theorizing her own untenable situation" can only reflect back to her "as in a mirror" her subjugation to the gaze.

The panoptic gaze defines, then, the *perfect,* that is, the total visibility of the woman under patriarchy, of any subject under any social order, that is to say, of any subject at all. For the very condition and substance of the subject's subjectivity is his or her subjectivation by the law of the society that produces that subject. One becomes visible—not only to others but also to oneself—only through (by seeing through) the categories constructed by a specific, historically defined society. These categories of visibility are categories of knowledge.

The perfection of vision and knowledge can only be procured at the expense of invisibility and nonknowledge. According to the logic of the panoptic apparatus, these last do not and (in an important sense) cannot exist. One might summarize this logic—thereby revealing it to be more questionable than it is normally taken to be—by stating it thus: since all knowledge (or visibility) is produced by society (that is, all that it is possible to know comes not from reality but from socially constructed categories of implementable thought), since *all* knowledge is produced, *only* knowledge (or visibility) is produced, or *all* that is produced is knowledge (visible). This is too glaring a non sequitur—the *then* clauses are too obviously not necessary consequences of the *if* clause—for it ever to be statable as such. And yet this lack of logical consequence is precisely what must be at work and what must go unobserved in the founding of the seeing/being seen dyad that figures the comprehension of the subject by the laws that rule over its construction.

Here—one can already imagine the defensive protestations—I have overstated my argument—there *is* a measure of indetermination available even to the panoptic argument. This indetermination is provided for by the fact that the subject is constructed not by one monolithic discourse but by a multitude of different discourses. What cannot be determined in advance are the articulations that may result from the chance encounter—sometimes on the site of the subject—of these various discourses. A subject of a legal discourse may find itself in conflict with itself as a subject of a religious discourse. The negotiation of this conflict may produce a solution that was anticipated by neither of the contributing discourses. Some film theorists have underlined this part of Foucault's work in an attempt to locate possible sources of resistance to institutional forms of power, to clear a space for a feminist cinema, for example.[6] I would argue, however, that this simple atomization and multiplication of subject positions and this *partes extra partes* description of conflict does not lead to a radical undermining of knowledge or power. Not only is it the case that at each stage what is *produced* is conceived in Foucauldian theory to be a *determinate* thing or position, but, in addition, knowledge and power are conceived as the overall effect of the *relations among* the various conflicting positions and discourses. Differences do not threaten panoptic power; they feed it.

This is quite different from the Lacanian argument, which states that that which is produced by a signifying system can never be determinate. Conflict in this case does not result from the clash between two different positions but from the fact that no position defines a resolute identity. Nonknowledge or invisibility is not registered as the wavering and negotiations between two certainties, two meanings or positions, but as the undermining of every certainty, the incompleteness of every meaning and position.[7] Incapable of articulating this more radical understanding of nonknowledge, the panoptic argument is ultimately *resistant to resistance,* unable to conceive of a discourse that would refuse rather than refuel power.

My purpose here is not simply to point out the crucial differences between Foucault's theory and Lacan's but also to explain how the two theories have failed to be perceived *as* different—how a psychoanalytically informed film theory came to see itself as expressible in Foucauldian terms, despite the fact that these very terms aimed at dispensing with psychoanalysis as a method of explanation. In Foucault's work the techniques of disciplinary power (of the construction of the subject) are conceived as capable of "materially penetrat[ing] the body in depth without depending even on the mediation of the subject's own representations. If power takes hold on the body, this isn't through its having first to be interiorized in people's consciousness."[8] For Foucault, the conscious and the unconscious are categories constructed by psychoanalysis and other discourses (philosophy, literature, law, etc.): like other socially constructed categories, they provide a means of rendering the subject visible, governable, trackable. They are categories through which the modern subject is apprehended and apprehends itself *rather than* (as psychoanalysis maintains) processes of apprehension; they are not processes that engage or are engaged by social discourses (film texts, for example). What the *Re-vision* editors force us to confront is the fact that in film theory these radical differences have largely gone unnoticed or have been nearly annulled. Thus, though the gaze is conceived as a metapsychological concept central to the description of the subject's psychic engagement with the cinematic apparatus, the concept, as we shall see, is formulated in a way that makes any psychical engagement redundant.

My argument is that film theory operated a kind of "Foucauldization" of Lacanian theory; an early misreading of Lacan turned him into a "spendthrift" Foucault—one who wasted a bit too much theoretical energy on such notions as the antithetical meaning of words, or repression, or the unconscious. It is the perceived frugality of Foucault (about which we will have more to say later), every bit as much as the recent and widely proclaimed interest in history, that has guaranteed Foucault's ascendancy over Lacan in the academy.

It was through the concept of the apparatus—the economic, technical, ideological institution—of cinema that the break between contemporary film theory and its past was effected.[9] This break meant that cinematic representation was considered to be not a clear or distorted reflection of a prior and external reality but one among many social discourses that helped to construct reality and the spectatorial subject. As is well known, the concept of the apparatus was not original to film theory but was imported from epistemological studies of science. The actual term *dispositif* (apparatus) used in film theory is borrowed from Gaston Bachelard, who employed it to counter the reigning philosophy of phenomenology. Bachelard proposed instead the study of "phenomeno-*technology*," believing that phenomena are not given to us directly by an independent reality but are, rather, constructed (cf. the Greek *technē,* "produced by a regular method of making rather than found in nature") by a range of practices and techniques that define the field of historical truth. The objects of science are materializable concepts, not natural phenomena.

Even though it borrows his term and the concept it names, film theory does not locate its beginnings in the work of Bachelard but rather in that of one of his students, Louis Althusser.[10] (This history is by now relatively familiar, but since a number of significant points have been overlooked or misinterpreted, it is necessary to retrace some of the details.) Althusser was judged to have advanced and corrected the theory of Bachelard in a way that foregrounded the *subject* of science. Now, although he had argued that the scientific subject was formed in and by the field of science, Bachelard had also maintained that the subject was never *fully* formed in this way. One of the reasons for this merely partial success, he theorized, was an obstacle that impeded the subject's development; this obstacle he called the imaginary. But the problem with this imaginary, as Althusser later pointed out, was that it was itself largely untheorized and was thus (that is, almost by default) accepted by Bachelard as a *given,* as external and prior to rather than as an *effect* of historical determinations. The scientific subject was split, then, between two modes of thought: one governed by historically determined scientific forms, the other by forms that were eternal, spontaneous, and almost purely mythical.[11]

Althusser rethought the category of the imaginary, making it a part of the process of the historical construction of the subject. The imaginary came to name a process necessary to—rather than an impediment of—the ideological founding of the subject: the imaginary provided the form of the subject's lived relation to society. Through this relation the subject was brought to accept as its own, to recognize itself in, the representations of the social order.

This last statement of Althusser's position is important for our concerns here because it is also a statement of the basic position of film theory as it was developed in the 1970s, in France and in England by Jean-Louis Baudry, Christian Metz, Jean-Louis Comolli, Stephen Heath, and others. In sum, the screen is a mirror. The representations produced by the institution of cinema, the images presented on the screen, are accepted by the subject as its own.[12] There is, admittedly, an ambiguity in the notion of the subject's "own image"; it can refer either to an image *of* the subject or an image *belonging to* the subject. Both references are intended by film theory. Whether that which is represented is specularized as an image of the subject's own body or as the subject's image of someone or something else, what remains crucial is the attribution to the image of what Lacan (not film theory, which has never, it seems to me, adequately accounted for the ambiguity) calls "that belong to me aspect so reminiscent of property."[13] It is this aspect that allows the subject to see in any representation not only a reflection of itself but a reflection of itself as master of all it surveys. The imaginary relation produces the subject as master of the image. This insight led to film theory's reconception of film's characteristic "impression of reality."[14] No longer conceived as dependent on a relation of verisimilitude between the image and the real referent, this impression was henceforth attributed to a relation of adequation between the image and the spectator. In other words, the impression of reality results from the fact that the subject takes the image as a full and sufficient representation of itself and its world; the subject is satisfied that it has been adequately reflected on the screen. The "reality effect" and the "subject effect" both name the same constructed impression: that the image makes the subject fully visible to itself.

The imaginary relation is defined as literally a relation of *recognition*. The subject reconceptualizes as its own concepts already constructed by the Other. Sometimes the reconstruction of representation is thought to take place secondarily rather than directly, after there has been a primary recognition of the subject as a "pure act of perception." This is, as we all know, Metz's scenario.[15] The subject first recognizes itself by identifying with the gaze and then recognizes the images on the screen. Now, *what* exactly is the gaze, in this context? Why does it emerge in this way from the theory of the apparatus? What does it add—or subtract—from Bachelard's theory, where it does not figure as a term?[16] All these questions will have to be confronted more fully in due course; for now we must begin with the observation that this ideal point can be nothing but *the signified of the image,* the point from which the image *makes sense* to the subject. In taking up its position at this point, the subject sees itself as *supplying* the image with sense. Regardless of whether one or two stages are posited, the gaze is always the point from which identification is conceived by film theory to take place. And because the gaze is always conceptualized as an analogue of that geometral point of Renaissance perspective at which the picture becomes fully, undistortedly visible, the gaze always retains within film theory the sense of being that point at which sense and being coincide. The subject comes into being by identifying with the image's signified. Sense *founds* the subject—*that* is the ultimate point of the film-theoretical and Foucauldian concepts of the gaze.

The imaginary relation is not, however, merely a relation of knowledge, of sense and recognition; it is also a relation of love guaranteed by knowledge. The image seems not only perfectly to represent the subject, it seems also to be an image of the subject's perfection. An unexceptional definition of narcissism appears to support this relation: the subject falls in love with its own image as the image of its ideal self. *Except* narcissism becomes in this account the structure that instruments the *harmonious* relation between self and social order (since the subject is made to snuggle happily into the space carved out for it), whereas in the psychoanalytic account the subject's narcissistic relation to the self is seen to *conflict with and disrupt* other social relations. I am attempting to pinpoint here no minor point of disagreement between psychoanalysis and the panoptic argument: the opposition between the unbinding force of narcissism and the binding force of social relations is one of the defining tenets of psychoanalysis. It is nevertheless true that Freud himself often ran into difficulty trying to maintain the distinction and that many, from Jung on, have found it easier to merge the two forces into a libidinal monism.[17] But easier is not better; to disregard the distinction is not only to destroy psychoanalysis but also to court determinism.

Why is the representation of the relation of the subject to the social necessarily an imaginary one? This question, posed by Paul Hirst, should have launched a serious critique of film theory.[18] That it did not is attributable, in part, to the fact that the question was perceived to be fundamentally a question about the content of the concept of the imaginary. With only a slightly different emphasis, the question can be seen to ask how the imaginary came to bear, almost exclusively, the burden of the construction of the subject—despite the fact that we always speak of the "symbolic" construction of the subject. One way of answering this is to note that in much contemporary theory the symbolic is itself structured like the imaginary, like Althusser's version of the imaginary. And thus Hirst's criticisms are aimed at our conception of the symbolic construction of the subject, in general. That this is so is made explicit once again by the *frugality of Foucault,* who exposes to us not only the content but also the emptiness of some of our concepts. For Foucault successfully demonstrates that the conception of the symbolic on which he (and, implicitly, others) relies makes the imaginary unnecessary. In a move similar to the one that refigured ideology as a positive force of the production, rather than the falsification of reality, he rethinks symbolic law as the *purely positive* production, rather than repression, of reality—and its desires. Although Foucault offers this conception of the law as a critique of psychoanalysis, psychoanalysis has itself never argued any differently.

What is the difference, then, between Foucault's version and psychoanalysis's version of the law/desire relation? Simply this: while Foucault conceives desire not only as an *effect* but also, as I have pointedly remarked, as a *realization* of the law, *psychoanalysis teaches us that the conflation of effect and realization is an error.* To say that the law is only positive, that it does not forbid desire but rather incites it, causes it to flourish by requiring us to contemplate it, confess it, watch for its various manifestations, is to end up saying simply that the law causes us to *have* a desire—for incest, let us say. This position recreates the error of the psychiatrist in one of Mel Brooks's routines. In a fit of revulsion the psychiatrist throws a patient out of his office after she reports having a dream in which, he relates in disgust, "she was kissing her father! Kissing her father in the dream!" The feeling of disgust is the humorous result of the psychiatrist's failure to distinguish the enunciative position of the dreaming patient from the stated position of the dreamed one. The elision of the difference between these two positions—enunciation and state-ment—causes desire to be conceived as realization in two ways. First, desire is conceived as an actual state resulting from a possibility allowed by law. Second, if desire is something one simply and positively has, nothing can prevent its realization except a purely external force. The destiny of desire is realization, unless it is prohibited by something outside it.

Psychoanalysis denies the preposterous proposition that society is founded on desire—the desire for incest, let us say once again. Surely, it argues, it is the *repression* of this desire that founds society. The law does not construct a subject who simply and unequivocably has a desire, but one who *rejects* its desire, wants not to desire it. The subject is thus conceived as split from its desire, and desire itself is conceived as something—precisely—unrealized; it does not actualize what the law makes possible. Nor is desire committed to realization, barring any external hindrance. For the internal dialectic that makes the being of the subject dependent on the *negation* of its desire turns desire into a self-hindering process.

Foucault's definition of the law as positive and nonrepressive implies both that the law is (1) unconditional, that it *must* be obeyed, since only that which it allows can come into existence—*being is,* by definition, *obedience*— and that it is (2) unconditioned, since nothing, that is, no desire, precedes the law; there is no cause of the law and we must not therefore seek behind the law for its reasons. Law does not exist in order to repress desire.

Now, not only have these claims for the law been made before, they have also previously and prominently been contested.[19] For these are precisely the claims of moral conscience that Freud examines in *Totem and Taboo.* There Freud reduces these claims to what he takes to be their absurd consequences: "If we were to admit the claims thus asserted by our conscience [that desire conforms to or always falls within the law], it would follow, on the one hand, that prohibition would be superfluous and, on the other, the fact of conscience would remain unexplained."[20] On the one hand, prohibition would be superfluous. Foucault agrees: once the law is conceived as primarily positive, as producing the phenomena it scrutinizes, the concept of a negative, repressive law can be viewed as an excess—of psychoanalysis. On the other hand, the fact of conscience would remain unexplained. That is, there is no longer any reason for conscience to exist; it *should,* like prohibition, be superfluous. What becomes suddenly *in*explicable is the very *experience* of conscience—which is not only the subjective experience of the compulsion to obey but also the experience of guilt, of the remorse that follows transgression—once we have accepted the *claims* of conscience that the law cannot fail to impose itself and cannot be caused. Foucault agrees once again: the experience of conscience and the interiorization of the law through representations is made superfluous by his theory of law.

Again: the claims of conscience are used to refute the experience of conscience. This paradox located by Freud will, of course, not appear as such to those who do not ascribe the claims *to* conscience. And yet something of the paradox *is* manifest in Foucault's description of panoptic power and film theory's description of the relation between the apparatus and the gaze. In both cases the model of self-surveillance implicitly recalls the psychoanalytic model of moral conscience even as the resemblance is being disavowed. The image of self-surveillance, of self-correction, is both required to construct the subject and made redundant by the fact that the subject thus constructed is, by definition, absolutely upright, completely correct. The inevitability and completeness of its success renders the orthopedic gesture of surveillance unnecessary. The subject is and can only be inculpable. The relation between apparatus and gaze creates only the mirage of psychoanalysis. There is, in fact, no psychoanalytic subject in sight.

Orthopsychism

How, then, to derive a properly psychoanalytic—that is, a split—subject from the premise that this subject is the effect rather than the cause of the social order? Before turning, finally, to Lacan's solution, it will be necessary to pause to review one extraordinary chapter from Bachelard—chapter 4 of *Le rationalisme appliqué,* titled "La surveillance intellectuelle de soi"[21]—where we will find some arguments that have been overlooked in more recent theorizations of the apparatus.[22]

Although Bachelard pioneered the theory of the institutional construction of the field of science, he also (as we have already said) persistently argued that the protocols of science never fully saturated, nor provided the content of, this field. The obstacle of the imaginary is only *one* of the reasons given for this. Besides this purely negative resistance *to* the scientific, there is also a positive condition *of* the scientific itself that prevented such a reduction from taking place. Both these reasons together guarantee that the concepts of science are never mere realizations of possibilities historically allowed and scientific thought is never simply habit, the regulated retracing of possible paths already laid out in advance.

To say that the scientific subject is constructed by the institution of science, Bachelard would reason, is to say that it is always thereby obliged to survey itself, its own thinking, not subjectively, not through a process of introspection to which the subject has privileged access, but *objectively,* from the position of the scientific institution. So far this *orthopsychic* relation may seem no different from the panoptic relation we have been so intent on dislodging. But there *is* a difference: the orthopsychic relation (unlike the panoptic one) assumes that it is just this objective survey that allows thought to become (not wholly visible, but) *secret;* it allows thought to remain *hidden,* even under the most intense scrutiny. Let us make clear that Bachelard is not attempting to argue that there is an original, private self that happens to find in objectivity a means (among others) of concealing itself. He is arguing, rather, that the very possibility of concealment is raised only by the subject's objective relation to itself. For it is the very act of surveillance—which makes clear the fact that the subject is external to itself, exists in a relation of "extimacy" (Lacan's word) with itself—that causes the subject to appear to itself as culpable, as guilty of hiding something. The objective relation to the self, Bachelard informs us, necessarily raises the insidious question that Nietzsche formulated thus: "To everything which a man allows to become visible, one is able to demand: what does he wish to hide?" It does not matter that this "man" is oneself. The ineradicable suspicion of dissimulation raised by the objective relation guarantees that thought will never become totally coincident with the forms of the institution. Thought will be split, rather, between belief in what the institution makes manifest and suspicion about what it is keeping secret. All objective representations, its very own thought, will be taken by the subject not as true representations of itself or the world but as fictions: no "impression of reality" will adhere to them. The subject will appear, even to itself, to be no more than a *hypothesis of being*. Belief in the reality of representations will be suspended, projected beyond the representations themselves. And the "impression of reality" will henceforth consist in the "mass of objections to constituted reason," Bachelard says here, and elsewhere: in the conviction that "what is real but hidden has more content than what is given and obvious."[23]

The suspicion of dissimulation offers the subject a kind of reprieve from the dictates of law. For these dictates are perceived as hypotheses that must be tested rather than imperatives that must be automatically and unconditionally obeyed. The subject is not only judged by and subjected to social laws, it also judges them by subjecting them to intellectual scrutiny; in other words, the subject directs a question, "*Che vuoi?* What do you want from me?" to every social, as well as scientific, law. Self-surveillance, then, conduces to self-correction; one thought or representation always advances another as the former's judge.

Bachelard's chapter ends up celebrating a kind of euphoria of free thought. As a result of its orthopsychic relation to itself, that is, before an image that it *doubts,* the scientific subject is jubilant. Not because its image, its world, its thought reflects its own perfection, but because the subject is thus allowed to imagine that they are all *perfectible*. It is this sense of the perfectibility of things that liberates thought from the totally determining constraints of the social order. Thought is conceived to police, and not merely be policed by, the social/scientific order, and the paranoia of the "Cassandra complex" (Bachelard's designation for the childish belief that everything is already known in advance, by one's parents, say) is thereby dispelled.

Curiously, the charge of guilt that is lodged, we were told, by the structure of surveillance has been dropped somewhere along the way.

It is now claimed, on the contrary, that surveillance enables thought to be "morally sincere." As it turns out, then, it is the very *experience* of moral conscience, the very feeling of guilt, that absolves thought of the very *charge* of guilt. How has this absolution been secured? By the separation of the act of thinking from the thoughts that it thinks. So that though the thoughts may be guilty, the act of thinking remains innocent. And the subject remains whole, its intentions clear. This is the only way we can understand the apparent contradictions of this chapter. Throughout his work Bachelard maintains that "duplicity is maladroit in its address"—that is, that they err who assume they cannot be duped, that no one is spared from deception. As a result, no thought can ever be perfectly penetrable. Yet, in chapter 4 he simultaneously maintains that the subject can and must penetrate its own act of thinking.

This scenario of surveillance—of the "joy of surveillance"—is consciously delineated in relation to Freud's notion of moral conscience. But Bachelard opposes his notion to the "pessimism" of that of Freud, who, of course, saw moral conscience as cruel and punishing. In Bachelard, surveillance, in seeming to offer the subject a pardon, is construed as primarily a positive or benign force. Bachelard, then, too, like Foucault and film theory, recalls and yet disavows the psychoanalytic model of moral conscience—however differently. Bachelard's orthopsychism, which is informed in the end by a psychologistic argument, cannot really be accepted by film theory as an alternative to panopticonism. Although Bachelard argues that a certain invisibility shelters the subject from what we might call (in the panoptic, not in the Lacanian sense) "the gaze" of the institutional apparatus, the subject is nevertheless characterized by an exact legibility on another level. The Bachelardian subject may not locate *in its image* a full and upright being that it jubilantly (but wrongly) takes itself to be, but this subject does locate *in the process of scrutinizing* this image the joyous prospect of righting itself. Film theory's correct subject is here replaced by a self-correcting one.

Yet this detour through orthopsychism has not led only to a dead end. What we have forcibly been led to consider is the question of deception, of the suspicion of deception that must *necessarily* be raised if we are to understand the cinematic apparatus as a *signifying* apparatus, which places the subject in an external relationship to itself. Once the permanent possibility of deception is admitted (rather than disregarded, as it is by the theory of the panoptic apparatus), the concept of the gaze undergoes a radical change. For, where in the panoptic apparatus the gaze marks the subject's *visibility,* in Lacan's theory it marks the subject's *culpability.* The gaze stands watch over the *inculpation*—the faulting and splitting—of the subject by the apparatus.

The Mirror as Screen

Film theory introduced the subject into its study, and thereby incorporated Lacanian psychoanalysis, primarily by means of "The mirror stage as formative of the function of the 'I.'" It is to this essay that theorists made reference as they formulated their arguments about the subject's narcissistic relation to the film and about that relationship's dependence on "the gaze." While it is true that the mirror-phase essay does describe the child's narcissistic relation to its mirror image, it is, nevertheless, *not* in this essay but in Seminar XI that Lacan himself formulates *his* concept of the gaze. Here, particularly in those sessions collected under the heading "Of the Gaze as *Object Petit a,"* Lacan *reformulates* his earlier mirror-phase essay and paints a picture very different from the one painted by film theory.

Lacan tells his tale of the relation of the subject to its world in the form of a humorously recondite story about a sardine can. The story is told as a kind of mock Hegelian epic, a send-up of the broadly expansive Hegelian epic form by a deliberately "little story" that takes place in a "small boat" in a "small port" and includes a single named character, "Petit-Jean." The entire overt plot consists in the sighting of a "small can." A truly short story of the object small a; the proof and sole guarantee of that alterity of the Other which Hegel's sweeping tale, in overlooking, denies.

The story sets Hegelian themes adrift and awash in a sea of bathos. A young (Hegelian) intellectual, identifying himself with the slaving class, embarks on a journey that he expects will pit him in struggle against the raw forces of a pitiless nature. But, alas, the day turns out to be undramatically sunny and fine, and the anticipated event, the meeting and match with the Master, never comes about. It is narratively replaced by what we can accurately describe as a "nonevent," the spotting of the shiny, mirrorlike sardine can—and an attack of anxiety. In the end, however, bathos gives way to tragedy as we realize that in this little slice-of-life drama there is no sublation of consumption, no transcendence, only the slow dying away, through consumption, of the individual members of the slaving class. The mocking is not merely gentle but carries in its wake this abrupt statement of consequence; something quite serious is at stake here. If we are to rewrite the tragic ending of this political tale, the relation between self and Other will have to be retheorized.

What is it that is at stake here? Plainly, ultimately, it is "I"—the I, the subject, that takes shape in this revised version of the mirror stage. As if to underline the fact that it is the I that is the point of the discussion, Lacan tells a personal story. It is he, in fact, who is the first-person of the narrative; this portrait of the analyst as a young man is his own. The cameo role in Seminar XI prepares us, then, for the starring role Lacan plays as the narcissistic "televanalyst" in *Television*. "What is at stake in both cases," Lacan says in *Television* about his performance both there and in his seminars, in general, "is a gaze: a gaze to which, in neither case, do I address myself, but in the name of which I speak."[24] What is he saying here about the relation between the I and the gaze?

The gaze is that which "determines" the I in the visible; it is "the instrument through which . . . [the] I [is] *photo-graphed*."[25] This might be taken to confirm the coincidence of the Foucauldian and Lacanian positions, to indicate that, in both, the gaze determines the complete *visibility* of the I, the mapping of the I on a perceptual grid. Hence the disciplinary monitoring of the subject. But this coincidence can only be produced by a precipitous, "snapshot" reading of Lacan, one that fails to notice the hyphen that splits the term *photo-graph*—into *photo,* "light," and *graph,* among other things, a fragment of the Lacanian phrase "graph of desire"— as it splits the subject that it describes.

Photo. One thing is certain: light does not enter these seminars in a straight line, through the laws of optics. Because, as he says, the geometric laws of the propagation of light map space only, and *not* vision, Lacan does not theorize the visual field in terms of these laws. Thus, the legitimate construction can*not* figure for him—as it *does* for film theory— the relation of the spectator to the screen. And these seminars cannot be used, as they are used by film theory, to support the argument that the cinematic apparatus, in direct line with the camera obscura, by recreating the space and ideology of Renaissance perspective, produces a centered and transcendent subject.[26]

This argument is critiqued in the seminars on the gaze as Lacan makes clear why the speaking subject *cannot* ever be totally trapped in the imaginary. Lacan claims, rather, that "I am not simply that punctiform being located at the geometral point from which the perspective is grasped."[27] Now, film theory, of course, has always claimed that the cinematic apparatus functions *ideologically* to produce a subject that *misrecognizes* itself as source and center of the represented world. But although this claim might seem to imply agreement with Lacan, to suggest, too, that the subject is *not* the punctiform being that Renaissance perspective would have us believe it is, film theory's notion of misrecognition turns out to be different from Lacan's in important ways. Despite the fact that the term *misrecognition* implies an error on the subject's part, a failure properly to recognize its true relation to the visible world, the process by which the subject is installed in its position of misrecognition operates without the hint of failure. The subject unerringly assumes the position the perspectival construction bids it to take. Erased from the process of construction, the negative force of error emerges later as a charge directed at the subject. But from where does it come? Film theory has described only the construction of this position of misrecognition. Though it implies that there is another *actual,* nonpunctiform position, film theory has never been able to describe the construction of *this* position.

In Lacan's description, misrecognition retains its negative force in the process of construction. As a result, the process is conceived no longer as a purely positive one but rather as one with an internal dialectic. Lacan does not take the single triangle that geometrical perspective draws as an accurate description of its own operation. Instead he rediagrams this operation using, instead, *two interpenetrating* triangles. Thus he represents both the way the science of optics understands the emission of light *and* the way its straight lines become refracted, diffused (the way they acquire the "ambiguity of a jewel") once we take into account the way the signifier itself interferes with this figuring. The second triangle cuts through the first, marking the elision or negation that is part of the process of construction. The second triangle diagrams the subject's mistaken belief that there is something behind the space set out by the first. It is this mistaken belief (this misrecognition) that causes the subject to *disbelieve* even those representations shaped according to the scientific laws of optics. The Lacanian subject, who may doubt the accuracy of even its most "scientific representations," is submitted to a *superegoic* law that is radically different from the optical laws to which the film theoretical subject is submitted.

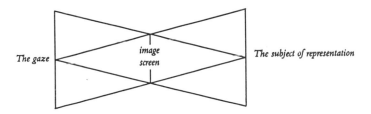

Graph. Semiotics, not optics, is the science that enlightens for us the structure of the visual domain. Because it alone is capable of lending things sense, the signifier alone makes vision possible. There is and can be no brute vision, no vision totally independent of language. Painting, drawing, all forms of picture making, then, are fundamentally graphic arts. And because signifiers are material, that is, because they are opaque rather than translucent, refer to other signifiers rather than directly to a signified, the field of vision is neither clear nor easily traversable. It is instead ambiguous and treacherous, full of traps. Lacan's Seminar XI refers constantly, but ambiguously, to these traps. When Lacan says that the subject is trapped in the imaginary, he means that the subject can imagine nothing outside it; the imaginary cannot itself provide the means that would allow the subject to transcend it. When he says, on the other hand, that a painting, or any other representation, is a "trap for the gaze," we understand this phrase as echoing the expression "to trap one's attention." That is, the representation *attracts* the gaze, induces us to imagine a gaze outside the field of representation. It is this second sense of trapping, whereby representation appears to generate its own beyond (to generate, we might say recalling Lacan's diagram, the *second* triangle, which the science of optics neglects to consider) that prevents the subject from ever being trapped in the imaginary. Where the Foucauldian and the film-theoretical positions always tend to trap the subject in representation (an idealist failing), to conceive of language as constructing the prison walls of the subject's being, Lacan argues that the subject sees these walls as *trompe l'oeil,* and is thus constructed by something *beyond* them.

For beyond everything that is displayed to the subject, the question is asked, "What is being concealed from me? What in this graphic space does not show, does not stop *not* writing itself?" This point at which something appears to be *in*visible, this point at which something appears to be missing from representation, some meaning left unrevealed, is the point of the Lacanian gaze. It marks the *absence* of a signified; it is an *unoccupiable* point, not, as film theory claims, because it figures an unrealizable ideal but because it indicates an impossible real. In the former case, one would expect to find at the point of the gaze a signified, but here the signifier is absent—and so is the subject. The subject, in short, cannot be located or locate itself at the point of the gaze, since this point marks, on the contrary, its very annihilation. At the moment the gaze is discerned, the image, the entire visual field, takes on a terrifying alterity. It loses its "belong-to-me aspect" and suddenly assumes the function of a screen.

Lacan is certainly *not* offering an agnostic description of the way the real object is cut off from the subject's view by language, of the way the real object escapes capture in the network of signifiers. He does not assume an idealist stance, arguing the way Plato does that the object is split between its real being and its semblance. Lacan argues, rather, that beyond the signifying network, beyond the visual field, there is, in fact, nothing at all.[28] The veil of representation actually conceals nothing; there is nothing behind representation. Yet the fact that representation *seems* to hide, to put an arbored screen of signifiers in front of something hidden beneath, is not treated by Lacan as a simple error that the subject can undo; nor is this deceptiveness of language treated as something that undoes the subject, deconstructs its identity by menacing its boundaries. Rather, language's opacity is taken as the very *cause* of the subject's being, that is, its desire, or want-to-be. The fact that it is materially impossible to say the whole truth—that truth always backs away from language, that words always fall short of their goal—*founds* the subject. Contrary to the idealist position that makes *form* the cause of being, Lacan locates the cause of being in the *informe:* the *unformed* (that which has no signified, no significant shape in the visual field) and the *inquiry* (the question posed to representation's presumed reticence). The subject is the effect of the impossibility of seeing what is lacking in the representation, what the subject, therefore, wants to see. The gaze, the object-cause of desire, is the object-cause of the subject of desire in the field of the visible. In other words, it is what the subject does not see and not simply what it sees that founds it.

It should be clear by now how different this description is from that offered by film theory. In film theory, the gaze is located "in front of" the image, as its signified, the point of maximal meaning or sum of all that appears in the image *and* the point that "gives" meaning. The subject is, then, thought to identify with and thus, in a sense, to *coincide with* the gaze. In Lacan, on the other hand, the gaze is located "behind" the image, as that which fails to appear in it and thus as that which makes all its meanings suspect. And the subject, instead of coinciding with or identifying with the gaze, is rather *cut off from* it. Lacan does not ask you to think of the gaze as belonging to an Other who cares about what or where you are, who pries, keeps tabs on your whereabouts, and takes note of all your steps and missteps, as the panoptic gaze is said to do. When you encounter the gaze of the Other, you meet not a seeing eye but a blind one. The gaze is not clear or penetrating, not filled with knowledge or recognition; it is clouded over and turned back on itself, absorbed in its own enjoyment. The horrible truth, revealed to Lacan by Petit-Jean, is that *the gaze does not see you.* So, if you are looking for confirmation of the truth of your being or the clarity of your vision, you are on your own; the gaze of the Other is not confirming; it will not validate you.

Now, the subject instituted by the Lacanian gaze does not come into being as the realization of a possibility opened up by the law of the Other. It is rather an impossibility that is crucial to the constitution of the subject—the impossibility, precisely, of any ultimate confirmation from the Other. The subject emerges, as a result, as a desiring being, that is to say, an effect of the law but certainly not a realization of it, since desire as such can never be conceived as a realization. Desire fills no possibility but seeks after an impossibility; this makes desire always, constitutionally, contentless.

Narcissism, too, takes on a different meaning in Lacan, one more in accord with Freud's own. Since something always appears to be missing from any representation, narcissism *cannot* consist in finding satisfaction in one's own visual image. It must, rather, consist in the belief that one's own being exceeds the imperfections of its image. Narcissism, then, seeks the self beyond the self-image, with which the subject constantly finds fault and in which it constantly fails to recognize itself. What one loves in one's image is something *more* than the image ("in you more than you").[29] Thus is narcissism the source of the malevolence with which the subject regards its image, the aggressivity it unleashes on all its own representations.[30] And thus does the subject come into being as a transgression of, rather than in conformity to, the law. It is not the law, but the fault in the law—the desire that the law cannot ultimately conceal—that is assumed by the subject as its own. The subject, in taking up the burden of the law's guilt, goes beyond the law.

Much of this definition of narcissism I take to be compacted in Lacan's otherwise totally enigmatic sentences: "The effect of mimicry is camouflage in the strictly technical sense. It is not a question of harmonizing with the background, but against a mottled background, of becoming mottled—exactly like the technique of camouflage practiced in human warfare."[31] The effect of representation ("mimicry," in an older, idealist vocabulary) is not a subject who will harmonize with, or adapt to, its environment (the subject's narcissistic relation to the representation that constructs him does not place him in happy accord with the reality that the apparatus constructs for him). The effect of representation is, instead, the suspicion that some reality is being camouflaged, that we are being deceived as to the exact nature of some thing-in-itself that lies behind representation. In response to such a representation, against such a background of deception, the subject's own being breaks up between its unconscious being and its conscious semblance. At war both with its world and with itself, the subject becomes guilty of the very deceit it suspects. This can hardly, however, be called mimicry, in the old sense, since nothing is being mimed.

In sum, the conflictual nature of Lacan's culpable subject sets it worlds apart from the stable subject of film theory. But neither does the Lacanian subject resemble that of Bachelard. For while in Bachelard orthopsychism—in providing an opportunity for the correction of thought's imperfections—allows the subject to wander from its moorings, constantly to drift from one position to another, in Lacan "orthopsychism"[32]—one wishes to retain the term in order to indicate the subject's fundamental dependence on the faults it finds in representation and in itself—grounds the subject. The desire that it precipitates *transfixes* the subject, albeit in a conflictual place, so that all the subject's visions and revisions, all its fantasies, merely circumnavigate the absence that anchors the subject and impedes its progress.

In contemporary analyses of the relation of psychoanalysis to politics, the real has no place; the psychical and the social are conceived as a realtight unit ruled by a principle of pleasure. I propose to show that *it is the real that unites the psychic to the social,* that this relation is ruled by the death drive. Taking seriously those formulations by which the subject and the unconscious are termed the *effect* of the social order, I will describe this relation as a causal one. But, reader, please beware: a definition of cause that depends on and is produced through a definition of the death drive will certainly not be familiar.

First, the real. How has it been evicted from current discussions? Within psychoanalysis the status of the real is problematic from the beginning. Once it is observed that pleasure is the goal of all psychic mechanisms and that the psyche is able to obtain pleasure by means of its own internal processes—that is, by producing a hallucinatory pleasure—the subject appears to be "independent of" what Freud calls "Fate,"[1] and what we will call the real. Psychical reality can indefinitely defer, and thus replace, the reality of brute fact. "Happiness" is therefore defined in *Civilization and Its Discontents* as "essentially subjective." This means that even if we were to imagine the most unhappy historical situations—"a peasant during the Thirty Years' War, a victim of the Holy Inquisition, a Jew awaiting the pogrom"[2]—it would be impossible to assume from the objective facts alone how, or even that, the victims suffered as a consequence of their situations. One would also have to recall that there is a whole range of psychic operations (to which we do not have direct access), which, by numbing, blunting, or distorting the harmful sensations, might shield the victim from pain.

It is nevertheless wrong to think that this Freudian description of the pleasure principle neatly separates psychical and social reality. The reality with which the reality principle puts us in touch is not simply a perceptual object, which can test the adequacy of the object of hallucination produced by the pleasure principle. That this is so is clear from the fact that Freud does not set social reality—civilization—*against* the pleasure principle, but rather defines the former as a product of the latter. Civilization does not test, but realizes our fantasies; it does not put us in touch with Fate (the real), but protects us from it. The social subject is thus pictured as "a kind of prosthetic God,"[3] whose fantasmatic, artificial limbs substitute for the inferior, natural ones Fate bestows. Civilization endows the subject with a fantasmatic body and fairytalelike powers. The subjects of modern cultures have telescopes, microscopes, cameras for eyes; microphones, radios, telephones for mouths; ships, trains, cars, and planes for legs; and all of these instruments-that-extend-our-grasp for arms.

For Freud, this definition of civilization does not, of course, end the question of the real; the real is not thereby banished from civilized existence, which brings discontent as well as pleasure. Although the real that is associated with discontent can no longer be conceived simply as that which opposes itself to the imaginary of the psychical, Freud retains the reference to the real.

For much of contemporary theory, however, the question *is* closed. Since the real is conceived as radically outside our ken, inaccessible to us, it is therefore thought to have no bearing on us. Between the subject and the real, civilization—the social order—is interposed. This order is now conceived not only as that which, in equipping the subject with a fantasmatic body, satisfies its desires, but more, as that which produces the desires it satisfies. Happiness is thus defined no longer as subjective, but as *objective*. For all the mirrors, cameras, telephones, microphones, planes, passenger lists, and statistics can be seen as so much social paraphernalia of surveillance by which alone the subject is made visible—even to itself. If we cannot judge immediately what measure of pain or pleasure belonged to a historical individual, this is not because we cannot project ourselves into her subjective position, her private mental sphere, but rather because we cannot so easily project ourselves into her objective *social* sphere in order to discern the categories of thought that constructed her expectations, narcotized her against disappointment, made her obtuse to her own suffering.

Consider, for example, certain analyses of the hystericization of women's bodies, of the "invention of hysteria." According to these, an investigation of turn-of-the-century medical practices, codes of photography, discourses of the Church and of psychoanalysis, and so on will tell us not how hysteria was looked at then but, more accurately, how it was constructed as a historical entity. From the point of view of the hysteric, however, how does this argument work? By assuming—implicitly or explicitly—that it is her "desire" that these practices construct. Her complicity and even her pleasure are secured as she looks at and constructs herself through the categories provided by these discourses.

Consider also the example of contemporary film theory. The concept of the gaze elaborated there is founded on assumptions similar to those just named. The gaze is conceived as a point constructed by the textual system of the film from which the subject is obliged to look; it is the condition of the possibility of the viewer's vision. The gaze acts as a kind of keyhold, the only opening into the visual pleasure the film affords. One sees and desires to see what it is given to see and desire; one assumes with pleasure—even if masochistic[4]—her own subjective position.

In these examples, the social system of representation is conceived as lawful, regulatory, and on this account the cause of the subject, which the former subsumes as one of its effects. The subject is assumed to be already virtually there in the social and to come into being by actually wanting what social laws want it to want. The construction of the subject depends, then, on the subject's taking social representations as images of its own ideal being, on the subject's deriving a "narcissistic pleasure" from these representations. This notion of pleasure, however vaguely invoked, is what makes the argument for construction stick; it "cements" or "glues" the realm of the psychic to that of the social. (Hume described cause as the "cement of the universe"—the metaphor helps to determine a certain conception of cause.) The point of insertion of the subject into society thus becomes a point of resemblance, convergence, attachment.

This is the understanding—by which the subject is thought to recognize itself in representations—that I intend to counter. I will begin by opposing to it two images meant to indicate the complexities that are currently razed. The first, taken from *Civilization and Its Discontents,* follows the description of the fairytalelike prostheses that define the contours of the modern bodily ego. "Man," Freud writes, first appeared on earth "as a feeble animal organism," and no matter how far the society into which he is born has succeeded in making this earth serviceable to him, "each individual of the species must once more make its entry ('oh, inch of nature!') as a helpless suckling."[5] It is the parenthetical phrase, "oh inch of nature!" that interests us particularly. This fraction is literally fractious, an oxymoron. For the very segmentation and measurement of nature denatures it; an inch of nature is itself unnatural, found not in nature but in the rods and rules by which culture calculates. It is perhaps this very unruliness of the image that *resists* the interpretation which claims that it provides the measure of the little man, who would thus be defined absolutely by the yardstick of the society into which he enters. The resistant image refuses to offer itself as the *equivalent* of the man, that little piece of nature that *is* man. Rather, the "inch of nature," we will argue, is that which is *not* incorporated into society, that which is sacrificed upon entry into the social.

The second image is opposed specifically to film theory's concept of the gaze, which asks us to assume the perfect functioning of apparatuses of surveillance. The image, taken from Samuel Beckett's *Watt,* describes the functioning of a five-man examining committee: "They then began to look at one another and much time passed before they succeeded in doing so. Not that they looked at each other long; no, they had more sense than that. But when five men look at one another, though in theory only twenty looks are necessary, every man looking four times, yet in practice this number is seldom sufficient."[6] And then it seems that several more pages describing the twistings, turnings, and other maneuverings of the five men is still not sufficient to establish that exchange of looks by which the committee would succeed in looking at itself. For some look always goes unreciprocated, spoiling indefinitely the perfect exchange.

Beckett's description is presented here as no mere anecdote; it is offered quite seriously as the means of rethinking the significance of the recalcitrant "inch of nature."

The Death Drive: Freud and Bergson

No one ever accused Freud of being a cutup,[7] except Fliess, as you will remember, who pointed out a resemblance between *The Interpretation of Dreams* and a book of jokes. Freud took Fliess's observation one step further by writing *Jokes and Their Relation to the Unconscious* in which he noted some more specific resemblances between his theory and that presented in Henri Bergson's "Laughter," published in the same year as *The Interpretation of Dreams*. Freud cites Bergson's essay several times, indicating always that he finds it both charming and canny. To support his own, economic view of pleasure, he quotes the following sentence from Bergson: "What is living should never, according to our expectation, be repeated exactly the same. When we find such a repetition, we always suspect some mechanism lying behind the living thing."[8] The constantly changing nature of life, Freud argues, demands a perpetual expenditure of energy by our understanding: repetition, then, the rediscovery of something already familiar, is pleasurable because it economizes energy. Laughter is the discharge of the excess of energy called up by our expectations of the new and made superfluous by the recognition of the same.

In addition to this specific reference, we find more general references and broader gestures of approval of Bergson's "plausible train of thought from automatism to automata," as Freud, like Bergson, considers the relation of jokes to the games of children.

Bergson's basic argument is that laughter is elicited by a perception of the mechanical encrusted on the living, of the "mechanization of life."[9] Where life is defined essentially by its "organic elasticity," as a ceaselessly changing, irreversible process of pure time and perpetual novelty, the mechanical is defined by its machinelike intractability, manifest in three different operations: repetition, inversion, and the reciprocal interference of series. These operations are illustrated by children's toys, automata, such as Jacks-in-the-box; puppets; a game of ninepins in which the ball rolls forward, upsetting the pins, and backward, restoring the pins to their upright position. Laughter is thought to serve a social function, not, as in Freud, by providing a potentially healing respite from the expenditure of energy, but rather by issuing a rebuke to every inelasticity of character, thought, and action. Laughter thus acts to restore us to social life and its constant demands for our alert attention and complete presence of mind.

The essay on laughter is supported by Bergson's larger metaphysical project: the assimilation of Darwin's theory of evolution to a nonmechanistic theory of mind.[10] The creative energy of the human mind, he maintains, is irreducible to the material conditions that triggered the mechanisms of selection. As part of this project, Bergson unfavorably contrasts the intellect (which relies on abstract concepts formed by language) with intuition (a kind of "auscultation," a sympathetic listening to the "throbbing of [life's] soul"). Intuition grasps the supple flow of life directly, while the intellect, distanced by its reliance on rigid and discontinuous spatial concepts, is doomed to let mobile reality slip forever through its categories.

The polemical force of this theory is aimed at the Eleatic philosophers, most notably Zeno. By Bergson's account, Zeno's paradox could be described as comic. This paradox is produced out of the inchmeal contemplation of an arrow in flight; the trajectory of the arrow is broken down into an infinite number of points in space and the result is offered as proof of motion's impossibility. Since the arrow's flight is composed of these points, the arrow that occupies one of them at any given moment must always be at rest. To this analysis Bergson responds with a laugh: it is not motion that is impossible, but the comprehension of motion, of life, by the intellect. The simple lifting of one's arm becomes grotesquely comic when contemplated by the intellect, which can only cut up movement, like a film, into hundreds of discrete moments. It is only the perception of motion from the *inside,* by intuition, that allows us to observe the former's completeness. (In a way, Bergson's theory of laughter seems tailor-made to account for the humorous, Tayloresque description of the five-man examining committee: it is the division of the completed look into a number of discrete glances that renders its accomplishment impossible.)

The similarities between Bergson and Freud turn out, however, to be superficial when we look more closely at the whole of Freud's work—especially its later development. We turn, then, to *Beyond the Pleasure Principle,* in which Freud returns to the subject of the relations among pleasure, repetition, and the games of children. At this point there can be no mistaking the differences between the two theorists of laughter. In his 1920 essay, Freud, still viewing children's games in the terms he did earlier, now sees adumbrated there the workings of the death drive, a principle beyond pleasure. The surprising turn of the argument hinges precisely on the term *organic elasticity,* the term used by Bergson to name the defining characteristic of the *animate,* of life. Freud, on the contrary, finds in this "organic elasticity" a pressure to return to an earlier, *inanimate* state. This is what he says: "*A [drive] is an urge inherent in organic life to restore an earlier state of things . . .* it is a kind of organic elasticity, or, to put it another way, the expression of the inertia inherent in organic life."[11] Allow me to state the obvious: there is simply no way to understand *organic elasticity* and *inertia* as synonymous as long as we hold to the Bergsonian model. Nor would we be able to understand why Freud, far from contrasting repetition with life, interprets repetition as the invariable characteristic of the drives that fuel life. The being of the drives, he claims, *is* the compulsion to repeat. The aim of life is not evolution but regression, or, in its most seemingly contradictory form, the aim of life is death.

The seeming contradictions of *Beyond the Pleasure Principle* can only be unraveled if we take it not as the biologistic myth it is often accused of being but as, in fact, an argument against such myths, including the one formulated by Bergson.[12] Freud's text is incomprehensible if one confounds instinct with drive, or—in a distinction made by Lacan, who finds it latent in Freud's work—if one confounds the first and the second death.[13] The first is the real death of the biological body, after which there is usually another, the second, exemplified by the various rituals of mourning that take place in the symbolic. It is with this second death that we are concerned when we speak of the Freudian concept of the death drive. This distinction between the two deaths separates the vital order of biological evolution—the order to which "process" or "evolutionary" philosophers, like Bergson, refer[14]—where events can be said to move only progressively forward, taking place once and for all time, from the order of the signifier, the symbolic, in which the text of human history is inscribed. In this second order, the past is *not* immortal. Since the signifier always receives its signification retroactively, what was done can always be undone; the past can, therefore, have no permanent existence. According to Bergson, the novelty of the present is assured only by the total survival of the past, novelty being defined as the moment's unique difference from its complete antecedent context. The persistence of the past in its entirety is thus necessary if the possibility of a recurrence of events is to be excluded. The death drive, then, which recognizes the possibility of the past's destruction, is inextricably linked to repetition.

The death drive and the compulsion to repeat are thus the inevitable corollaries of *symbolic* life.

Cause: Lacan and Aristotle

In his elaboration of Freud's concept of the death drive, Lacan does not, however, make explicit reference to Bergson but rather to Aristotle. The connections between these last two are nevertheless clear, starting with the fact that they articulate their arguments in opposition to the same theoretical foes. Aristotle, too, took the Eleatics—metaphysical materialists who asserted that Being is immutable and change impossible—as his primary philosophical enemy. Contrary to the Eleatic position, Aristotle, like Bergson, based his philosophy on the primacy of change, of a becoming that is not divisible into parts exterior to each other. One of the major differences between them is to be found in their positions with respect to teleology. Aristotle argued for the validity of teleological explanation, while Bergson argued most adamantly against it on the grounds that the concept of an internal finalism destroyed time and annihilated novelty. But Aristotle, for his part, was careful to distinguish his position from the idealist one in which form is thought to be given at the outset and to guide from an ideal space; form in Aristotle is always the terminus of change in the natural world. And time for him, as for Bergson, is what retards; it hinders everything's being given in advance, all at once. The teleological argument was advanced, then, in an attempt at a *nonmechanical* explanation of change.

This is merely to say that when Lacan, in his explanation of Freud's death drive, names the signifying network that is its only domain *automaton,* he mounts an argument that answers Bergson as well as Aristotle, even though it is to the latter's use of the word that we are referred. In *The Physics* and elsewhere in Aristotle, the term *automaton* appears as part of an attempt to define cause. His basic position is that natural, living substance (as opposed to the inanimate) has an internal principle of change.

Yet because Aristotle must coherently argue that there is a diversity as well as an eternity of change, he is led to suppose that a natural substance changes according to it own nature *and* that it depends on something else for the realization of change. This something else is, of course, the well-known Prime Mover.

Automaton, the general category of chance or coincidence, occurs, by contrast, not through some inner principle of change but as a result of the collision of separate events, each with its own independent cause. None of the events occurs because of any other, and there is no cause, no connected cause or explanation, for their simultaneity. Their conjunction is therefore not, properly speaking, an event. One example given is that of the man who goes to the market to buy something and happens to meet there a debtor who repays his loan. Aristotle argues that since the first man did not go to the market for the sake of recovering his money but rather for some other reason, the meeting with the debtor demonstrates a certain *failure* of final cause as explanatory principle: that which results occurs not for some purpose but *in vain*.[15] It is this notion of failure that Lacan will systematically explore, linking it to Aristotle's general assertion that accidental causes are indeterminate. In *The Four Fundamental Concepts,* Lacan says clearly, "Cause is to be distinguished from that which is determinate in a chain," and, a bit later, "Whenever we speak of cause . . . there is always something indefinite."[16]

Before we can understand Lacan's intervention, we must recall again the difficulties of Aristotle's argument. As we have said, what must be maintained is both the diversity of finite change and the eternity of change in general. The universe cannot be thought to stop and start without sacrificing this last requirement. We have also said that this dictates the solution of the doubling, in effect, of the cause of change. It also dictates the distinction between an underlying substance and its attributes, or properties. The substance is that which continues, remains the same, while the attributes register change by coming to be or falling away. The sentence "the uncultured man became a cultured man"[17] serves as illustration. Man, we see, is constantly present throughout the transformation in which the attribute of culture comes to replace its absence. The parts of natural substance must always be of this order; they must be qualities rather than mechanical parts, if the per se unity of the substance is to be safeguarded. (I need not add, I think, that the concept of underlying substance is the point of Lacan's attack.)

And yet at points, especially in the *De Motu Animalium,* when Aristotle attempts to detail a simple process of locomotion, this unity seems to break down, as the movement in a film breaks down when the projection is slowed. In order to make room for the Prime Mover (who must himself be unmoved), the description of physical movement is forced to take on a remarkably mechanistic tenor: "The origin of movement, qua origin, always remains at rest when the lower part of a limb is moved; for example, the elbow joint, when the forearm is moved, and the shoulder, when the whole arm; the knee when the tibia is moved, and the hip when the whole leg."[18] Things grow still worse when Aristotle places an instrument, specifically a stick, in the hand whose movement he contemplates. Seeking the "true original" of the stick's movement, the analysis makes its way up the arm joint by joint, rejecting each with the declaration that it is something "higher up" that can always initiate the motion even if each joint were to stiffen and thus each section of arm go rigid as the stick. The arm itself is in this way turned into an instrument.

It is to this passage, or some similar one, in which Aristotle determines the necessity of the Prime Mover on the basis of the corporeal experience of raising one's arm (the same experience that Bergson claims can only be grasped by intuition) that Lacan refers in his seminar on anxiety when he summarizes the classical philosophical position on the question of cause:[19] Seeing myself as self-moving (as *automatē*), I focus my attention on some appendage, my arm, say, which I can move at will. But once I have isolated my arm by considering it the intermediary between my wish and my act, it becomes necessary to modify the fact that, if it is an instrument, it is not free. It is necessary to ensure myself against the fact not of my arm's amputation immediately but of my losing control of it, of its coming under the power of another, or of my simply forgetting it—as if it were some common umbrella—in the metro. Paradoxically, I reassure myself that I maintain control over myself through one form of determinism or another. I hold to the belief that even in the absence of my conscious attention, my arm will move automatically, according to a whole system of involuntary reflexes or to an ultimate guiding presence.

In other words, the whole sum of the body functions, the entire corporeal presence, is assumed in order to maintain man's freedom of thought and will. But ironically this sum depends for its existence on our supposing the intervention of some supernatural power, some power beyond us: Aristotle's Prime Mover, Bergson's Spirit.

In opposition to this, Lacan argues that we think not as a consequence of our engagement with the totality of our bodily presence but rather as a consequence of the fact that "a structure carves up [man's] body. . . . Witness the hysteric."[20] Now, this plain hortatory may, I fear, prove misleading. For one thinks first of all of the vivid, visible symptoms of hysteria—the hystericization by which the body and its movements become an erotic spectacle: the passionate attitudes, the arcs of circle, the pregnancies. And by now, with the help of the theory of psychoanalysis, one recognizes "hysterogenic zones" as symptoms inscribed by language. The body is written, it is constructed by language and not pregiven; all the work on the "technologies of the body" have repeated this often enough. Lacan would not deny this—in fact, it is largely his theory that enables this position to be taken. Yet I would suggest that when Lacan tells us that language carves up the body, *"Witness the hysteric,"* he is speaking of a more unkind cut than that which merely carves *out* (or defines) a body image through which the subject will assume its being. The cut to which Lacan refers instead carves *up* (divides) the body image and thus drives the subject to seek its being beyond that which its image presents to it; it causes the subject always to find in its image something lacking. Lacan is asking us to witness the *paralyses* and *anesthesias* of the hysteric, those blind spots in consciousness, those spaces of inattention that mark the point where something is missing in the hysteric's image of herself. The fact that she is constructed by society's language means *to the hysteric* that part of her body will *not* be visible, or present to her. The inert limbs and the facial paralyses of the hysterics are testimonies of a cut too often ignored by those who would turn Lacan's theory into a linguistic or cultural determinism. Those who speak of the "invention of hysteria" as the pure imposition on the subject of an identity formed by the social neglect to consider that hysteria is conceived by psychoanalysis as a challenge to the subject's social identity: hysteria is the first analyzed instance of the subject's essential division, its questioning and refusal of social dictates.

We are now in a position to reconsider the matter of the *failure* of identity. Earlier, we cited the example of Beckett's five-man examining committee which fails infinitely in the exchange of looks that would establish its identity. Immediately we turned to Bergson's theory of laughter, which would account for the impossibility of the look's completion by its limitless segmentation. Indeed, the almost complete degeneration of movement in Beckett's fiction in general seems to result from its division into endless inventories of its exact spatial possibilities. The humor seems to result from the overly analytic attempt to grasp movement. Yet, at the outset of the Beckettian hero's trajectory, a desire is expressed that can be seen to impel the whole narrative machine. This desire gives us an entirely different understanding of the fiction's relation to failure. This desire is expressed by Murphy, who yearns, it is revealed, to participate in the bliss he imagines to be the hysteric's own: "And it would not surprise me if the great classic paralyses were to offer unspeakable satisfactions. To be literally incapable of motion at last, that must be something! And mute into the bargain! And just enough brain intact to allow you to exult!"[21]

It is this identification with the hysteric, more specifically with her paralyses, that yields the succession of heroes who slough off more and more of their bodies, their possessions, their positive existence, and approach asymptotically their own oblivion, without ever being able to reach it. Something always remains, uneffaceable. Let us now reconsider Zeno's paradox in its proper, psychoanalytic perspective. The immutable being in which Zeno believes is not, as Bergson maintains, the consequence of the illusion that our being is only equal to the "practical" or "abstract" definitions that languages imposes on it. It is the consequence, rather, of the illusion that part of our being resides beyond language's limits. For Lacan it is the being beyond, not the being within language, that is perceived as immutable, as the inert pound of flesh, the "inch of nature," which the blank in memory or sight signals as missing from our own self-image. The subject constructed by language finds itself detached from a part of itself. And it is this primary detachment that renders fruitless all the subject's efforts for a reunion with its complete being. The arc of its strivings appears to the subject as Zeno's arrow—an endlessly interrupted flight that can only asymptotically approach its goal. It is the cutting off of the subject from a part of itself, this part being the object-cause of its desire, that accounts for the cutting up of the subject's movements and the *reductio ad surdum,* that is, the reduction to infinite series of its replaceable objects. While Bergson argues that the Eleatic tradition errs by making the future, all time, present at once, and thus abolishing time, change, and succession, Lacanian psychoanalysis shows that, on the contrary, it is the nonpresence of the subject to its whole self that determines the formulation of the Eleatic paradoxes.

Bergson and Lacan are in agreement, however, on one point at least: they both oppose the logico-implicative notion of language. But while Bergson understands language according to this notion and thus attacks language for its tenselessness, for being able to derive consequence only as something already contained in a premise, Lacan takes the logico-implicative as a *mistaken* notion of language. His task becomes, then, the clarification of the way consequence *is,* in fact, derived from language. He will thus define the subject not as an effect contained within language but as a surplus product of it, the excess that language appears to cut off. Lacan will say, in short, that it is this missing part—this additional nothing—that *causes* the subject; the subject is created ex nihilo.[22]

This position could not be more directly opposed to that of Bergson, for whom, recall, duration (*dureé,* the name Bergson gives to his progressive temporality) is thought to "grow" out of all that precedes it. The process he describes is one of "intususception," in which the present is conceived not as something added to the past but as something incorporated into it. The present, and all that comes into being, depends absolutely on the existence of everything that comes before it. Nothing comes from nothing. For Bergson, nothing is simply a meaningless concept. There is no difference, he maintains, between thinking of something and thinking of it as existing. He believed, as many have, that existence is an attribute of all that can be thought. It is this assumption that must be discredited if one is to imagine creation ex nihilo.

Lacan, as we know, believed in the priority of social discourses, of language, over the subject. In referring to the signifying chain as *automaton,* he declares this belief in the fact that language "produces effects . . . in the absence of intention; [that] no intentions intervene to animate and fill up speech." As Derrida has written, the classical *condemnation* of the machine is a denial of this fact. Now, to say that language exceeds the intentions of the subject is to say that signifiers are opaque to intentions. But this opacity prohibits not only their being used for the communication of intentions, it also prohibits their reflection of an exterior reality. We have returned, then, to the place where we began, with the observation that a certain definition of the social being of language seems only to founder on this impasse, to trap us wholly in a socially constructed reality in which and with which we are bound to be happy. Or perhaps more simply, in which we are bound. For if we begin by assuming that the subject is the effect of a particular social organization in the sense of being a *realization* or *fulfillment* of its demand, then pleasure becomes a redundant concept and the need to theorize it is largely extinguished. It becomes merely the subjective synonym of the objective fact of the subject's construction. An exclusive reliance on the pleasure principle as the only available form of the subject's relation to the social ends in the elimination of the need for pleasure.

It is at this point that *delay*—that which prevents everything's being given at once—becomes a crucial concept in Lacan's argument, much as it was in Aristotle's and Bergson's. But whereas in Bergson delay is called on to refute the claims of language, to overturn it in favor of duration, in Lacan (following Freud) it is understood as prolonging the pleasures of language; it introduces the reality principle, which psychoanalysis defines as that which delays the pleasure principle, or which maintains desire beyond the threats of extinction presented by satisfaction. The death drive does not negate the pleasure principle, it extends it.

We have said that the opacity of signifiers means that language does not reveal a reality or truth behind them. This logic must now be extended to take note of the fact that this very opacity also guarantees that whatever reality or meaning is produced by them will never be able to convince us of its truth or completeness. *Since signifiers are not transparent, they cannot demonstrate that they are not hiding something behind what they say—they cannot prove that they do not lie.* Language can only present itself to the subject as a veil that cuts off from view a reality that is other than what we are allowed to see. To say that the mechanisms of language acquire a certain *organic elasticity*—recall the point on which Freud turned the Bergsonian argument against itself—is to say that in stretching beyond, or delaying, determinate meaning, language produces always something more, something indeterminate, some question of meaning's reliability. It is this question that suspends the automatic attribution of existence to everything that is thought and instead raises the possibility of conceiving nonexistence: nothing. Signification gives rise inevitably to doubt, to the possibility of its own negation; it enables us to think the annihilation, the full-scale destruction of our entire signified reality.

When, therefore, Lacan says that the subject is created ex nihilo, he acknowledges the fact that any statement prepares the possibility of its own negation, the fact that the pleasure principle (the subject's independence from fate) leads inexorably beyond itself, outstrips itself by producing doubt, which in turn produces the belief that there is a reality lying behind language. The subject can only question whether what it has been given to enjoy is truly what there is, or whether there isn't something missing in what has been offered. Desire is produced not as a striving for something but only as a striving for something else or something more. It stems from the feeling of our having been duped by language, cheated of something, not from our having been presented with a determinate object or goal for which we can aim. Desire has no content—it is for nothing—because language can deliver to us no incontrovertible truth, no positive goal.

The Lacanian aphorism—desire is the desire of the Other—is often taken to mean that the subject fashions itself in the image of the Other's desire. It is this that I have been taking as a problematic political position, but my particular interest is in the problem this position presents for feminism. For when this assumption is combined with the uncovering of a masculinist bias in the ordering of social relations, then woman can only be comprehended as a realization of male desires; she can only be seen to see herself through the perspective of a male gaze. Lacan's answer to this mistaken interpretation of his formula is simply that we have no image of the Other's desire (it remains indeterminate), and it is this very lack that causes our desire. It is first of all an *unsatisfied* desire that initiates our own, one that is not filled up with meaning, or has no signified. That that desire is *unsatisfiable* is a secondary truth resulting from this primary condition.

To all those who describe the subject as a fiction of extravagant prostheses, a prosthetic god manufactured by (and in the image of the desire of) a cultural order, we must now issue a reply. It is not the long arm of the law that determines the shape and reach of every subject, but rather something that escapes the law and its determination, something we can't manage to put our finger on. One cannot argue that the subject is constructed by language and then overlook the essential fact of language's duplicity, that is, the fact that whatever it says can be denied. This duplicity ensures that the subject will *not* come into being as language's determinate meaning. An incitement to discourse is not an incitement to being. What is aroused instead is the desire for nonbeing, for an *in*determinate something that is perceived as *extra*discursive. This indeterminate something (referred to by Lacan as object *a*) that causes the subject has historical specificity (it is the product of a specific discursive order), but no historical content. The subject is the product of history without being the fulfillment of a historical demand.

Achilles and the Tortoise

That Zeno's paradoxes are still relevant to any semiotically based theory of the subject is demonstrated in an important essay by Samuel Weber entitled "Closure and Exclusion."[23] Here Weber explores how an acceptance of the Saussurian dictum, "in language there are no positive terms, only differences," forces us to confront the specter of Zeno and the problem of infinite regress. For, once one breaks up the signifying chain, the statement, into a series of minimal units, of diacritical terms or signifiers that take their meaning only from their reference to another signifier, which in turn refers to another, and so on and on, and once this endless deferral is no longer considered to be grounded in some external reality (language being conceived as autonomous, as self-sustaining), we are obliged to wonder how it is possible to produce any statement at all. It would seem that this deferral would suspend meaning indefinitely. Intimidated by this problem of infinite and therefore de-determining regress, Saussure eventually retreated from his original path-breaking notion of pure difference and replaced it with a notion of determinate oppositions by isolating a moment within this process of deferral. That is, Saussure temporarily limited the differential play of signification to the moment of understanding, when the open-ended diachrony of the system was bracketed and a synchronic closure was supposed to be operative. The signifier, then, no longer awaited a future signifier that would give it meaning but received its value from a signifier with which it was co-present. Past *and* future, temporality and change dropped out of the system of signifiers that now were assumed to determine each other mutually, simultaneously.

Charles Sanders Peirce, Weber points out, could not be satisfied with such a solution and thus developed an alternative theory of signs that did not retreat from the belief that signification had to have a temporal dimension. As a result, Peirce was plagued throughout his life by the paradox of Achilles and the tortoise. How is it, he continued to ask himself, that a process of meaning's deferral can produce meaning; how does deferral overtake the limit that it can never reach? Peirce obtained a solution to this paradox by joining his "pragmaticism" to his semiotic investigation, that is, he came gradually to see that the other "sign" to which a sign addresses itself is "not entirely or simply some other *thought*" but entails as well "practical bearings," "effects that engage behavior." Pragmatic fact, then, leapfrogs over semiotic division, just as Achilles, despite the infinite, geometric division of his movements, does, in fact, overtake the tortoise. At first Peirce conceived these behavioral effects of language as "habit," but finally, feeling that an emphasis on habit would bring to a standstill the whole *process* that he took semiotics to be and would reduce thought to a kind of *automatism* ("something like Freud's repetition compulsion," Weber adds),[24] he settled instead on "habit-change" as the only possible ultimate sign and the only solution to Zeno's paradox.

Weber is quite right to note the similarities between this notion of habit-change and Derrida's notion of iteration, the continuous alteration and difference in which repetition results. What should be clear, however, from this discussion and the emphases we have given to it, is how dangerously similar habit-change and iteration can seem to be to those notions of self-change and perpetual novelty that support evolutionary philosophy's notion of the subject. This similarity does not escape the notice of Weber, who carefully tries to dissociate the subject of self-*division* implied by Peirce and Derrida from a notion of the self-present and self-*changing* subject that can be found in Bergson. But these dangerous similarities remain a threat, even if recognized here. The contamination of modern thought by Bergsonian evolutionism is so thorough that it often goes unnoticed and unquestioned. The Derridean notion of difference has, as a consequence, been employed all too often in support of an apolitical (naive) optimism regarding the inevitability of change: nothing can ever appear twice the same because the context that determines meaning is always different from the context of a moment before. The "subject-in-process" is often accorded this sense of perpetual and progressive self-changingness that gives the slip to the rigidifying structures of the social order.

The problem, however, is not *simply* a lack of vigilance or an abuse of Derridean theory. One can locate in Derrida himself, and in even the best of his interpreters, a certain leap in the argument:

> Does the absolute singularity of signature as event ever occur? Yes, of course, every day.[25]

> Having established as certain structural instability in the most powerful attempts to provide models of structuration, it was probably inevitable that Derrida should then begin to explore the other side of the coin, in fact that *undecidability notwithstanding,* decisions are *in fact* taken, power *in fact* exercised, traces *in fact* instituted.[26]

The fact or effect (the signature effect, the institution effect, the subject effect) is posited, then, in the face of and against ("the other side of the coin") the deferral installed by semiotic difference, but—and this is strikingly the case—the mechanism by which these effects take effect is never foregrounded and always remains obscure. A symptomatic silence installs itself time and again. Take, for example, Derrida's critique of J. L. Austin's theory of speech acts. While Derrida rightfully deconstructs the contention that the performative depends on a determinable context, he safeguards, in the end, Austin's major premise: words do (and do not merely describe) things. They construct subjects, produce signatures. Yes, but how? Similarly, in "Closure and Exclusion," for all the astuteness of his arguments concerning Peirce's solution of the paradox that afflicts his theory, Weber curiously fails to link up successively the various points of Peirce's intervention: *semiotic,* in which the linguist posits the notion of a community without limits in place of Saussure's temporally defined "collective consciousness"; *pragmatic,* in which he supplements thought, or reason, with purposeful behavior, and *phenomenological,* in which he introduces the notion of a real that is not at the disposal of human thought. This last, which Peirce calls "secondness," defines the realm of cause and thus indicates that he did not believe cause was conceptual. Despite the lucidity with which Weber discusses all three points, one cannot help feeling that he never explains how the paradox is solved. This failure is not to be ascribed to Weber's carelessness but is symptomatic of the fact that Derridean theory cannot *but* encounter an obstacle to the formulation of this solution.

This obstacle, I would suggest, is precisely its commitment to deconstruction, to the undoing of every totality, to betraying the illusory character of the whole. A notion of the whole, deconstruction would have us believe, always disguises the infinite play of difference. During the period in which this Derridean tenet was embraced by film theory, for example, the closure of "mainstream cinema" was denegrated as ideologically compromised, while the disruption of every spatial, aural,

or narrative continuity was automatically celebrated as politically progressive. What this gross dichotomy was incapable of conceiving was a
more complex notion of closure and totality that was not simply illusory
and that, far from suppressing difference, was the very condition of its
possibility. This unthinkable notion is the very basis of the solution to
Zeno's paradox: only a closed totality can be considered infinite; only a
limit guarantees that the production of meaning will continuously be
subject to revision, never ending. Rather than baring the device of difference behind the illusion of totality, Lacanian theory reverses these terms
and shows the infinite play of difference to be dependent on a limit, a
closed totality. In order to assert this truth, Lacan continuously resorts to
the paradoxes of Zeno to make the same claim that Peirce himself made:
"To the extent that a number has a limit, it is infinite. Clearly, Achilles
can only overtake the tortoise, he cannot catch up with her. He rejoins
her only in infinity."[27]

The paradox derives from a definition of the whole such that one
of its essential features is its superiority to its parts.[28] The fallacy of this
reasoning rests on its forgetting the limit toward which Achilles pro-
gresses. The series of his steps is thus not a diverging, but a converging
series; the set to which they belong is, in other words, closed. It is the
closure of the set that gives rise to the performative dimension, allowing
Achilles to *overtake* the tortoise, to *overcome* the impasse of the diverging
series she represents. The performative cannot come into existence without this internal limit.

Subsequent chapters will explore the way Lacan develops and
makes use of this paradoxical logic of the whole within his psychoanalytic
theory—the theories of suture, of groups, of sexual difference, all emerge
from this logic. For the moment, however, we want only to note one
difference between Lacan and Derrida on this point. Lacan allows us to
see that the Derridean deconstruction of the subject errs by conflating the
infinity of the subject's desire with the subject itself. The psychoanalytical
subject is not infinite, it is *finite,* limited, and it is this limit that causes

the infinity, or unsatisfiability, of its desire. One thing comes to be substituted for another in an endless chain only because the subject is cut off from that essential thing that would complete it.

Cause and the Law

Although Lacan's position must be differentiated from others with which it has been confused, it should not be seen as simply idiosyncratic, for it shares many insights with other current theories of cause.

The dominant philosophical position, held for some time, was that cause is implied by an invariable sequence or the constant conjunction of events ruled by a covering law. Causal explanations were thought to establish a formally determinable, deductive relation between statements describing the effect to be explained, the initial (causal) conditions, and a law allowing the deduction of the former from the latter. It is to this position that Lacan refers in *The Four Fundamental Concepts of Psychoanalysis* when he says that his concept of cause is to be distinguished from that which sees it as *law*. He gives as an example of that to which his theory is opposed the invariable sequence or constant conjunction of action and reaction, whose covering law, as we know, was defined by Newton.[29]

In recent years much effort has gone into contesting the covering-law theory of cause. Some of the most fruitful efforts have, ironically, been inspired by Aristotle. For although Aristotle maintained that a substance's nature was revealed only through specific or typical sorts of changes, he did acknowledge that atypical changes could be described. These were thought to be due to a mere interference with the natural course of things and to give, therefore, no information about the substance's nature. Nevertheless, Aristotle does lend considerable attention to these interferences and, in fact, ends up defining voluntary movement— say, once again, the lifting of one's arm —*negatively,* in terms of the absence of interference or of "excusing circumstances." He thus devotes a lot of space to the examination and full description of the context of an event and the excuses that contribute to the *failure* of natural change to be exhibited by cause.

In 1956, J. L. Austin was able to create a philosophical stir by writing ceremoniously and approvingly of this fascination with failure for which Aristotle had so long been chided.[30] A few years later, two of Austin's colleagues at Oxford, H. L. A. Hart and A. Honoré, published *Causation in the Law,*[31] a work which has, through its detailed attention to context and failure, proved to be extremely influential in the development of theories of causality that connect cause not to law but to failure. The book offers convincing arguments against "the doctrine that the generalizations of law which it is the business of experimental sciences to discover, constitute the very essence of the notion of causation." It also offers an indictment (though by no means centrally or extensively considered) of the bodily metaphor—of the experience of exerting bodily pressure or force on an object in order to move it—which Hart and Honoré assume to underlie the notion of cause that their book repudiates. It is because of this underlying and unanalyzed metaphor, they argue, that cause comes to be conceived as a positive force and nonevents, accidents, and failures are eliminated from consideration as possible causes.

Causation in the Law makes the basic distinction between conditions or occasions, the normal and inconspicuous factors surrounding effects, and cause itself, conceived as a deviation from normal circumstances, as something that goes wrong and thus stands in need of explanation. By way of illustration, Hart and Honoré offer the example of a fire breaking out.[32] Normally one would refuse to attribute the cause of the fire to the presence of oxygen, though certainly no fire can occur without it. One looks for cause, rather, in some abnormal circumstance, in something that has gone wrong.

Even this summary description of their argument should be sufficient to suggest ways in which Lacan can be seen to share and improve on the insights of Hart and Honoré.

1. Lacan also focuses on the bodily metaphor that underlies a particular conception of cause, but he makes this metaphor more central to his theory and demonstrates why it is invalid. The body in Lacan is more clearly a symbolic construct that is never fully complete.

2. Lacan makes failure independent of the static and problematic norm/deviation distinction.

3. By making the questions that require us to seek after cause arise not from the subject but from the materiality of language, Lacan eliminates the psychologism that plagues all (including Hart and Honoré's) conflations of cause and explanation.

The principle of sufficient reason, the belief that everything must have a cause, is absolutely central to the psychoanalytic project, which would have been inconceivable before the historical assertion of this principle. Yet psychoanalysis is just as intimately tied to the belief that the cause which must necessarily exist is never present in the field of consciousness that it effects.

G. G. de Clérambault was a well-known and respected French psychiatrist who, through his concept of mental automatism, completely revised our notion of psychosis and disassembled the category of effort or will upon which the study of the psyche had been based since the beginning of the nineteenth century. Yet, immediately after his death in 1934, the newspapers saluted his memory by publishing "a handful of hasty and inaccurate gossip."[1] Reporting, above all, an "astonishment"—at his "taste for rare cloth, Indian, madras, Oriental fabric brocaded with gold and silver" and at his possession of the several wax mannequins that were found in his home, a journalistic fantasy fashioned Clérambault as a "new Caligari."[2] The gossip ended only when interest in him waned.

Interest in Clérambault—whom Jacques Lacan once hailed as his "only master"[3]—has recently reawakened, but not without raking up at the same time all the old smirky astonishment, the old fantasy of the public figure with a very private perversion. Catherine Clément, for example, in her *Lives and Legends of Jacques Lacan,* feels justified in summarizing Clérambault as "a rather unusual psychiatrist who was mad about fabrics and woolens,"[4] and a few years ago, the book *La passion des étoffes chez un neuro-psychiatre*[5] was published, treating us, at last, to a documentary look at this eponymous passion.

The case of *La passion des étoffes* is instructive. What the book does is intersperse several "speculative" essays with documentary evidence of Clérambault's passion; fragments of lectures, case studies, obituaries, and a number of photographs are all exhibited to the reader. But despite this documentary alibi, one cannot fail to see that it is around what is not—and, it is suggested, *cannot*—be placed in evidence that the book ultimately turns. Although the essays by the editors are, ostensibly, attempts to analyze the data, they seem to delight in posing many more questions than they answer: Clérambault, dispassionate observer or impassioned fetishist? Aesthete or man of the world? His suicide, was it motivated by his failing sight, dwindling finances, or rising insanity? A swarm of questions form the obscure center of each aspect of Clérambault's life; they indicate the limit points of our knowledge. Conspicuously, it is the unfortunate loss of so much of the record (lectures never published, witnesses never located) that makes these questions unanswerable, but one senses that there is an underlying presumption that no amount of documentation, however extensive, will ever resolve them. For it is the very undecidability of any and all evidence that is at the core of this particular construction of Clérambault that we will now title the "psychological" construction.

Confronted by the possibility of any fact's being able to provide proof not only of a specific psychological intention but also of its contrary, unable to extract from any single or mass of facts a guarantee about our suspicions about the person these facts surround, the psychological fantasy supposes a subject behind the facts who has unique access to his or her own psychological intentions, who uniquely knows by virtue of being the living experience of those intentions. The psychological fantasy constructs an *inscrutable* subject, a kind of obstacle to all archival work, a question that historical research will never be able to answer.

This psychological construction is one that psychoanalysis sets out to disperse, its primary target being the supposed subject of knowledge. Against this supposition psychoanalysis argues not that we can ultimately penetrate what had previously seemed the unfathomable secret of the subject but that there is nothing to fathom; the subject has no secret knowledge, or, to quote the famous Hegelian quip: the Egyptian secrets were also secret from the Egyptians themselves.[6] What does this mean in the terms of our argument so far? Psychoanalysis, like the psychological fantasy, acknowledges that no fact is unequivocable. This is so because no fact exists outside a signifying chain and no signifier is unequivocable.

All photographs in this chapter by G. G. de Clérambault, courtesy Musée de l'homme, Paris.

And since this is so, psychoanalysis reasons, the subject, affected by the facts of its life, is affected by meanings that it never lives, never experiences. This is what psychoanalysis means when it speaks of the overdetermination of the subject: the subject is subject to the equivocations of the signifier. It is for this reason that Freud was led to defend constructions of analysis, those analytic imagining of events that affected the subject even though they never happened *as such,* were never experienced and thus could never be remembered *as such.*

Needless to say, not only will the subject be unable to bear direct witness to such constructed events, no other such witness or document will ever be found to perform this task either. This does not mean that psychoanalysis renounces history to maintain a truth that no history can uncover. Psychoanalysis requires history; it can begin only by gathering the facts. What it renounces is what we can now term the "historicist" construction. Historicism is faulted not because it is, in fact, not possible to recreate historical experience (this is, again, a psychologistic objection), but because this construction operates with the belief that it is *experience* that must be recreated, that the truthful and logical statements we make about a historical period are empirical generalizations about the ways in which people thought. A new historicism has, in recent years, provided detailed accounts of the everyday life of the *pathological* subject,[7] but it has been unable to account for, or describe the everyday life of, the subject inasmuch as it resists this reduction to the pathological. We know now, more concretely than every before, what goods men and women of various classes were supposed to find pleasurable, which of these were denied them, which allowed, and how the inequalities in the distribution of goods affected the actions of these men and women. We learn nothing, however, of the historical effects of the fact that men and women often act to avoid pleasure, to *shun* these goods.

Having stated these distinctions, I would like to return to the case of Clérambault to see if history will allow us to dislodge the fantasmatic notion of his "nasty secret" that is even now being revived. At the literal center of this fantasy (i.e., reproduced in the middle of *La passion des étoffes*) is a series of photographs that Clérambault took between 1914 and 1918 while he was in Morocco recuperating from a war wound. During these years in Morocco Clérambault learned Arabic and began a study of Arab dress; these photographs are obviously a part of that study.

The photographs, in other words, were taken at the very height of the "golden age" of French colonialism. Our postcolonialist knowledge of this fact and of this historical period is relied on to form the backdrop of the current revival of the Clérambault "scandal." *La passion des étoffes* offers constant invocations of familiar Orientalist myths, but it neither clarifies Clérambault's relation to them nor deconstructs them. Thus, the image of exotic sexuality these myths create becomes something Clérambault vaguely "participated" in. The historical period is so sketchily recalled and so underexamined that it cannot be conceived to wield any real determining force.

If we, on the other hand, would like to delineate the relation between the photographs and French colonialism, its *production* of myths, we might best begin by comparing Clérambault's to other photographs that have been exhibited as emblematic of this production. In *The Colonial Harem,* for example, postcards of Algerian women are narratively ordered as a kind of striptease, though the running commentary argues, of course, that the stripping is performed by the colonialist gaze acting out a will to knowledge and power that had been temporarily obstructed by the women's veils.[8] In the light of this very familiar scenario of the colonialist project, Clérambault's photographs might seem to exemplify a sort of failure of the "will to unwrap," an unaccountable defaulting of desire or halting at the initial stages of the complete sexual scenario. Although there is a clear difference between Clérambault's and these other photographs, the terms of this difference, I will argue, are not these. Nor should the mere recognition of this difference, of this discrepancy between our expectations and the photographs themselves, be used to sustain the psy-

chologistic argument: that the very opacity of the images indicates the opacity of the man who took them—his idiosyncratic passion for cloth.

Colonies and Colonnades

In opposition to this, I will claim that this passion was not a purely idiosyncratic phenomenon but one conditioned by historical circumstances, and I will begin, then, my historical investigation by focusing on the year 1923. This was the year that Clérambault began a series of courses—which would go on regularly until 1926—at the Ecole des Beaux-Arts. As a renowned psychiatrist and spellbinding teacher, Clérambault thrived in the atelier mode of the Ecole; his were the most popular courses offered.[9] The subject of these courses was—drapery. Clérambault would arrive at the lecture hall carrying a valise from which he would pull out wax dolls and a variety of cloths with which he would, during the course of the lecture, drape the dolls. He would often also use live models—whom he would drape with the same materials and whom he would ask to execute certain movements of the arms or body—in order to demonstrate his points.

The next question, of course, arises automatically: what were these points? It is here that the record is most wanting, for the Beaux-Arts lectures were never published. But two addresses made to the Société d'Ethnographic were published, and they provide important clues to the historical dimension of his fascination with fabric. In one of these addresses, Clérambault demonstrated that a characteristic North African manner of fastening cloth, a ligature, was, in fact, also used by classical Greeks and Romans and was reproduced in their sculpture.[10] Before his discovery, this fastening of the tunic was incorrectly interpreted as a fibula. In addition, Clérambault was able conclusively to demonstrate, by pointing to a marginal thickness in some of the bas-reliefs at the Louvre, that scalloped hems existed in Greek drapery. This finding directly contradicted the pronouncements of the most prominent scholar of antique costumes, who had been formally denying that Greeks used hems.[11] In the resume of the second article, we are given a clearer sense of the larger outlines of Clérambault's ambitious ethnographic project.[12] The nature and originality of this project is indicated by one of his contemporary defenders: "Clérambault," he insisted, "was the first to consider the flowing folds of clothes as the signature of a race, a tribe. He conducted his research on Assyrian tunics, Greek chlamys, Roman togas, Arab cloth. He studied their curve and their sense; he made them speak."[13] Although this project may seem from our vantage point dismissably bizarre, an absolute novelty, it was, as we shall see, consonant with a range of concerns of the Ecole des Beaux-Arts.

Every year the Ecole set a different project for the Grand Prix competition; in 1923, the year Clérambault began his course on drapery, the project was a residence for the representative of France in Morocco.[14] Once, in 1862, in a very famous incident, the Ecole had been attacked for specifying in the program, and awarding the prize to, a design rendered in the classical style, even though the project was a palace for the governor of Algeria, for which many thought an indigenous Islamic style would have been more appropriate.[15] But in 1923 the Ecole still steadfastly favored the classical style, which it had so long championed and so "magnanimously" disseminated throughout France and its colonies.

There is no doubt that the Beaux-Arts obsession with classical architecture and sculpture sprang, in part, from its conviction that Greece and Rome represented the imperial origins of France's high degree of civilization, or that this myth of origins helped propel France's imperialist, civilizing mission. No doubt that the transposition of neoclassical architecture to the sites that had become the *goals* of this mission euphemized the brutal process of the erasure of the colonies' own beginnings. Nor is there any doubt that Clérambault's lectures and photographs assisted this process. Moroccan drapery was not merely being used to reinterpret classical sculpture, classical sculpture was also being used to reinterpret Moroccan drapery—to reinvent it for the West. But this superficial de-

scription of the relation between an interest in drapery and the advance of colonialism not only leaves much about this relation and about Clérambault's photographs unexplained, it also simplifies the notion of origins that operated in this context.

It is necessary to pinpoint, then, what I take to be a more fundamental beginning for our understanding of the photographs; it is Clérambault's succinct pronouncement that "a draped costume must be defined by the scheme of its construction."[16] At the end of the lecture in which this pronouncement is delivered, Clérambault notes that this mode of definition "leaves open" the question of genesis, but by this point in the presentation we will have noticed that description of drapery in terms of its structure or construction actually vacates this question; his mode of analysis *replaces* description of the genesis or the sensuous or symbolic characteristics of costume. Clérambault will attempt to correlate a description of dress with a description of national identity on the basis of a relatively new manner of describing clothing type. My claim is not only that Clérambault's passion for cloth was a passion (in some measure) socially shared but also that it was a residue of the revolution in the definition of "type."

Let us, by way of explanation, take up the discussion again where we left off, with the year 1923. This was the year that Le Corbusier's *Towards a New Architecture* was published, along with its critique of the Ecole des Beaux-Arts. It might seem that by beginning his lectures at the very moment when Le Corbusier and other modernists were making the Ecole an anachronism, Clérambault was showing himself to be merely "an adept lingerer in [the] nineteenth century."[17] spouting an ideology and participating in a project whose end had already arrived. But in terms of one matter at least, modernism must be considered the *culmination* or a *variation* of (rather than the break from) the Beaux-Arts tradition; this matter is the appropriate manner of characterizing buildings.

Far more fundamental than the differences between the modernism Le Corbusier represented and the academicism he attacked was the

rupture introduced at the beginning of the nineteenth century by a completely new notion of building type, one that would operate continuously
not only throughout the century but also throughout modernism. One
architectural historian has dramatized this rupture by contrasting a classification of buildings written in the middle of the eighteenth century
with one written at the beginning of the nineteenth. The first, taken from
Jacques-François Blondel's *Cours d'architecture,* lists these architectural
genres: "Light, elegant, delicate, rustic, naive, feminine, grandiose, au-
dacious, terrible, dwarfish, frivolous, licentious, uncertain, vague, bar-
baric, cold, poor, sterile or futile"; the second, from J.-N. L. Durand's
Collection and Parallel of Buildings of Every Genre, Ancient and Modern, offers
a much different list: "Amphitheaters, aqueducts, triumphal arches, . . .
baths, bazaars, belltowers, libraries, . . . colleges, . . . granaries, grottoes,
. . . villas, markets, . . . pagodas, palaces, . . . light houses."[18] Between
the first list and the second, there has clearly been a revolution in thinking
building kinds. Adjectives providing sensuous description of a building,
its character or physiognomy, are surrendered and replaced by nouns
designating a building's *use;* at the beginning of the nineteenth century,
for the first time in history, a building's nature is thought to reside not
in its relation to some primitive or ideal form, not in its symbolic value,
but in its function. From this point on, utility will define architectural
type, and all questions of form, construction, and ornamentation will
refer themselves to and resolve themselves according to the dictates of
use.

The isolation of utility as the essential parameter of a building's
definition resulted not only in the assigning to style and ornament the
task of *expressing* this essential definition, of linking themselves to use, it
resulted as well in the underlying assumption that obliged this task:
namely, that style and ornament were separate from and secondary to
function. It is at this point that style and ornament began to be considered
precisely as *clothing;* their connection to the building, in other words, was
taken as arbitrary rather than necessary, and they were thus viewed, for

the first time, as the wrapping or covering of an otherwise nude building. It was, of course, their altogether inessential status that made them vulnerable to the obsessive economy that ruled functionalism—ornament was eventually banished as crime, and stylistic eclecticism (the borrowing of styles from different historical periods) was outlawed by architecture's cultivation of a new indifference to all history except that of the building's own process of construction; style, in short, disappeared as an independent entity as it merged with construction. Functionalism, in the form of architectural purism, peaked, then, in a rending of clothing. Nevertheless, between this conclusion and the early nineteenth-century introduction of utility as the criterion of classification, fabric was for architecture not only an issue passionately pursued but a concept that owed its very existence to that of utility.

Eschewing any discussion of the symbolic power of cloth, focused instead on its construction, its articulation of structural and functional elements, Clérambault would not have been out of place in the architectural world of the 1920s. Clothing style (Moroccan, Greek, Roman) had for him, it is clear, no existence apart from the structure of clothing's technical composition. Drapery is defined as what it does. Clérambault divided and subdivided the "scheme of [the drapery's] construction" into basic elements whose combination determined the costume's appropriate classification. Three orders of elements are noted: (1) the principle point of support (the head, neck, shoulders, etc.); (2) the movement of the cloth from this point; and (3) the zones of the body covered and the various means of fastening, twisting, and folding the cloth.[19] The awkward and unnatural poses of the figures in many of the photographs attest to Clérambault's determination to analyze the articulation of these elements. In the photographs and in the written reports, description remains fixed on this matter of technical form charged, ultimately, with the carrying out of a specific function: the wrapping of the body or (as Clérambault says of head drapery in one of the rare moments when his commentary goes beyond the dry tabulation of minute differences and myriad combinations) protection against the sun or against the weight of various burdens.

Now, while this focus on the union of utility and construction may partially account for the Moroccan photographs—especially those in which the form of the clothed body is visible—it does not yet fully account for them. Those in which the bodily form has completely disappeared retain their enigmatic quality, for what is thus obscured in these cases is the very prop on which the drapery's purpose hangs. And though his desire for scientific exactitude—his stated fear that photographs taken without an analytic goal will fail to register all the components of the cloth's structure—may explain why Clérambault took a great number of photographs of draped costumes, few will feel that it justifies his taking 40,000 of them!

Guilty versus Useful Pleasures

Corbusier once noted that in French the word *type* has a double sense; it refers not only to a kind—of building, say—but also to a man: a *type* is a "man." But it was more than this pun that allowed him to argue that

> from the point that the type becomes a man, we grasp the possibility of a considerable extension of the type. [This is] because the man-type is a complex form of a unique physical type, to which can be applied a sufficient standardization. According to the same rules one will establish for this physical type an equipment of standard habitation.[20]

What makes these statements possible is the historical fact that at the very moment when buildings were being reclassified according to their use, man was undergoing a similar reclassification. Sensations had ceased not only to provide the basic facts about buildings, they had also ceased to be seen as the basic facts of the mind that considered these buildings. The

rise of the industrial regime initiated a privileging of "the industrious character of the human species"[21] that resulted in utility's becoming a *psychological* as well as an architectural principle. This meant that effort or *will* (rather than sensation) would henceforth be taken as the basic fact of the human mind and man himself would be seen as a tool, his vocation "to be set in his place and to be set to work,"[22] like a machine. Man was seen as that being who directs himself toward work, not, as was formerly thought, toward contemplation.[23] This led to a kind of externalizing of the psyche, for this meant that the mind could not apprehend itself directly, but rather perceived itself reflected in the traces left behind by its efforts. This definition of man was thus well suited to empiricism.

And in the human sphere, as in the architectural, this redefinition occasioned considerable attention to questions of clothing.[24] Before the debut of industrialization, clothing had been an important indicator of social status; it had served to mark the division of classes into distinct groups. But once "man" became vested with a functional definition, the old vestiary regime collapsed and man was submitted to a new one. Sartorial distinctions among men were abolished, and all classes accepted a uniformity and simplification of style. The egalitarianism that defined the political agenda of the day and permitted man to define himself through his work rather than his birth was thus evidenced in the leveling and unmarking of his clothing.

But we must be careful to note that it was, in fact, specifically *man* (and not actually mankind) who was defined by his labor, and that he alone was required to choose his wardrobe by its fitness for work. Woman, on the other hand, came at this same time to be subjected to a new, modern notion of fashion: the rapid and seasonal renewal of clothing before any functional wearing out. From the middle of the nineteenth century and into the twentieth, the image of the modern woman was defined and redefined several times over by the vicissitudes of vestiary codes. While the image of man remained steady and stable, hers was constantly reshaped behind the accelerated changes of clothing styles.

This modern history of clothing is detailed most famously in a book called *The Psychology of Clothing,* written in 1930 by J. C. Flugel. This book is best known for its designation and analysis of "the great masculine renunciation"—by which man surrendered the field of fashion to women and came to occupy, instead, that of function. What has, however, received little attention is the following corollary of this renunciation: "In sartorial matters," Flugel writes, "modern man, because of his devotion to principles of duty, has a far sterner and more rigid conscience than modern woman."[25] Now, what is to account for this surging up of the superego in the sartorial field? What is the logic of this encounter between ethics and dress? Flugel's surprising observation depends on there being a connection between duty and dress, while we have so far discussed only the relation between dress and *function* or *use.* Though it is clear that the equation of man's plain and uniform costume (his functional attire) with his stern and rigid conscience hinges on our accepting use and duty as equivalent, it is also clear to us that *duty* has an ethical sense that *use* does not, at least not necessarily. So either his argument is simply sleight of hand, or *use* had acquired, at the time Flugel wrote, a sense that was ethical. The latter turns out to be the case. The sleight of hand is demonstrably historical.

We now know how Freud must have felt when in *Civilization and Its Discontents* he complained that the discussion of the superego spoiled the framework of his paper, for all of a sudden it seems that our previous discussion has implicated us in an ethical dimension that has so far gone unacknowledged. Looking back, we see that one concept in particular—that of pleasure—has been elided, and yet this is precisely the concept that presided over the conversion of functional issues into issues of morality. Let me illustrate:

Having made the historical claim that an ethics of clothes must proceed by evaluating their function, Flugel spells out in bold what their ultimate function must be: "to secure the maximum of satisfaction in accordance with the 'reality principle.'"[26] In this case, it turns out that the reality principle is that principle that allows us to abandon a false, narcissistic pleasure in favor of the true pleasure that only a love of others can bring. It turns out, in other words, that Flugel's reality principle is a principle of (maximum) pleasure.

We began, you remember, by citing the work of Durand. In architecture it is he who is credited with inaugurating the redefinition of type in terms of use. Turning to his famous *Précis des lécons d'architecture,* we stumble almost immediately over a statement that will now be impossible to disregard: "In all times and in all places, the entirety of man's thoughts and actions have had their origin in two principles: the love of well-being and the aversion to every sort of pain."[27] Well, then, does man's construction of architecture, like everything else, have its origins in the principles of pleasure and pain; or does it originate, as we said earlier, in the principle of use? Durand answers economically that it originates in both, and he thereby erects modern architecture on the same equation that Jeremy Bentham used to formulate his utilitarianism.

Durand may not have wavered, as Bentham did, on the question of whether to call his founding precept the principle of utility or the principle of pleasure, but he was far from dismissive about the necessity of pleasure in architecture. Contrary to all the criticism that we have heard about the failure of functionalism, or modernism, to consider the importance of pleasure, it would be more accurate to say that pleasure was from the beginning taken as fundamental—*as long as it could be used.* To state it in this way, however, is to give too much away too soon. Durand did not start out from the proposition that pleasure is usable; he began his *Précis* instead with the assumption that use is pleasurable. His argument is essentially this: because we seek pleasure, we therefore seek to surround ourselves with useful things, since they alone can and do necessarily provide us with pleasure—or, at least, with the only pleasure worth considering. For, in fact, there is more than one pleasure in Durand's text, though only one is accepted as legitimate, the other is discounted as a false pleasure.

Like Bentham, Durand attempts to justify his principle of utility by imagining its subversion. Putting us in mind of the Venus de Medicis and the Farnese Hercules, he conjures up a person who thinks the head of one is more graceful than that of the other and who thus places the head of Venus on the body of Hercules and vice versa.[28] The result, he says, would be ridiculous. It is easy to see that the strategy here is to make the alternative to utility seem as self-evidently stupid as possible, to reduce it to an absurdity. It is also easy to see that this argument for functionalism relies on our having already accepted the necessity and appropriateness of familiar, finished forms. In fact, we can say that our belief in functionalism follows from our belief in total form, that *it is only by imagining a determinate goal or form than utility can even be thought.*

Bentham's defense of utility proceeds in a similar way. The alternatives to utility are presented as purely destructive *or* as purely capricious. Finally, however, Bentham argues that all alternative principles are one, all—he says, using a term that coalesces the two sorts of objections— are "despotic."

One of the virtues of Lacan's seminar on ethics is that it allows us to see Bentham's charge as an instance of the kettle calling the despot black. Like Durand, Bentham begins descriptively, with the observation that man finds use pleasurable. Man seeks those things that are most useful in maximizing his own pleasure and minimizing his own pain. Bentham then converts this description of what is into a prescription of what should be: pleasure, he says, must be maximized and pain minimized. We must convert man's self-interest into dutiful commitment to the common good—the greatest happiness for the greatest number. The maximization of pleasure becomes a duty. Society can be held together only if men can be made to sacrifice their immediate, local gratifications for longer-term and greater ones. Now, it is precisely this maneuver that occasions the attack by Lacan, who sees it as the source of utilitarianism's unethical "penchant for expansion";[29] and, in similar vein, Jacques-Alain

Miller will later describe this maneuver as part of the "despotism" of utility.[30]

These attacks on utilitarianism find immediate support in already familiar observations. We understand to what Lacan and Miller refer when we recall that colonialism was the historical partner of functionalism's rise. We think of the "extensive benevolence" of industrialized nations, the "civilizing mission," the desire to dispense "charity and humanity" that carried imperialism forward. We picture the "international style" as the attempt panoptically to house the whole world under the same roof. But the Lacanian critique of utilitarianism goes beyond these standard observations by locating the mainspring of use's elasticity in its allied principle of pleasure. Lacan's seminar on ethics allows us to see at work beneath utilitarianism's proposition that use is pleasurable a second proposition: pleasure is usable. It is because it imagines that it can place pleasure in the service of the common good, the social whole, that utilitarianism becomes (1) so much a matter of technique, and (2) so extensible.

Once it was decided that the goal of man was known (that goal being pleasure), utilitarianism thought it could regulate and manipulate man through this goal, or motivation. The belief that man is basically and infinitely manageable turned the utilitarian into an engineer, a designer of machines that would quadrate man's pleasure with his duty. It is surely this entangled belief that troubled Corbusier's previously cited sentences. While the designer of "machines for living" was arguing that buildings must be tailored for man's use, he was simultaneously saying that man himself could be tailored by building. The social project of functionalism (Le Corbusier's "revolution or architecture") was, like that of utilitarianism, based on the notion that man was fundamentally *ruly*. Le Corbusier's own words accurately state the precondition of functionalism's utopian agenda: "the possibility of a considerable extension of the *type*."

Bentham's derivation of ethics from a descriptive psychology is often described as the derivation of *ought* from *is*. It now seems more fitting to say that, in utilitarianism, *ought* is derived from *ought*. The

imperative to extend benevolence infinitely stems from the notion that
man can be counted as zero. Defined as essentially pleasure seeking, he
becomes total compliance. For, once his motive is established, his manip-
ulability is assured. The ambitious imperialism of functionalism does not
expect to encounter resistance. Since it arrives bearing what man wants—
happiness—it expects its subjects to submit to its embrace. For this reason,
French colonialism adopted a policy of "assimilation."

Lacan's seminar should be read not only as a critique of utilitarianism but also of the "liberal" criticisms aimed at functionalism and
utilitarianism. The problem is not simply that it is presumptious to think
we know what another man—a colonial subject, for example—wants,
because only he can know that for himself. Nor can we say that the
problem is that man is *more* than the rationalist engineers will allow. Lacan
does not begin by adding qualities, filling out the picture of man, but
rather by noting that man is, in a manner, *less* than the utopians realize.
What makes him less is the fact that he is radically separated from, and
cannot know, what he wants. The difference between the utilitarian and
the Lacanian subject is the difference between zero and minus one, between a subject who is driven to seek the maximization of his pleasure
in his own greater good, and a subject for whom pleasure cannot function
as an index of the good, since the latter is lost to him. The psychoanalytic
subject, in short, being subject to a principle *beyond* pleasure, *is not driven
to seek his own good*. This obliges psychoanalysis to reformulate its ethics
on the basis of another principle, that of the death drive. This Freud does,
adducing the superego from the collapse of utilitarian logic. He begins
"The Economic Problem of Masochism" (1924) with one of his charac-
teristically concise and devastating observations: if the *aim* of life were
the obtaining of pleasure and the avoidance of pain, then the pleasure
principle itself would become dysfunctional, and masochism, including
the "moral masochism" that rules our ethical conduct, would be incomprehensible. This reasoning is extended in *Civilization and Its Discontents,*
where Freud founds the superego not on some "oceanic" impulse to merge

our destiny with the destiny of others (i.e., to seek our happiness in the happiness of all), but in the horrified *recoil* from this impulse, in the moral revulsion it elicits in us.

Beyond the Good Neighbor Principle

We can most profitably pursue the psychoanalytic critique of utilitarianism by returning simultaneously to our discussion of Clérambault and his Moroccan photographs. We were, recall, troubled by the fact that our account of the historical privileging of utility did not generate an adequate description of the photographs; too much was left unexplained. What was it that thwarted our project?

In 1924, immediately after beginning his Beaux-Arts course in drapery, Clérambault published his first—and, basically, definitive—description of what he called *mental automatism*.[31] He was, almost from the beginning, uncomfortable with the term, which he treated as a kind of found object. For a while he simply abbreviated it to "A.M.," but eventually he substituted a term of his own invention, *syndrome of passivity,* which he in turn abbreviated to "S." Yet, if Clérambault did first think through his theory under the borrowed term, this is because it designated the key concept of French psychiatry at the time he wrote, and his thought—however much it would diverge from that of his contemporaries—was initiated by the problem this concept signaled.

In the nineteenth century, as we have said, mind was defined as will, in the sense of effort, or work. This definition reversed the supposed relation between the body and the mind. Where formerly man had been understood as "an intelligence served by organs," he was now understood as "a living organization served by an intelligence."[32] The mind was primarily something that served—it became an instrument with a function. But once it had, through this definition, brought the mind more in line with a machine, psychiatry was very quickly beleaguered by doubts and questions about where to draw the boundaries *between* mind and

machine. It is this still-troubled situation that placed "psychic automatism" at the top of the docket of French psychiatric theory in the early part of the twentieth century. The fact that discussions of the ambiguity of the word *automatic*—which can mean either "operating by itself, on its own volition, spontaneously, as in acts of creation or invention" *or* "an implacable unfolding, mechanical, without consciousness or will"—were almost de rigueur in theoretical essays of the time is only one of the most handy signs that psychiatry was having a great deal of difficulty negotiating a definition that did not threaten to lose the mind altogether—to its own definition.[33]

Although the attempts to resolve this difficulty preoccupied much of psychiatric theory and produced a number of different positions, the predominant direction of resolution lay in conceiving the mind as hierarchically structured and thus as ranging from lower levels of tension and synthesizing power to higher levels, from lesser to greater levels of will. Pathological automatism resulted when, because of a weakening of tension or a failure of will, the mind regressed to a lower, more lax level of operation. At the lower levels, the mind produced habitual, mechanical responses; at the higher levels, creative, willful ones. This hierarchy provided the means by which psychiatry thought its own self-defined object: "the pathology of freedom."[34] Freedom was considered an essential and *positive* characteristic of the forward-moving will, which became shackled only when the psyche fell ill and regressed to a lower level of energy.

Yet even with this solution, the boundary between willful and mechanical functioning could not be easily or consistently drawn—which is not to say that it was more easily drawn elsewhere. With the advent of the industrial revolution in his definition, it was no longer possible to be sure that man was *other* than machine, and thus the concept of *counterfeitable* man, of man as that which could be simulated by a machine, was soon derived from his primary definition.[35] In fact, in 1950, Alan Turing would demonstrate that if one proceeded axiomatically from this definition, one could devise a game which would prove that the differences between man and machine were undetectable.[36]

The simple point is that from the moment man was submitted to redefinition according to use, he was also submitted to the trauma of the fact that this definition would not definitively, unambiguously enclose him. In part, he escaped definition. There opened up, then, in the heart of the symbolic universe of utilitarianism a gap, a hole through which man, at least partially, slipped. If a volatile ambivalence characterized our relation to technology during the first half of this century, this is due not simply, as the familiar account has it, to the fact that technology was associated both with progress and—through war, industrial and railway accidents, and so forth—with destruction. The traumatic collision of the concepts of man and machine robbed man of a little bit of his existence, and technology, I would suggest, came to be symbolized as the embodiment of the very impossibility of man's complete identity. Technology incarnated the limit of man not merely because of its role in actual events but—in a more primary way—because it interfered with man's comprehension of himself.[37]

Though this fundamental failing of comprehension may always, as here, attach itself to historically contingent conditions, it is, nonetheless, a structural necessity, and, as Freud argues in *Civilization and Its Discontents,* it is what falsifies the principle on which the utilitarian project is based. Confronted with utilitarianism's moral command "Thou shalt love thy neighbor as thyself," Freud reacts with undisguised and unabashed *incomprehension,* with feelings of "surprise and bewilderment"—"Why should we . . . ?"[38] One should not mistake this reaction for a lack of altruism. Freud does not hesitate to agree with Bentham that we are basically altruistic, that we would be willing to sacrifice for the Other. But would the Other be willing to sacrifice for us? This is the question upon which the ethics of psychoanalysis turns.

This question does not remain in *Civilization and Its Discontents,* however, an empty point, a simple void in our understanding; rather, it is filled out with a shocking, a scandalous, image—that of a malign, noxious neighbor who will spare us no cruelty in the accrual of its own pleasure. This neighbor, Freud tells us, is our superego, sadistic source of our moral law. He thus shatters all our images of a humane and equitable law that would proscribe acts of violence and oblige acts of charity and installs instead this principle—strictly outlawed by Bentham as *un*principled—of caprice, arbitrariness, destruction. Moral order is established, according to psychoanalysis, not in obedience to some reasonable or compassionate command to sacrifice our pleasure to the state but because we recoil before the violence and obscenity of the superego's incitement to *jouissance*,[39] to a boundless and aggressive enjoyment. The recoil before the commandment to love thy superego as thyself does not open up the floodgates of our aggression or our enjoyment; on the contrary, it erects a barrier against them, and places out of reach the object of our desire. In resisting the superego, then, we insist on separating ourselves from, rather than surrendering to, this incomprehensible part of our being; we insist, in other words, on prolonging the conflict with ourselves. The sole moral maxim of psychoanalysis is this: do not surrender your internal conflict, your division.

This is an extraordinary account of moral law, which we can understand only by continuing to clarify its opposition to utilitarianism. We passed perhaps too quickly over the utilitarian rejection of caprice. Recall Durand's example of the person who would tamper with classical sculpture. Finding the head of one preferable to that of another, this person would switch them; admiring the form of one of the limbs, he or she would multiply it, producing, for example, a statue with four arms or four legs, creating, as Durand says, a "monster." What is it that is being rejected here, and on the basis of what assumptions? Clearly the horror evoked is that of an erratic instability, one that depends not only on an image of arbitrary change, the possibility that some form already familiar to us could suddenly and whimsically be altered, but also on the disequilibrium of the altered form itself, its upsetting of classical proportions and its "unfair" (inexact and improper) distribution of limbs. This is a horror of disharmony produced by what? An untrammeled will. The underlying assumption is that individual will, left to its own devices, would result in the disordering of society. Ethics then becomes a matter of the reconciliation of the equality of men—the freedom of their individual wills—with the equilibrium of society.

Reciprocity is offered as the only resolution of this ethical conundrum. Durand's example implicitly relies on the symmetry of the bodily form to secure the rightness of reciprocity; it also depends on there being a consensus of opinion about the value of classical sculpture, on its seeming, therefore, to be *objectively* preferable to whatever form would be confected by the whimsy of personal taste. Similarly, Bentham argues in *An Introduction to the Principles of Morals and Legislation* that caprice is as a principle inferior to utility, since only utility is subject to public debate and verification; caprice relies on unfounded and nondiscussable tastes. The communities of Bentham and Durand are intersubjective orders bound together by the sharing and exchange of objects: language, opinions, property, services and—most notoriously—women. For, in fact, Claude Lévi-Strauss makes use of this same modern model of ethics. In his famous analysis of kinship relations, he conceives the incest taboo as a kind of utilitarian command: man must renounce the *immediate* pleasure of endogamy for the greater pleasure of exogamy and the stability his sacrifice avails him.

Psychoanalysis's opposition to this ethical model is predicated on a very different understanding of the prohibition of incest as the foundation of society. Unlike utilitarianism, which tacks onto the interdiction of pleasure a list of rewards—extended kinship relations, women, property, trade routes, *Unités d'Habitations, Seidlungen,*[40] happiness itself—psychoanalysis detaches its interdiction from any promise of pleasure, it razes the ethical field, sweeps away all good objects. The psychoanalytic interdiction does not make reward the *condition* of sacrifice; one must obey the interdiction unconditionally. *Pleasure is,* then, *of no use* in securing commitment to moral law.

What is crucial for psychoanalysis is not the reciprocity of individual subjects in their relations to a contingent realm of *things* but the nonreciprocal relation between the subject and its sublime, inaccessible *Thing;* that is, that part of the subject that exceeds the subject, its repressed desire. Nor is the figure of the woman central to moral law the daughter, who will be exchanged and thus made accessible to the larger community, but rather the mother, who must remain, according to the interdiction, inaccessible to the subject. The moral interdiction bears, in other words, on an *impossible* object (not, as in utilitarianism, on an actual object that one might otherwise possess), the mother, who is impossible because she is already unattainable. It is because the good object is *already* lost, desire has *already* been repressed, that the law forbids access to it. This means that repressed desire is the cause, not the consequence, of moral law. The subject does not *surrender* its desire in order to gain the rewards society offers as incentives; instead, the subject *maintains* its desire rather than succumb to these "pathological" motives for giving it up. Far from offering any benefit, the sadistic law of psychoanalysis offers the subject only further suffering, a prolongation of its separation from the object of its desire.

What happens in this account to the notion of psychical will? No longer conceived as a purely positive force opposed to or manipulated by external social laws, will comes to be conceived as a force in which the law is always already immanent. It is not the facile opposition between individual will and social world that rules moral order, but rather the opposition internal to will, by which it turns against its own fulfillment. This is a morbid will, but one whose morbidity is essential rather than accidental. We are not here resuscribing to evolutionary psychology's notion of a "pathology of freedom," whereby the basic freedom of will is restricted through some accident.

Psychoanalysis looks askance at this notion of a freedom that is not only regularly infringed but also *defined* by contingent causes and conditions. For, this freedom is always conceived as the subject's ability to act in its own best interest, while this interest is always determined by specific circumstances. It is freedom itself that is reconceptualized by the psychoanalytic concept of will: the subject's only freedom consists precisely in its ability to *disregard* all circumstances, causes, conditions, all promises of reward or punishment for its actions. The subject determines itself not by "choosing" its own good (an illusory freedom, since the good determines the choice, not the other way around), but by choosing *not* to be motivated by self-interest and thus by acting contrary to its own good—even to the point of bringing about its own death.

It should be obvious from this discussion that Freud was not the first to define the freedom of the ethical subject in this negative way, as the freedom to resist the lure of the pleasure principle and to submit oneself to the law of the death drive. Kant paved the way for psychoanalysis by placing the ethical imperative in a realm radically beyond the phenomenal and thus by splitting the subject between two realms, one subject to the determinations of historical conditions, the other not. Yet he also partially sealed up again the gap he so dramatically opened. Treating the categorical imperative, correctly, as a statement, he abridged linguistic law by neglecting to consider the statement's enunciating instance. While utilitarianism argued that one must act in such a way that everyone would benefit from one's actions, Kant argued that one must act in such a way that no one would benefit. In fact, psychoanalysis tells us, someone—the Other—always benefits from the sacrifice of enjoyment—and always at the subject's expense. By making this point, psychoanalysis means to reinstate the superegoic Other as the enunciator of the law and to restore the division of the subject that Kant's gesture threatens to conjure away. For, when the marks of enunciation are erased from a statement and it thus appears to come from nowhere, its addressee can presume to occupy the vacant enunciative position: the addressee

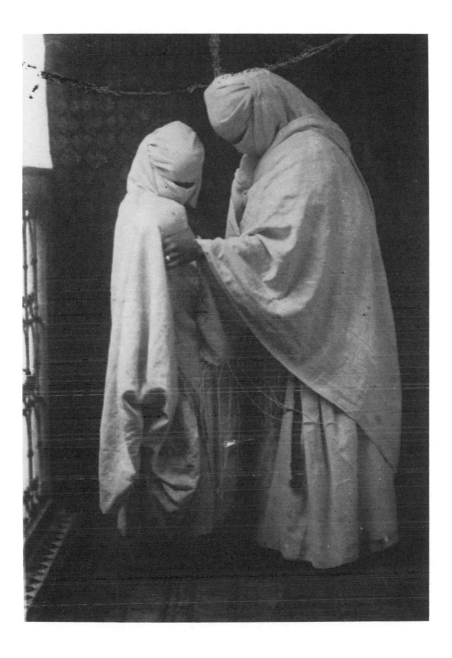

takes itself as the source of the statement. This is precisely what happens in Kant. He supposes that the ethical subject hears the voice of conscience as its own.[41]

Why does psychoanalysis insist on exposing the cruel enunciator, the sadistic superego, who speaks the moral law? Because it wishes to demonstrate the ethical necessity of hearing the otherness of this voice and of maintaining our distance from it. It is always and only this division of the subject that psychoanalysis insists on, not only because the attempt to establish an ethics on the basis of its disavowal is *mistaken* but—more importantly—because it is *unethical*. The principle of the maximization of happiness on which the ethics of utilitarianism is based is a product of this disavowal; it is also responsible for some of the most violent aggressions against our neighbors.

Fantasy and Fetish

In a finely argued essay on "The Nuclear Sublime,"[42] Frances Ferguson deals with the same relationship that concerns us here: the relationship between the egalitarianism that propelled the utilitarian demand for an extension of property relations and the aesthetics/ethics of the sublime relation of the subject to an "extimate"[43] object that is in the subject, yet more than the subject. As part of her argument, Ferguson offers a fascinating reading of Mary Shelley's *Frankenstein* in which she suggests that Victor Frankenstein's invention of his sublime monster must be seen against the background of his family's "philanthropic, territorial imperialism," its steady assimilation of more and more wards into the family. In this light it seems that the invention of Frankenstein represents his attempt to construct an object that cannot be shared, an inalienable object that would depend solely on his consciousness and would thus attest to its uniqueness. The invention of the monster, in other words, bespeaks a dissatisfaction with the limitations imposed by the "labours and utility" of the overcrowded world of the nineteenth century at a point when the "rights of man" had been so massively extended that "Victor seems to imagine his identity ebbing because his rights, his freedom have to be shared." "Recoil[ing] at the way the notion of individual freedom seems stretched too thin to accommodate its various claimants,"[44] Frankenstein flees the claustrophobic world fostered by utilitarian values and seeks refuge in the sublime "dream of self-affirmation." It is more broadly suggested that Frankenstein's path is paradigmatic, that the sublime becomes in the nineteenth century a kind of escape from the Gothic over-crowding of the intersubjective world of property relations.

Following Freud, I will argue that the reverse is true. What the nineteenth- (and twentieth-) century world of "labours and utility" recoils from—primarily—is not the nearness of its neighbor but the principle that moral law must be founded on a recoil from the Neighbor. It is, in other words, precisely its attempt to flee the sublime law inflicted by the superego, to elude the the cruel rigors of the immanent law of morbid will, that defines the social world of utilitarianism. The utopian dream of a society in which relations of exchange would be harmonious and universal was dreamed up in the nineteenth century as an evasion of the recognition of the failed—and forbidden—relation of the individual subject to its terrifying, superegoic Other—its Neighbor. Rather than recoiling from the obscene/sublime part of itself, utilitarianism refused to recognize it, setting itself up on the erasure of its self-contesting aversion.

What is in question here is not the observation that we have experienced, since the beginning of the nineteenth century, a steady increase in our sense of intersubjective claustrophobia. What is in question is the description of the genesis of this social hell. For, if a proliferation of the rights of individuals has made the world seem stiflingly overpopulous, this is due to the way these rights have defined the individual and *not* to a sheer increase in the number of other subjectivities.

It might be helpful at this point to recall that, in the 1930s, Walter Benjamin attributed the modern perception of a contraction of space to the decay of the aura. Defining the aura as "the unique manifestation of

a distance, however near [an object] might be,"[45] Benjamin initially seems to celebrate this decay. Since the loss of distance can be considered the loss of the priority and authority the thing has over others, this loss becomes a sign of the dawn of a new era in which the universal equality of things is being sought. To celebrate the decline of the aura is to embrace the new ethical order based not, as formerly, on a master/acolyte model but on the equality and sovereignty of individuals.

Yet it is clear from the start that Benjamin is ambivalent about the disappearance of this auratic quality, that he would like to see it restored in some way. Through his notion of the "optical unconscious"—which bears witness to something in the photograph, the film, the person, that lies beyond the photograph, film, or person—he begins to give back to the object its aura, its distance. And in his description of Eugène Atget's photographs, his ambivalence appears especially acute. Praising them for initiating a liberation of the object from the aura, he pinpoints the power of these photographs of empty locations in terms that suggest their *possession* of an aura. He likens these locations to scenes of crimes, to places that harbor some guilty secret. Notice, these photographs contain no *evidence* of crime; it is precisely of evidence that they are empty. This lack does not lessen our suspicions about the crime, rather it is the source of them or, to put it another way, it is not the evidence of suspense but the suspension of evidence that grips us in these photographs. Benjamin finds the photographic practice of Atget exemplary, makes it the proper definition of the task of the photographer, which he gives as follows: "to uncover guilt . . . in his pictures."[46]

Benjamin thus calls for the inscription of what Lacan refers to as a symbolic relation. For what is Benjamin describing if not the very phenomenon Lacan invokes thus: "With a machine, whatever doesn't come on time simply falls by the wayside and makes no claims on anything. This is not true for man, the scansion is alive, and whatever doesn't come on time remains in suspense."[47] Through language, the human subject maintains a symbolic relation to the world, which is to

say that the subject comes to believe in a real that *exceeds* all its traces. If a friend does not show up at the appointed hour, we wait for her and wonder where she is. Our waiting does not depend on prior evidence of her existence; it is not empirical evidence—but rather the symbolic—that lends her her stability and thus leads us to expect her when there is no sign of her presence. When Parrhasios painted a veil on the wall, thus causing Zeuxis to wonder what was behind it, he demonstrated the fact that we require no evidence of a thing in order to anticipate its existence. Through the symbolic relation, we are able to take a certain distance from the evidence immediately presented to us, supposing the real to have recessed from it as well.

It is precisely this symbolic relation—this aura, or distance—that was in decline in the nineteenth century. Why? Because of the utilitarian definition of the subject which declared that the subject was indeed equal to its traces, that it could be fully grasped in its use or function. Not only did work democratize society, it also "exposed simulation."[48]

Now, the condition of this utilitarian definition is not simply—as the usual complaint would have it—its elimination of the subject's *interiority,* but more exactly its elimination of the subject's *interior lack,* or fault. Utilitarianism is not incompatible with a notion of interior will, as we have seen; it is, however, incompatible with a notion of a will that would impede itself, block its own realization. What utilitarianism flees from, above all, is the fact of repressed desire—or, for that matter, the crime whose scenes Atget photographed—for they do not exist, even though we see clearly their effects, in the subject's feeling of guilt and in the photographs. Because desire and the crime are posited *retroactively* as causes of these effects and never did exist in any realized form, this cause/effect relationship is *not* an indexical—that is, not an existential—one. Such a relation confounds utilitarianism, which depends on seeing in every effect evidence of some actually existing cause.

The functional definition of the subject, therefore, is also a definition of the subject as a pure, positive drive toward realization and self-affirmation. When Ferguson describes, then, the flight *toward* the sublime as a flight toward self-affirmation, she makes the sublime consubstantial with this utilitarian definition, the *cause* of claustrophobia and not, as she argues, the means of escape from it. For claustrophobia, or the decay of the aura, results not only from the fact that a definition according to use reduces our distance from the real by seeing the object as *present* in its traces but also from the fact that the guilt thus internally denied the subject comes to saturate its surroundings. Because the guilt has not been uncovered *in* the photographs of empty environments, the environment itself becomes guilty. That which exists outside the subject threatens, by virtue of the fact that it is outside, to oppose the subject's drive toward fulfillment.

From the nineteenth-century phobia of crowds[49] to our current obsession with the dangers of passive smoking (a symptom aptly highlighted by Ferguson), it is clear that the historic deterioration of the symbolic relation has forced our environment—the space, people, things around us—to carry the burden the modern subject will not internally bear. We feel the pressure of other people because they are part of this environment, not simply because they are other people. The rise, since the nineteenth century, of historicism, biologism, sociologism are all indications of this modern suspicion—paranoia, even—about a context that has been handed the power to corrupt us.

Paradoxically, then, the utilitarian fantasy of the maximization of pleasure, of the universalization of the principle of the sovereign and equal rights of individuals, seems to be sustained by the structural suspicion that somewhere—in the other—the principle has defaulted. Included, and necessarily so, in the fantasy of a perfect reciprocity of social relations is the negation of the principle that produces the fantasy. For someone— the other—must structurally be supposed to oppose this principle, by the very assertion of its own will. The system of utilitarianism only constitutes itself as such, only thinks its totality by including within itself an element that gives positive form to the impossibility it otherwise excludes.

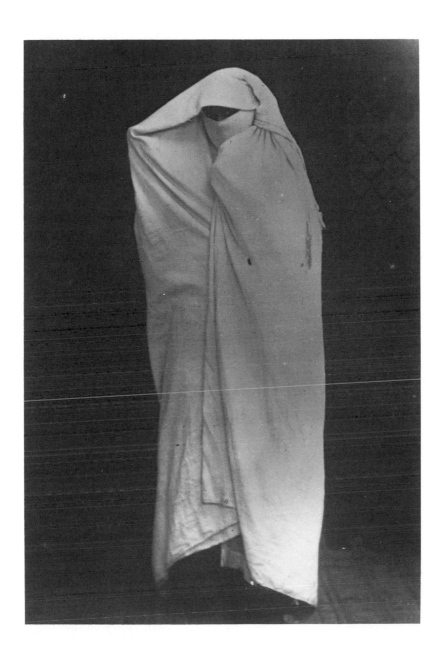

This element is the positive will of the other; it is, in psychoanalytic terms, utilitarianism's symptom.[50]

Nowhere is this symptom more visible than in the well-documented fantasy of an erotic and despotic colonial cloth. For, on the margins of the utilitarian renunciation of useless enjoyment and all but functional clothes, on the borders of the whole cloth of the greatest happiness, there emerged a fantasmatic figure—veiled, draped in cloth—whose existence, posed as threat, impinged on our consciousnesses. There are countless witnesses to this fantasy, countless accounts of the special fascination colonial cloth held for Western eyes and of the singular and sustained effort of imperialism to remove the veils that covered its colonial neighbor.[51]

Several self-contradictory reasons, ranging from the humane to the strategic, are given for this effort. Yet no rational explanation will account for this fantasy, which can only be understood as the positive bodying forth of the lack utilitarianism denied. What was capital in this fantasy was the surplus pleasure, the useless *jouissance* that the voluminous cloth was supposed to veil and the colonial subject, thus hidden, was supposed to enjoy. Every effort to strip away the veil was clearly an aggression against the bloated presence of this enjoyment that would not release itself into the universal pool. Isn't this fantasmatic figure of the veiled colonial subject a kind of objectified, sartorial form of the superego? Hasn't the obscene, superegoic neighbor, abandoned by utilitarianism, returned in the form of those who lived in literal proximity to its project, its colonial neighbors?

All that remains is for us to consider the relation of this figure to the photographs taken by Clérambault. Does this historical fantasy of colonial cloth underlie his photographs? Do we see in them not, as some of them seemed to suggest, a cloth defined by its utility but rather by the way it curtains off an inaccessible pleasure? There is some reason to believe that

this is so, for we discover in Clérambault's work the rudiments of just such a fantasy.

Cloth was of interest to Clérambault not only as an ethnographic issue but also as a clinical one, for in the course of his psychiatric studies, he noticed that several of his women patients expressed a peculiar passion for cloth. On the basis of these observations, he isolated this passion as a definable clinical entity: a specifically female perversion that resembled, in many respects, the male perversion of fetishism. Clérambault wrote very confidently, however, about why the two perversions ought not to be collapsed, stating the fundamental distinction thus: while for the male, fetishism represents an "homage to the opposite sex," and thus puts into play an entire fantasy of love, of union with the opposite sex, the perverse female passion for cloth is rooted in the very refusal of this fantasy. The dream of union, of shared love, plays no role either in the genesis or in the sustaining of the perversion. "With no more reverie than a solitary gourmet savoring a delicate wine,"[52] the woman enjoys the cloth—*for itself,* not for any imagined connection it might have with the opposite sex. Not because it has any existential or symbolic relation to a male object of desire.

In other words, Clérambault conceived the female passion for cloth as selfish. The perversion that simply *uses* cloth to obtain orgasmic pleasure is seen as useless in terms of its ability to secure the common happiness of men and women. It is for this reason that Clérambault refers to the perversion as an *asexual* fetishism; what is missing from it is the sexual relation.

Is this not, *mutatis mutandis,* a clinical version of the colonialist fantasy of a cloth that acted as a barrier to union, of a surplus sexuality? Is this symptom not the *exception,* the surplus sexuality that makes the utilitarian dream of reciprocal relations possible? And are we not, then, presented with this very fantasy in Clérambault's photographs? My brief answer is, Yes and no. Although this fantasy does indeed provide the historical basis of the photographs, we find in them, I would argue, not simply another a version of the fantasy but precisely a *perversion* of it. For these 40,000 photographs focused on one rigidly-adhered-to object choice—cloth—betray not simply a fantasy of cloth but a fetishization of it. But how is such a distinction to be drawn?

Freud formulated an exact, if too concise, definition of the difference between neurosis and perversion. Neurosis, he said, is the *negative* of perversion. It is perhaps this definition that Lacan had in mind when he distinguished the neurotic fantasy from perversion thus: perversion, he said, is "an inverted effect of the phantasy. [In the perversion] the subject determines himself as object in his encounter with the division of subjectivity."[53] Starting from the formula for fantasy: $\$ \lozenge a$, that is, the split subject ($\$$) in some form of relation ($\lozenge$) to an object (a), we can easily derive the formula for perversion: $a \lozenge \$$. But what does this mean?

In the fantasy, the subject establishes a relation to the object-cause of its desire (a), that "presentifies" the subject's loss. Although this loss is presented in an externalized form and represents a misrecognition of the subject's internal impossibility, the subject does, nevertheless, constitute itself in relation to this objective lack. In the colonialist fantasy of cloth, for example, the utilitarian subject developed a desire to see what lay behind the veil or to stop the excess pleasure concealed by it.

The pervert, however, refuses all recognition of his own lack, even in external form. The pervert places himself in the position of "never being deprived with regard to knowledge, and most particularly knowledge concerning love and eroticism."[54] Or, as Freud says of one variety of pervert, "What other men have to woo and make exertions for can be had by the fetishist with no trouble at all,"[55] for he is certain about love, about what the Other wants. The pervert, then, places himself in the real, the only place where nothing is lacking, where knowledge is certain. That is, rather than position himself in relation to the imaginary form of the object a, he positions himself *as* the object a, in its real form.

While imagining itself whole, the neurotic subject of the fantasy becomes split in relation to the doubled form—imaginary and real—of

the object *a*. The pervert, on the other hand, evades this division by making himself the *agent* of a division outside himself. This is why fetishism is, as Freud claimed, "particularly favourable"[56] for studying the splitting of the ego in the process of defense; as a perversion, it *ex-planes* it, unfolds the split onto a flat surface and thus conveniently displays it for the analyzing eye. "I know very well, but just the same [I] . . ."—here we see laid out before us the splitting of the two I's in the *statement,* but what we do not see is the *instance of enunciation,* the pervert, who positions himself safely outside this division. To take another example: if the Chinese man mutilates the woman's foot *and* reveres it, it is the foot that wears the mark of this division, not the Chinese man.

My thesis is that in taking his photographs, Clérambault did *not* always position himself as the colonialist subject confronted with an objectified image of his own loss. He also sometimes positioned himself as the gaze of the Moroccan Other. (This must not be interpreted in a psychologistic sense as an instance of empathy or compassion for one's neighbor. It must first of all be recalled that this Moroccan neighbor is a structural *supposition,* not a reasonable or compassionate presumption. Second, it is a disavowal of lack, not a feeling of "fraternity," that precipitates the perverse positioning.) Entering into a kind of complicity with this Other, photographing the cloth to meet the satisfaction of its gaze, he turned himself into an instrument of the Other's enjoyment.

Clérambault was certain about just what sort of cloth the Other preferred: usually it was silk, not for whatever "connotative" value silk had, but for its *stiffness.* Stiffness, solidity, these were the characteristics most consistently sought. Clérambault recorded his admiration of the North Africans for the way they left their clothes out after washing them, allowing them to become stiff and dry.[57] This same admiration is expressed, apparently, in the photographs, for here we see not a cloth that flows from or hugs the outline of the body, not a cloth elaborately embellished, symbolically erotic, but a material whose plainest, best-photographed feature is its stiff construction.

Viewed from the vantage of the supposed Moroccan Other, from this perverse, fetishistic position, the cloth of the photographs is *not* (as it is in the fantasy) the object-cause of desire; it does not beckon us to peer behind it, or to imagine a hideous enjoyment concealed by it. This is why there are no photographs of the unveiling of the figures or, indeed, of any action taken toward them. There is no—or strikingly little—fantasy space in these photographs, that is, no virtual space suggested by the figures. No promise of a future knowledge to which they may provide the key. The photographs are precisely *cut off* from such a space, which would only be generated if the cloth were to occupy the place of the object *a.* The cloth is not a presentified image of loss, but rather a solid *presence,* a barrier against any recognition of loss. If the perverse beholder of these images remains still, inert, before them, this is due not to the failure of any will to know but, on the contrary, to a refusal of failure, a refusal of subjectivity that turns the pervert into an inert object devoted to the fulfilling of the will of the Other.

But if Clérambault, as fetishistic photographer, refused to assume his subjective division, he did—in typical perverse fashion—make himself, through his photographs, the *agent* of this division. Who—or what— became the subject of this split? In order to answer this question, it is important to recall Freud's several warnings against possible misunderstanding: the construction of the fetish does not itself reveal, except in certain "very subtle" cases,[58] the subject's simultaneous affirmation and denial of loss. The split usually occurs between the disavowal that produces the fetish object and the avowal that allows the subject to do without it. In Clérambault's photographs we see just such a division between images of fetishized cloth and images in which the "nonfetishized" cloth illustrates the characteristics of its utilitarian construction.

What these photographs *ex-plane,* I am now claiming, what they display for us, is the utilitarian fantasy itself. The fantasy, we have said, is ultimately supported by the supposition that there is an Other who enjoys a certain and useless pleasure. We might say, then, that this *useless*

pleasure becomes *useful* in securing and sustaining the utilitarian effort. In other words, the pleasure of the Other is "very subtly" affirmed and denied when, in the utilitarian fantasy, it is retroactively posited as cause of the subject's desire. This simultaneous affirmation and denial is what splits the subject of the fantasy.

In the fetishistic photographs of Clérambault, however, the enjoyment of the Other is only affirmed; it is not turned to Clérambault's, the beholder's, advantage. For these photographs are, like all fetish objects, "marked with the seal of uselessness."[59] The whole point of the construction of the fetish is to satisfy the Other, not oneself. The fetish, then, must be "rigorously of no use" to the pervert, who makes no claims on any rights to enjoyment and who busies himself with them only for the sake of the Other. What becomes split over the broad range of these photographs, therefore, is not Clérambault but the utilitarian fantasy. For the division of these photographs into two groups—those that demonstrate the usefulness of cloth and those that rigorously deny it any usefulness—corresponds to the division between the statement or fantasy of utilitarianism (of the ethical value of useful pleasure) and the useless pleasure of our neighbor, which enables, at the same time as it is neglected by, the fantasy. By not converting the Other's supposed enjoyment into an image useful to utilitarianism, by laying the two alternatives side by side, the photographs taken by Clérambault expose what the fantasy obscures: its strict dependence on the supposition of the Other's obscene enjoyment. Not an enjoyment that can be corralled by use, but one threateningly outside the bounds of utility. This is not to say that these photographs constitute a radical, deconstructive practice. Clearly, they participate in the utilitarian project; but they do so in a way that makes one of the fantasy's necessary preconditions more obvious—less subtle.

In 1926, three years after they began, Clérambault's lectures on drapery were abruptly stopped by the authorities at the Ecole des Beaux-Arts. Since the popularity of the lectures had not diminished, Clérambault was at a loss to understand his dismissal. He therefore wrote an incredulous letter to the authorities in which he reiterated the full scope and originality of his project. His teachings, he stressed, aimed not merely at a comprehension of the drapery but also at an exact rendering of the Fold![60] (*Fold* was capitalized in that curious way Clérambault had of allowing ordinary words to pop up in upper case.) From their refusal to revoke their decision, we can only guess that the authorities saw only too clearly what Clérambault meant, that his doubling and splitting of his project into a consideration of cloth's usefulness and his fetishization of its useless, overbearing presence were precisely the problem. Clérambault's lectures, his explanations, were perhaps too painfully clear in their demonstration of a split to which utilitarianism had to remain blind.

5   Vampires, Breast-Feeding, and Anxiety

Jean-Jacques Rousseau, *Emile:*

> Do you wish to bring everyone back to his first duties? Begin
> with mothers. You will be surprised by the changes you will
> produce. Everything follows successively from this first deprav-
> ity [mothers who despise their first duty and no longer want to
> feed their children]. The whole moral order degenerates. . . . But
> let mothers deign to nurse their children, morals will reform
> themselves, nature's sentiments will be awakened in every heart,
> the state will be repeopled. This first point, this point alone, will
> bring everything back together.[1]

Mary Wollstonecraft, *Thoughts on the Education of Daughters with Reflections
on Female Conduct in the more important Duties of Life:*

> I conceive it to be the duty of every rational creature to attend
> to its offspring. . . . The mother (if there are not very weighty
> reasons to prevent her) ought to suckle her children. Her milk is
> their proper nutriment, and for some time quite sufficient.[2]

Let these two—probably the most prominent—examples stand as indications of a phenomenon that was widespread in the eighteenth century,
an insignia, we might even say, of Enlightenment thought: the advocacy
of breast-feeding. This phenomenon is currently the subject of much
speculation by historically informed literary theorists intent on establishing its links with the political, philosophical, and literary themes of the
period. While I, too, will urge a consideration of these links, I do not

propose to attempt an explication of either the external causes or the meaning of the phenomenon. For to do so would be to ignore its most essential aspect: *the aura of anxiety that surrounds it.* It is this aspect that allows us to observe the unexplored historical coincidence and close correspondence between this phenomenon and a form of literature that emerged in the eighteenth century. I am speaking, of course, of vampire fiction, in all its Gothic forms. I will argue that the political advocacy of breast-feeding cannot be properly understood unless one sees it for what it is: the precise equivalent of vampire fiction.

It is necessary, first of all, to say something about anxiety. If its cause cannot be determined, this is because it is the most primitive of phenomena. It is that which nothing precedes. One could also say, conversely, that that which nothing precedes, that which follows from nothing, is what awakens anxiety. Anxiety registers the non sequitur, a gap in the causal chain. It was the difficulty of trying to think this very priority of anxiety that made *Inhibitions, Symptoms and Anxiety* the confused text that it is, with Freud switching from his "first theory" (in which repression precedes anxiety) to his "second theory" (in which anxiety precedes repression) and back—several times—and quarreling with Otto Rank about whether or not birth can be the occasion of anxiety. Freud says that it cannot, but he also seems to incorporate Rank's arguments at points.

And yet a definition does clearly emerge from Freud's text: anxiety is a signal of danger. This signal is extraordinary because it works without the use of any signifiers. Since a signifier can always be negated, the message it sends can always be doubted. Rather than a signifer, then, anxiety is an affect—a special sort of affect—and as such it cannot be doubted. Common usage notwithstanding, anxiety is connected to certitude rather than doubt. This is also a way of saying that what anxiety signals is real. As we have just remarked, Freud—like Kant, who gave both respect, a signal of moral law, and terror, a signal of the sublime, a special status—sets anxiety apart from all the other affects, feelings, sentiments that are caused by objects acting on the subject.[3] If anxiety can be considered a presentiment, it is only in the etymological sense of the term; it appears *prior* to any sentiment in the "normal," "pathological" sense.[4]

Anxiety—again, like respect and terror—is not only not caused by any object, it is not even caused by any loss/lack of object (which is why anxiety can be distinguished from disappointment, say, or grief). Rather than an object or its lack, anxiety signals a lack of lack, a failure of the symbolic reality wherein all alienable objects, objects that can be given or taken away, lost and refound, are constituted and circulate. Somewhat perversely, however, Lacan does refer to this encounter with a "lack of lack" as an encounter with an *object:* object *a.* But this object is unique; it has neither an essence nor a signification. It cannot be communicated or exchanged. It has, in short, no *objectivity.* The danger that anxiety signals is the overproximity of this object *a,* this object so *inalienable* that like Dracula and all the other vampires of Gothic and Romantic fiction it cannot even be cast as a shadow or reflected as a mirror image, and yet so *insubstantial* that like Murnau's Nosferatu it can disappear in a puff of smoke.

Now, if the signal of anxiety cannot lie, if we cannot be misled as to its message, it stands to reason that any *interpretation* of anxiety is superfluous and inappropriate. But if interpretation is not the proper response, what is? The best way to answer this question is to look once again at that overinterpreted anxiety dream, the dream of Irma's injection. Lacan's commentary on this dream is designed to demonstrate how we must act—and how we must not act—in the face of anxiety.[5] The dream is divided by Lacan into two parts, each of which is marked by its own climax. In the first part, Freud appears as a man free of any "Oedipus complex"; his research is driven entirely by his desire to know, whatever the cost.[6] Propelled by this desire, he stalks his party guest, Irma, and, struggling against her resistances, peers curiously down her throat, only to make his truly horrible discovery. What he witnesses is the very "origin of the world," the equivalent of the female genitals. It is clear that the uncanny appearance of what ought to have remained hidden is a sickening, noxious sight. But what is it, really? "A large white spot . . . curled structures . . . white-grey scabs." Almost nothing. This is the climax of the first part of the dream, the anxiety-filled encounter with the object *a*.

After this encounter the dream abruptly switches into another mode. The dream space becomes fantasmatically populated with Freud's doctor friends: Dr. M., Otto, Leopold; in other words, the space becomes "Oedipalized." By this I mean, first of all, that the second part of the dream is defined by a *turning away from* the object *a* that erupted in the first part. In the second part, Freud no longer wants to know; his primary desire is a desire *not* to know anything of the real that provoked in him so much anxiety. The abruptness of the transition indicates that Freud *flees* from the real—Irma, her white scabs, the unconscious—into the symbolic community of his fellow doctors.

So, the proper response to anxiety is, according to this dream, flight. But is it not the height of absurdity to say that the founder of psychoanalysis, of the study of the unconscious, based the whole of this discipline (recall how proudly Freud thought of a future commemoration of this dream, as though it were the cornerstone of the edifice of psychoanalysis) on a turning away from the unconscious? On a desire to know nothing about it? Some further clarification of the character of the second, Oedipalized space is necessary before our suspicions can be allayed. Filled with paternal figures, this space is infused with an air of interdiction, of rules, regulations, and prescriptions, and yet it offers relief from the constricted asphyxiating space that *zusammenchnuren,* that chokes, Freud as well as Irma. In what, then, does this relief consist, and how is it secured? Most simply put, it consists in the setting up of the symbolic as rampart against the real; the symbolic *shields* us from the terrifying real. The climax of the second part, the triumphant pronouncement of the word *trimethylamine,* indicates that it is the word itself, or the symbolic itself, that is our salvation.

But in order for the symbolic to evict the real and thereby establish itself, a judgment of existence is required; that is, it is necessary to *say* that the real is absented, to *declare* its impossibility. The symbolic, in other words, must include the negation of what it is not. This requirement is not without its paradoxical effects, for it means ultimately that the symbolic will not be filled with only itself, since it will also contain this surplus element of negation. According to this reasoning—which is to be found in Freud's 1919 essay "Negation"—that which is impossible must also be prohibited.

It should be immediately evident that this negation of the real by the symbolic presents a special problem. The real that is to be negated cannot be represented by a signifier, since the real is, by definition, that which has no adequate signifer. How, then, can this negation take place *within* the symbolic as the requirement demands? The answer is, Through repetition, through the signifier's repeated attempt—and failure—to designate itself. The signifier's difference from itself, its radical inability to signify itself, causes it to turn in circles around the real that is lacking in it. It is in this way—in the circumscription of the real—that its nonexistence or its negation is signified *within* the symbolic.

This is also the explanation of the Lacanian thesis that *doubt is a defense against the real.* Doubt—which emerges from the signifier's non-coincidence with itself, its incapacity to guarantee itself—registers the impossibility of the real and thereby defends us against its intrusion into the symbolic. Dr. M., Otto, Leopold, the three sorry figures of authority in the dream of Irma's injection, will illustrate this argument. Their supposedly professional probings and pronouncements are simply ridiculous. Whatever principle of diagnosis one may represent is quickly transgressed by the other, who proposes a different and contradictory principle. These fellows are simply not credible as standard bearers of their profession. But have we not entered here into that place so often evoked by

Lacan, the place where tracks are made *in order to be taken as false*? As so many, including Foucault, have noted, laws are made to be broken, prohibitions to be transgressed, but through its very violability the law simply binds us closer to it. The law has an irrefutably *positive* force to which every transgression, which defines itself in terms of the law while dreaming itself beyond it, attests. It is wrong to assume, however, as so many, including Foucault, have, that the fundamentally *negative* character of the law is in this way refuted. For the transgression of the law's interdiction of specific, named acts in no way violates the law's other, more basic interdiction—of the real. This interdiction, unlike the first type, is never *named* by the law but is inscribed in it nevertheless: in the law's very inability to authorize itself.[7] The Foucauldians have simplified the Freudian thesis about negation by rendering it as "that which is negated must be named" and by failing to realize that that which is impossible must be negated *without being named*.

In the psychoanalytic version, the symbolic order defends against the real by substantifying its negation in the interdictions and doubt that define symbolicity as such. We have thus described the space of the second half of Freud's dream as an Oedipalized space both because it instantiates an avoidance of the real, a desire not to know anything about it, and because this avoidance necessitates an impotent, violable (that is, Oedipal) law. It is now necessary to confess a considerable complication of this argument. We have called that from which Freud takes flight the object *a,* but though we have refrained until now from saying so, that which marks his avoidance of this traumatic point, the absence of the real, is also called object *a.* The object *a* is both real and a positivization of the symbolic's failure to say the real; it is both real and imaginary. What is the explanation for this terminological condundrum? If the symbolic must inscribe its lack of foundation in the real, the inaccessibility to it of some knowledge of this real, then, we are obliged to admit that it also thereby inscribes the real itself, since it is precisely there where we do *not* know, that enjoyment, *jouissance* (a pleasure in the real) arises. *Jouissance* is a kind of "secondary gain" obtained where knowledge fails.[8] As Lacan says at the beginning of *Television,* "Saying it all is literally impossible: words fail. Yet it's through this very impossibility that the truth holds onto the real."[9] This statement demonstrates a Möbius strip kind of logic, for in the last analysis it means that the real *is* its own negation, its own prohibition. The real encounters itself in its own lack, its exclusion from the system of signifiers.[10]

In his dream of Irma's injection, then, Freud does not simply flee from the unconscious or from the real of Irma's desire: *he holds onto them.* This is the reason psychoanalysis can claim to found itself on the unconscious and on the desire of the woman, precisely because it so rigorously registers their inaccessibility. We could say, then, using the Lacanian definition of sublimation, that psychoanalysis "raises" the unconscious and the woman's desire "to the dignity of the Thing." It is in its refusal to interpret them that psychoanalysis maintains them, for there where they are interpreted they cease to be.

But if in order to preserve itself psychoanalysis has to register its own radical inability to know, does it not consign itself to skepticism? Must we place Freud among his foolish mentors, equal to them in his ignorance of the truth? No, psychoanalysis is not a skepticism. By not declaring merely that the good (which would be a standard of our actions) *cannot* be known but insisting further that it *must* not be known, psychoanalysis commits itself to what Lacan refers to as a "belief without belief," to a belief in an Other whose very existence is dependent on our lack of knowledge.

"The problem of evil is only worth raising as long as one has not fixed on the idea of transcendence by some good that is able to dictate to man what his duties are. Till that moment the exalted representation of evil will continue to have the greatest revolutionary value."[11] It's because radical doubt undermines the position of every would-be master and every stated good that the problem of radical evil must be raised. Psychoanalysis shares this position with a certain strain of Enlightenment thought, which celebrated evil while attempting to secure the individual subject's freedom from authority. For both psychoanalysis and this mode of thinking that originated in the eighteenth century, the exalted evil referred to is synonymous with the subject itself, since it is the subject that seems to pose the greatest threat to the established social order. One should not be too quick, however, to equate this conception with the standard reading of the Romantic opposition between the individual and society. Romantic notions are fundamentally recast by this conception, which sees neither the subject as the external cause of society's corruption, nor society as the corruptor of the pure, innocent subject. Instead of an external opposition between the subject and society, we must learn to think their necessary interrelation: the very existence of the subject is simultaneous with society's failure to integrate, to represent it.

It is its rendering of this peculiar interrelation that makes *Frankenstein* such an exemplary text and Frankenstein's monster such a paradigmatic example of the modern subject. While it gives reign to the fantasy that things might have turned out otherwise, that society would have been spared the monster's maleficence if only it had treated him with more kindness, if only the young De Lacey had not rushed into the cottage just as the monster was about to reveal his true character to the blind, old De Lacey, *Frankenstein* also exposes the truth on which this fantasy depends: the monster is, constitutionally, he whose character cannot be revealed. He, like the modern subject in general, is located there where knowledge of him is omitted. His monstrosity is therefore structural, not accidental.

This is why the common belief that Victor Frankenstein invented the monster is in error. If the monster were, in fact, the product of a scientific invention, he would have awakened at the end of chapter four, but he does not; it is only at the very beginning of chapter five that the baleful yellow eye first opens. If Frankenstein had *succeeded* in his scientific project, this success would have been recorded as the climax of a series of steps and discoveries, as the end product of a causal chain of effort and effect. But at the end of the chapter in which these discoveries are re-corded, the invention remains uninvented. That Frankenstein has failed is apparent in the opening of the following chapter where the thing that he strove to animate lies lifeless at his feet. It is only *then* and in the absence of any indication or sense of agency on Frankenstein's part—the inventor is described as a passive witness of the event—that the monster comes to life. There seems to be only one reading of this narrative pacing: Frankenstein's invention did not go awry, as the standard reading claims, it *failed*. It is only insofar as it failed, only inasmuch as Frankenstein's scientific efforts fell short of their goal, that the monster appears, the embodiment of this failure. It is therefore misleading to call the creature "Frankenstein's monster," as though it were the hero's botched invention, rather than the botching of his invention, as though it were not precisely the *lack* of that "belong to me aspect so reminiscent of property" (in Lacan's phrase) that provided the creature with its essential definition—and made him so uncanny.

In response to anxiety's signal of danger, one flees or avoids the real. But one flees into a symbolic whose hedge against the real is secured only through its negation of the real, that is, through its failure to coincide with itself, to guarantee itself. The subject—like the Frankenstein mon-ster—*is* the failure that maintains the symbolic, prevents it from collapse. But we claimed earlier that in his discussion of the dream of Irma's injection, Lacan made clear not only the proper but also the improper manner of accomplishing this avoidance. Despite the many insights with which Lacan credits him, Erik Erikson is, to some extent, used to illustrate an improper response, a certain deafness, to the signal sounded by the dream. There is, of course, a major difference between Erikson and Freud regarding the characterization of the second space of the dream. Lacan's understanding of this space as symbolic reality in its function as shield against the traumatic real, as being simultaneously salutary for the subject and the place of its *nonintegration,* would make no sense at all to Erikson for whom reality is that into which the healthy ego is integrated. He therefore comprehends this space differently: as the place of the regression of the ego. Rather than focus on all the broad and basic differences between Lacanian psychoanalysis and ego psychology, however, let us note that Lacan chose to derogate Erikson's *interpretation* of Freud's dream with the term *culturalist*. What most disturbs Lacan is Erikson's digging into Freud's life and culture in the hopes of finding some additional facts that will push the interpretation beyond the limit demarcated by Freud. Against this endless ransacking of the archives, Lacan maintains not that history is unimportant but that historicism can only bring about the destruction of history: that some limits are meant to be observed. In the middle of making this point, something wonderful happens: a member of the audience intervenes to make the point for him, *a contrario*. At the very moment Lacan asks us to confront the horrifying real that threatens to choke Irma and Freud, the moment Lacan points to the suffocation, the gasping for breath that evidences the overwhelming presence of the real, Mme. X—we can give her a more descriptive name, Mme. Culturalist, or Mme. Historicist—interjects the following observation, "In the old days, three or four people were needed to pull on the laces of a corset to tighten it."[12]

Here we have a clear example of an avoidance of the real, but not of the sort at which we have been aiming. In place of a negative judgment of existence (the establishment of a second symbolic space that would announce its nonreal status: "I am no longer anything," is the way Lacan phrases it), Mme. Historicist offers *no judgment* on the real's existence. She *forecloses* rather than repudiates it. No anxiety disquiets her, nothing signals the danger that faces Irma and Freud. What Freud confronts in his moment of anxiety is a gap in symbolic reality, a point that interpretation, the logic of cause and effect, cannot bridge. In response, he does not bridge it; he records its unbridgeability and in this way circumscribes it. Mme. Historicist does not come up against a gap, she sees only an uninterrupted chain of signifiers that she interprets by assigning them a place in another causal chain.

The Drying Up of the Breast

Now, it is precisely this sort of historicist interpretation that we must guard against while considering the eighteenth-century advocacy of breast-feeding. For there is ample evidence that this advocacy expressed a profound anxiety, that it situated itself at the very limit of interpretation. If we return to the Rousseau and Wollstonecraft texts previously cited, we will find that each utters its plea for the maternal breast as a safeguard against what? Against the suffocation, the strangulation the child will suffer without it. Rousseau thus rails against the child's "being prevented from breathing," its being more cramped, more constrained, more compressed than "in the amnion," its being "garroted,"—all as a result of its being deprived of its mother's breast.[13] And Wollstonecraft speaks of such a child as being "overloaded," as being in a state of unalleviated bodily pain, and later contends that "it is easy to distinguish the child of a well-bred person [that is, of a mother who honors her duty to breast-feed her child] if it is not left entirely to the nurse's care. These women are of course ignorant, and to keep a child quiet for the moment, they humour all its little caprices. Very soon does it begin to be perverse, and eager to be gratified in everything."[14] Both Rousseau and Wollstonecraft understand the deprivation resulting from the mother's neglect of her "duty to breast-feed" as a *deprivation of deprivation*. This understanding is then reiterated in their subsequent warnings against the *excesses* of motherly devotion. It is a "cruel" mother, Rousseau warns, who "plunge[s her] children in softness." The encouragement of breast-feeding seeks to submit the child not to the mother but—quite the contrary—to social law.

But we have promised to come to terms with this phenomenon by establishing its corollary in vampire fiction. That the encounter with the vampire is always anxiety-ridden would seem to be undebatable. And yet even this seemingly obvious fact is in danger of being lost by those analyses that attempt to define the Gothic depiction of this encounter as a form of sentimental fiction. As we argued earlier, anxiety is not an affect or a sentiment like others; it has, for the reasons stated, an exceptional status. The Gothic world is, in fact, only conceivable as the elimination of sentiment. If vampirism makes our hearts pound, our pulses race, and our breathing come in troubled bursts, this is not because it puts us in contact with objects and persons—others—who affect us, but because it confronts us with an absence of absence—an Other—who threatens to asphyxiate us. And rather than making us more at home in our bodies, rather than anchoring us to bodies conceived as the agents of our intelligence, the makers of sense, vampirism presents us with a bodily double that we can neither make sense of nor recognize as our own.

In what, essentially, does the phenomenon of vampirism consist? The first thing to note is that it is a matter of an *oral relation,* of a *jouissance* attained through sucking. One might spontaneously think of the child in its oral-parasitic relation to its mother as the image of vampirism. But as Lacan—along with all the narratives and iconography of vampirism—makes clear, it is not the child who is the vampire.[15] The image of the child at the mother's breast is not one that elicits anxiety. Vampirism is located beyond this point where the child maintains itself in relation to a partial object, an object of desire. It is only at the point where the fantasy enabling this relation to the partial object no longer holds that the anxiety-ridden phenomenon of vampirism takes over, signaling, then, *the drying up of the breast as object-cause of desire,* the disappearance of the fantasy support of desire. The drying up of desire is the danger against which vampirism warns us, sending up a cry for the breast that would deliver us from this horror.[16]

The breast—like the gaze, the voice, the phallus, and the feces—is an object, an appendage of the body, from which we separate ourselves in order to constitute ourselves as subjects. To constitute ourselves, we must, in other words, throw out, reject our nonselves. Our discussion of the Freudian concept of negation has taught us, however, that this rejection can only be accomplished through the inclusion within ourselves of this negation of what we are not—within our being, this lack-of-being. These Freudian objects are, then, not only rejected from but also internal to the subject. In brief, they are *extimate,*[17] which means they are in us that which is not us.

It is precisely because the subject is defined in this way—or, as we will argue later, *when* the subject is defined in this way—that it stumbles into the dimension of the uncanny. The special feeling of un- canniness is a feeling of anxiety that befalls us whenever we too closely approach the extimate object in ourselves. In his theorization of the uncanny, Freud, influenced by the literary works on which he drew, underlined the privileged relation uncanniness maintained with the gaze. But as vampire fiction demonstrates, the uncanny can also manifest itself as an overproximity to the "extimate" breast.

Normally, when we are at some remove from it, the extimate object *a* appears as a lost part of ourselves, whose absence prevents us from becoming whole; it is then that it functions as the object-cause of our desire. But when our distance from it is reduced, it no longer appears as a partial object, but—on the contrary—as a complete body, an almost exact double of our own, except for the fact that this double is endowed with the object that we sacrificed in order to become a subject. This would mean that the vampire is not only a creature that menaces the breast as object-cause of desire, but that it is also a double of the victim, whose distorted bodily form indicates its possession of a certain excess object: the breast once again, but this time as source of *jouissance*. The most vivid confirmation of this thesis concerning the double is given in Bram Stoker's *Dracula,* in that horrifyingly obscene moment when we are startled to witness Mina Harker *drinking from the breast of Dracula.* Desire, society itself, is endangered by Mina's intimacy with this extimate object. But it is Alfred Hitchcock's *Rebecca*—a twentieth-century version of an eighteenth-century form, the "female Gothic"[18]—that best illustrates the fact that the object which "completes" the subject, filling in its lack, is also always a disfiguring surplus. In this film the paradox functions as a plot device when the baby with which Rebecca was supposed to have been pregnant when she died is revealed to have been a fatal cancer.

The reference to *Rebecca* reminds us that the breasted, vampiric double is not only a creature with "too much" body, it is also a "body too much"; that is, as a double of the subject, it always stands in the way of or crowds out the subject's own actions. In *Rebecca,* her personal possessions, her ubiquitous initial, the constant references to her talents and accomplishments create the sense of the continuing presence of Rebecca at Manderley. Because the dead-without-knowing-it Rebecca refuses to relinquish her place, the nameless Joan Fontaine character cannot assume hers—she is unable to enter the symbolic network of the household. What releases the younger woman, finally, is the *exteriorization* of her battle with the excess body, the double. That is, at the moment when Rebecca's body is found at the bottom of her boat, thus raising questions about the other body buried in her name and in her grave, at the moment when the "body too much" becomes objectivized as a narrative conflict rather than the psychical conflict it had been up until this point, the second Mrs. de Winter begins to escape the hold of the first. At this moment it becomes possible and necessary to reject one of the bodies as a false claimant.

One other film needs to be mentioned in this context, since it is one of the most compelling examples one will ever find of the anxiety that attends the experience of the uncanny. The film's title, *La Jetée* (Chris Marker, 1964), names the primary location of the narrative—the jetty at Orly airport—as well as the danger that threatens completely to overwhelm not only the diegetic characters but the diegesis itself: a "little piece of reality," a childhood memory that has not been rejected, thrown out, by the hero. Despite the fact that the film is often viewed as a film about the hero's need to remember, it is clear that the opposite is true; this is a film about the necessity of forgetting.[19] At the end of World War III, the world in which the hero lives is on the edge of complete extinction, it cannot "take flight," remains stuck in place. Why? The world has survived, barely, the nuclear war, but what it cannot survive is the hero's refusal to reject this memory. It is he who has condemned his world to destruction; the world is in danger as long as the memory endures.

On every level *La Jetée* reproduces the phenomenon of "running in place" so typical of the anxiety dream: not only in the film's insistence on still, unanimated images (there is no illusion of movement in this "photo-novel" composed of still photographs, except at one point where the woman whose image the hero refuses to surrender opens her eyes to look at the hero—an image of desire rather than anxiety) but also in the dark backgrounds that limit the visual field to a very small part of the frame, in the narrative suggestion that the world that has at least temporarily survived is restricted to the narrow corridors of an underground existence, and, finally, in the time-loop structure of the narrative itself. The hero travels back in time to a traumatic scene that he witnessed as a child; there he learns that he is the man whose death he witnessed. A primal scene, but one in which death is substituted for birth. Here, as in the primal scene, the problem is the presence of a body too much. Instead of $\$ \lozenge a$, the formula for fantasy, we get $\$a$: the shriveling up of the distance separating the two terms results in the collapse of the fantasy structure.

La Jetée should make it clear, however, that the procrastination or *postponement*,[20] again the phenomenon of running in place that typifies the reaction to the uncanny, is not to be understood, as theorists from Otto Rank on have understood it, in *epistemological* terms. The hesitation is not a matter of uncertainty but of "illegality." The presence of the uncanny registers an abandonment of prohibitions, an unabandoned embrace of *jouissance*. In *La Jetée* the hero allows himself to enjoy the woman. But things do not work out very well for those who enjoy, for, as it turns out, when nothing is prohibited, then everything is prohibited. The negativism of psychotics is proof of this;[21] libidinal cathexis is withdrawn from the world, producing the psychotic experience of the "end of the world." Since every affirmation is founded on a negation, no future is possible in *La Jetée* as long as the hero clings to rather than negates the image of the woman.

Officially, of course, I am not claiming that *La Jetée* is a vampire film, only that it is a pedagogically useful illustration of the anxiety, hesitations, postponements, digressions that characterize vampire fiction. But why *do* those superimpositions, those curious, distorting superimpositions of images (there is a frequent overlapping of images that produces a doubling *rather than* movement) so often assume those winglike—batlike—shapes?

One final point must be made concerning the phenomenon of anxiety, and I will make it by returning to *Rebecca*. Like so many of the "female Gothics" of the eighteenth and early nineteenth centuries, this film centers on a woman's encounter with a female double who haunts an old, ruined, or anachronistically styled house. The manner of haunting obeys a formula: while the whole house is rendered uncanny by the presence of the "undead" female double, there is one room in the house, one forbidden, barred room, that is the *particular* site of uncanniness. One could understand this formula as exemplifying an *en abyme* structure: a part of the house, the closed-off room, replicates in a miniaturized, condensed form the house as a whole. Thus, within it, the experience of the uncanny is particularly intense. But this reading misses the point entirely. In *Rebecca,* however, the point is more difficult to miss. Which is the forbidden room here? The first answer that suggests itself is the beach house. This is the one place that Max places off-limits. This answer is extremely odd, however, since the beach house is not a room, not, properly speaking, a part of the house; it is—strangely—a *supernumary space* that has, as it were, *subtracted* itself from Manderley. But if this were so, if the beach house were subtracted from Manderley, then it follows that Manderley would be missing a space, that all the remaining rooms would fail to "fill up," to complete the house. And this is precisely the case. Within Manderley there is one room, one exceptional space whose primary function is to mark this emptiness; this space is Rebecca's bedroom. Both the beach house and Rebecca's bedroom have an exceptional status, but while the beach house marks a surplus, Rebecca's room marks an absence, a deficiency.

By clearly delineating these two spaces, *Rebecca* simply reveals the paradoxical function of the forbidden room in Gothic fiction generally: this room marks simultaneously a surplus *and* a deficit, an outside *and* an inside, a particular room within the house *and* the house as a whole. What the barred room bars, first of all, is the rest of the house; that is, by withdrawing itself from the rest of the house, it marks the limit that allows the house to constitute itself as a whole—but a whole from which this room is absent. It is the opening up of this empty space that makes the wind whistle and the living dead blow through the uncanny house. It is also this loss that creates the sense peculiar to the ruined Gothic mansion that all its known rooms do not exhaust its space, that there is always one more room, one uncannily extra space lying hidden from sight. The child's unwitting witticism so often repeated by Lacan bears repeating in this context—"I have three brothers, Paul, Ernest, and me"— because it is an accurate description of this uncanny phenomenon of the barred room that subtracts itself from the others only to appear among them in the form of an excess. To complete the argument begun a moment ago: the element, the room, does not *contain* the set, the house, by *reproducing* it in condensed form, it *constructs* the house by *negating* it. The barred room is an extimate object, the most horrible part of the house— not because it is a distillation of all its horrifying features but because it is without feature, the point where the house negates itself.

But let us return to the two forbidden spaces in *Rebecca,* for their differences will help us to make our final point. The bedroom is ruled over by Mrs. Danvers, Rebecca's devoted private maid, who keeps every- thing just as her mistress left it. In one scene in the bedroom, Danvers encourages the new Mrs. de Winter to sit before the vanity as Rebecca always did upon her return from an evening out. A photograph of Maxim faces Rebecca's empty seat, her brushes are arranged within reach. As

Danvers relates the details of how she would brush her mistress's hair, she begins to act out the gestures she describes. What is the effect of this scene?—A very strong sense of Rebecca's *absence*. A relation is set up between Danvers, all the personal items in the frame, and the seat in front of the vanity where Rebecca does *not* sit, that is, the place where her absence is signified. As we know from Saussure's famous example of the 8:45 Geneva-to-Paris train, something can be registered as missing only if it is assigned a place in a differential network; it is only absent as a signifier in relation to other signifiers. It is therefore not the unique presence of Rebecca that we miss in this scene but the way she fits in with the other objects. If Danvers were fired, the room rearranged, we would no longer half expect Rebecca to return. She would then be fully dead, and not simply absent. Her absence, in other words, is registered as a matter of sense, of signification—not of being as such.

A parallel scene is played out in the beach house. Here as well things are as Rebecca left them—almost. Dust has settled on everything here, cobwebs have formed. The differential network has begun to deteriorate. Max begins to narrate to his new wife, the second Mrs. de Winter, the events of his final confrontation with Rebecca. So far the scene is strikingly similar to the one we just examined. But this time, instead of remaining stationary and allowing Max to act out his own movements (as Danvers had acted out hers), the camera acts out, that is, it appears to "follow," the movements of Rebecca. The effect of this scene is quite different from the one in the bedroom, for here we have a sense not of the *absence* of something missing from its place but of the *presence* of something that is out of place. This scene is, in the precise sense, uncanny. What makes it uncanny is not the fact that we do not see Rebecca but the fact that the camera movement that indexes her presence *does not see us,* that is, it is a *unique* camera movement that does not "respond" to any establishable pattern of movement. It cannot be placed into any differential system of movements, any field/reverse field, moving/stationary, or other system. Without any assignable position within such a system of differences, the movement is devoid of sense. This, then, is our final definition of the anxiety that attends the uncanny: it is an affect aroused in reaction to an existence, to *pure existence, without sense*.[22] The camera movement that traces Rebecca's path is pure indication; it expresses a *purely thetic proposition,* "there is," and nothing more. If one were to fill this movement with meaning by inserting it into a differential system, the "there is," pure being would cease to be.

If the Frankenstein monster is—as most readers agree—the uncanny double of Frankenstein, why then is he allowed to speak, to try to make sense of his existence for us? Wouldn't speech, wouldn't the very signifying display of his existence destroy it?

Breast-Feeding and Freedom

In *Architecture civile,* a portfolio of drawings by the eighteenth-century "visionary" architect Jean Jacques Lequeu, we find the famous image of a rather robust woman lying on her back under an archway. The angle of the drawing is designed to profile her breasts; a bird in flight is visible at the top of the arch. The drawing, whose title is *He is free,* turns the image of vampirism inside out—replacing the terrifying vampire with the simple bird and the horror of the drying up of the breast with these full breasts—and returns us to our main concern: the relation between the advocacy of breast-feeding and a new, revolutionary definition of the subject as free. We have been arguing that this advocacy must be viewed as a manifestation of anxiety, especially similar to that expressed in vampire fiction. We have also argued that anxiety must not be interpreted, that we must not seek an external cause for it. This does not prevent us, however, from asking why there seems to have been so much anxiety in the late eighteenth and early nineteenth centuries, for we can answer this question without recourse to any external phenomenon. It was the very definition of the subject *as* free that ensured this increase of anxiety. That is, the eighteenth century detached a double of the subject that it made

inaccessible to annihilation; this double, unlike older notions of the immortal soul, allowed the subject to become detached from the world
without becoming attached to some otherworldly principle—the unfortunate consequence of the conception of the double as soul. Rather than
another principle, the Enlightenment double was conceived as nothing,
nothing but the negation of the subject's attachment to the world. This
double, then, guaranteed the *autonomy* of the subject, its freedom from a
pathetic existence in which it could be manipulated by other things,
persons, or traditions. But once this double was thus detached, once it
was set loose in the world, it was inevitable that the subject would
occasionally "run into it," approach it a little too closely. Whenever this
happens, anxiety signals us to take our distance once again.

This suggests that there are times when the real overtakes us
without warning, that we are sometimes not provided with an opportunity
to protect ourselves from it. Freud himself makes this suggestion: there
are occasions, he says, when anxiety is omitted, when it does not arise
to prepare us from the real's overproximity. In these cases, the results are
always catastrophic. We would argue that anxiety increases with the
emergence of the modern subject, that it is this inclusion of the real *within*
the symbolic, this negation within reality, that sounds the warning which
not only unsettles society but also allows it to take steps against a more
catastrophic confrontation.

The steps we must take have also already been spelled out: we
must not stop writing the impossibility of the real, the impossibility of
"saying it all." As Lacan pointed out in *The Ethics of Psychoanalysis,* it is
Kant's conception of the beautiful that writes this impossibility most
eloquently. The symbolic world—the second space of Freud's dream of
Irma's injection—is strictly parallel to the Kantian conception of the aesthetics of the beautiful. The question of aesthetics, as we know, assumed
a priority during the eighteenth century. In the widespread investigations
of this topic an important shift is discernible: the aesthetic field is regularly
conceived as *excluding* the subject. Think, for example, of Diderot's influ-

ential dictum: "Act as though the curtain never rose"; that is, subtract the subject from the aesthetic field and focus on establishing its unity and homogeneity. But while others excluded the subject in order the better to *affect* him/her, in order to attain the maximum emotional effect, Kant completely revolutionized aesthetic theory by excluding the subject in order to *protect* him/her—in order to hold onto the subject as free. This he did by defining the beautiful object as one that could not be subsumed under any determinate concept, as one about which we could not say all. Kant thus made the beautiful the signifier of a limit, a barrier against the real. With this the object *a,* the nothing that guarantees the subject's freedom, was prohibited from being spoken—and thus from being lost.

Before the Kantian revolution, as we know, the question of rights was determined "vertically"; rights were assigned and assured by a power beyond man. With the Kantian revolution, some have argued, this question was determined "horizontally"; it was assumed that the rights of one individual were only curtailed by those of another.[23] This made one subject the limit of his neighbor, that which prevented him from achieving all that he might. The problem with this conception of rights—which is, admittedly, *a* modern if not *the* modern conception, and certainly *not* the one that issues from the Kantian theorization of the subject—is that it perceives rights only as a series of *demands,* fully expressible in language and fully known to the subject who insists on them. This notion of rights pits one subject, one consciousness,[24] against another and decides all conflicts by determining which demand will best benefit the *general will.* What this reduction of rights to demands results in is the elimination of the question of the subject's desire. It eliminates the question of the subject's attachment to what language cannot say, to the unspeakable double that is the indestructible support of our freedom. For it is only if the "lonely hour" of the S_2, the final signifier that retroactively determines our meaning, "does *not* arrive," that our actions can be determined by anything other than self-interest.

So, if the advocacy of breast-feeding, as I have argued, is not to be understood as a demand but as a cry for the object-cause of desire, then it could only have been properly answered by assurances of the subject's freedom. It would be naive to suppose, however, that the historicism which turns a deaf ear to anxiety is only a current danger; it is clear that this same historicist response was a possibility contemporaneous with the anxiety-filled cry itself. It is certain that there were many who understood this anxiety about the drying up of the breast as a demand that the woman be subsumed under the category of the mother, that the biological family becomes the primary cell of society, even though these demands—that the woman cede her desire, that one place one's faith in the sexual relation—are absolutely antithetical to the political project whose possibilities had only just been opened up.

Victor Frankenstein is probably one of the most instructive illustrations of this sort of contemporary historicist reaction to the celebration of breast-feeding. As many critics have pointed out, *Frankenstein* is a novel about motherhood in which Frankenstein plays the role of an extremely bad mother. But what is it that makes him so bad? Not the fact that he refuses the demand of "his child," but that he interprets his cry as a demand. Earlier we asked, rhetorically, if the monster's attempt to justify his existence wouldn't entail the destruction of that existence—knowing well that it would. Now we must note that it is no coincidence that it is to Frankenstein that this justification is offered; it is he alone who hears the monster's long speech, the whole of which is set out in quotes, since it is from Frankenstein (and not the monster) that *we* (along with Walton) hear it. If Frankenstein is able to quote this long tale verbatim, we can only imagine that this is because *he takes the monster literally;* he refuses to question the words of the monster in order to discover what he *wants* to say, what he desires.

In other words, to Frankenstein, the monster is *not* the uncanny being we have taken him to be; to Frankenstein, the scientist, there is no pure being without sense, no desire. After the initial shock of seeing this monstrous embodiment of his failure, Frankenstein treats the creature as just another being whose rights threaten to abridge his own. It is no wonder, then, that he interprets the monster's cry as a demand, and of a very specific sort: a demand for a sexual relation. If he refuses to grant this demand, it is not because he doubts its validity or attainability. In fact we can surmise that he believes in this relation, that he believes that one subject must complement the other or engage him in a battle to the death. This last is the only relation he can imagine having with the monster, and so he refuses him, thinking the monster's profit can only mean his loss.

Under the circumstances, the novel could only have ended as it did—with Frankenstein's melancholy journeying to the ends of the earth. For, deprived of the ballast of the object *a*—the object-cause of desire that lends things their only value, their desirability—the subject is condemned to wander in pursuit of one thing after another, without any hope of freedom; that is, without any hope of choosing a path that is not dictated by the objects themselves. At one point Frankenstein refers to the monster as "my own vampire." We know that what he had in mind was closer to the vulgar image of the child sapping its mother's strength with its demands than to the horrifying Gothic image of the menacing double. We now see that he would have been better off had he felt some of the anxiety that vampires aroused in many of his contemporaries.

The *Unvermögender* Other: Hysteria and Democracy in America

The Teflon Totem

You don't have to know the plan of a building in order to bang your head against its walls; as a matter of fact, it is precisely through your ignorance that you *guarantee* such accidents. I couldn't help recalling Lacan's observation—a kind of ironic reechoing of Dr. Johnson's refutation of Bishop Berkeley—as I watched the various episodes of television's comically repeated battle with what it called the "Teflon President." Every idiotic blunder, every bold-faced lie that was caught by the cameras was played and replayed on the nightly news, juxtaposed with an image that directly contradicted, and thus exposed the falsity of, the president's words. But though by this means it could decisively refute one statement after another, the medium could not—by its own incredulously tendered admission—menace the position of the president himself. Ronald Reagan emerged virtually unscathed by all these proofs of the incompetence and mendacity of his speech. It was as though America had acquired its own Shroud of Turin, immune to all the doubts produced by fiber analysis.

Let's not stoop to lazy name-calling by noting merely that it was television that proved the bigger imbecile here; analysis is doomed unless one can name the precise failing involved. In this case we must point out (more precisely) that it was its own "*realist* imbecility" that television ended up exposing.[1] This malady received its clinical designation in "The Seminar on 'The Purloined Letter,'" where Lacan used it to explain the police's failure to locate the object of its methodically misdirected search: the Queen's stolen letter. Why couldn't the police find this object so obviously displayed? Because they were looking for it in the wrong place. The only time something can be hidden in plain sight (which is where,

in fact, the letter was hidden) is when its invisibility is a psychical condition and not merely a physical one. The police comb geographic space
and neglect completely the "intersubjective"[2] or signifying space, which
is where the letter remains unobserved. The realist imbecility, then, is
just this sort of error committed in the service of a "referential plenitude."
As Barthes describes it in his essay "The realistic effect," this imbecility
results from a tampering with the "tripartate nature of the sign," a sacrificing of the signified—the dimension of intersubjective truth—in favor
of the referent.[3] This sacrifice of the signified is, moreover, strictly dependent on the effacement of a statement's marks of enunciation. In other
words, the particularity of the enunciator must be abolished for the
"referential illusion" to take hold, for it to become possible to believe that
it is the referent alone that determines the truth value of a statement. The
reign, since the nineteenth century, of "objective" history is a consequence
of this belief, of this effacement of the signifying trace of the authorial
voice. Reality thus appears to be free standing, to be independent of and
prior to any statements one can make about it. History, then, follows
reality; it emerges from the fact that something happened then, something
existed there. The sole function of history is to tell the tale of what once
had been.

Barthes, who wrote his essay on the "reality effect" in 1968, cites
the then-current success of the Tutankhamun exhibit to illustrate the way
this "having-been-there" quality that history attributes to things continues
to induce the most massive response, the way it continues to structure
our world and dictate our actions. His excellent example of the modern
rage for the referent lacks only the properly ludicrous dimension of a
more recent example, again provided by American television. Toward
the end of December 1989, major and local television networks all at once
dispatched their camera crews and news staffs to Aspen, Colorado. What
was the purpose of this not-insignificant expenditure of time and money?
In each case it was to obtain one very specific image: that of the now-
empty spot in front of Bonnie's restaurant where Ivana had confronted

Donald Trump. Now, it is precisely this imbecilic devotion to the referent
that made television news the dupes in their battle with Reagan. So
absorbed were the news staffs in pinning down the president's lies and
errors—his referential failures, let us call them—that they neglected to
consider the intersubjective dimension of the whole affair; they forgot to
take account of the strength of the American audience's *love* for Reagan.
If you know anything about love, then you perforce know something
about Lacan; you know what he means when he says that love is giving
what you do not have. He means that what one loves in another is
something more than the other, some unnameable thing that exceeds any
of the other's manifestations, anything he has to give. We accept someone's gifts and ministrations because we love him; we do not love him
because he gives us these gifts. And since it is that something beyond the
gifts that we love and not the gifts themselves, it is possible to dislike the
gifts, to find fault with all the other's manifestations, and still love the
other—as the behavior of the hysteric makes clear. The unnameable excess, the exorbitant thing that is loved, is what Lacan calls the object *a,*
and so we might say that television didn't have to know anything of
Lacanian theory in order to bang its head against this object. What television attacked was the president's statements; what it left intact was the
object *a,* the instance of enunciation—that very thing which the "realist
imbecility" always and necessarily (as the condition of its possibility)
disregards. It is this object that allowed Reagan to be Reagan; it was in
this object—and obviously not in his statements—that his consistency was
to be found. American didn't love Reagan for what he said, but simply
because he was Reagan.

   It is important not to confuse the object *a* with some poetical or
essentialist notion of the subject. This object does not precede the statement but is instead its retroactive effect, the surplus that overruns what
is said and that "always comes back to the same place," always designates
the same thing—again, retroactively—no matter how self-contradictory
the statements that produce it. This is why it cannot be dispersed by any

simple appeal to the referent, by any refutation of the subject's speech—because it posits a subject that is the same without being self-identical.

Counterbalancing America's love for Reagan was its often-noted lack of regard for the news media. It has also been noted that "liberal bourgeois states" (states with long-standing democracies) such as Britain, France, and America do not regard the police very favorably.[4] These observations may not be unrelated, for it might be supposed that it is precisely because the news *acts* like the police that it meets with such disfavor. But just what it means to "act like the police" requires clarification, and so we refer to a certain type of fiction—produced first, and primarily, in Britain, France, and America[5]—which has always been intent on denigrating these actions: it is called detective fiction. This fiction systematically differentiates the law of the police from the law of the detective in order to valorize the latter. My hypothesis is that *detective fiction is a product of modern democracy,* and thus I will argue that the law of the detective is that which subtends democracy and that it is shown to be jeopardized by the law of the police, that is, by the law of scientific realism.

There are, of course, some who continue to insist on tracing detective fiction back to Greek drama, but most critics are willing to acknowledge that detection is a historically specific form of fiction that began only in the 1840s, with writers such as Edgar Allan Poe. Those who hold to the former belief, however, usually argue that the genre is occasioned by the rise of scientific reason and the establishment of the laws of evidence. They then propose that detective fiction is a celebration of scientific reason, that the detective is an exemplar of positivist thought. What proponents of this argument ignore is the fact that scientific reason is only there in detective fiction to be ridiculed and subverted. What they remain blind to is the "symbolic mutation" in which detection participates, a mutation otherwise referred to as the democratic revolution.[6] This is not to say, however, that there is no relation between the scientific and the social revolutions, for indeed there is.

To understand this relation—and the subtlety of the difference between the two terms—let us return to the phenomenon of the "Teflon President." It is possible to conceive of a different argument from the one we proposed. One might have supposed instead that by continuing to believe in the president even as it grew more and more suspicious of the president's statements, the American television audience was repeating— in a peculiar, twentieth-century way—the gesture of a late-seventeenth-century philosopher: René Descartes. For what, in fact, did Descartes do if not reveal that there is an instance (which we have been calling, according to linguistic theory, the enunciating instance) that exceeds all the enunciations, or statements, a subject may make? The cogito is nothing but this enunciating instance, and its isolation by Descartes is what allowed him to make his remarkable, historically consequential argument: even if every thought one thinks, every statement one utters, can be doubted, can be shown to be guilty of some error or deception, the *instance* of doubt—of thought or speech—*cannot* be doubted; it remains innocent of all charges of error.

This would not be the first time Americans were suspected of Cartesian sympathies. At the beginning of part 2 of *Democracy in America,* for example, Alexis de Tocqueville declares Cartesianism to be the natural mode of thought in democracies.[7] Rather than relying on the authority of others, on a tradition of knowledge established by ancestor-scholars, de Tocqueville claims, democratic peoples prefer to base their thinking on common sense, on those clear and distinct ideas that are, in principle, available to anyone who will submit his thinking to radical doubt, who will purge himself of all subjective particulars. What is, of course, precipitated out by this radical operation is a pure mode of the subject, denatured, universal, the subject, in short, of modern science. Some might object that there is, on the contrary, a good deal of unscientific hocus-pocus in Descartes, that he uses God as a gimmick to cheat science, but this is to misunderstand that his God is merely the principle that the Other is just like you and that this is the very same principle—that of the possibility of total consensus—upon which modern science is founded.

But not only science. This principle also unleashed the great democratic revolutions of the eighteenth century, making Descartes the father not only of science but of the American revolution as well. For no one would have thought of fighting for the rights of a universal subject— a subject whose value is not determined by race, creed, color, sex, or station in life—no one would have thought of waging a war on behalf of liberty and justice for *all* subjects if Descartes had not already isolated that abstract instance in whose name the war would be waged: the democratic subject, devoid of characteristics.

America's sense of its own "radical innocence" has its most profound origins in this belief that there is a basic humanity unaltered by the diversity of the citizens who share in it. Democracy is the universal quantifier by which America—the "melting pot," the "nation of immigrants"—constitutes itself as a nation. If *all* our citizens can be said to be Americans, this is not because we share any positive characteristics but rather because we have all been given the right to *shed* these characteristics, to present ourselves as disembodied before the law. I divest myself of positive identity, therefore I am a citizen. This is the peculiar logic of democracy. It is also a logic that can be used to explain the phenomenon of the Teflon President. An American public made sentimental about the flag redoubled its belief in the fundamental democratic principle for which it stands. Reagan, who was largely responsible for stirring up this sentiment, became the emblematic repository, the most visible beneficiary of this increase of belief that beyond all its diverse and dubious statements there exists a precious, universal, "innocent," instance in which we can all recognize ourselves.

We now have, then, two different explanations for the same phenomenon. In both cases we claim that the charges against Reagan did not stick because they were aimed exclusively at the concrete man—his class-belonging and alliances (the Bloomingdale friends), his professional background as an actor, his "psychological make-up" (the unwillingness to "meddle" in administrative affairs, the inability or unwillingness to recall details), etc. But by establishing these parallels between the object *a* and the cogito, the psychoanalytic and the philosophical explanations, have we not invited the reiteration of one of the most common charges against psychoanalysis: that it is ahistorical, that it disregards the concrete individual in favor of an abstract, universal subject? How much of *this* charge can be made to stick?

One must first recall that the concept of the universal subject is not itself ahistorical; introduced, as we have said, by Descartes only at the end of the seventeenth century, it must instead be acknowledged as a modern, historically specific concept—one without which psychoanalysis would have been unthinkable. For psychoanalysis, too, addresses itself to a nonconcrete subject; it founds itself on the denial of the nominalist claim that all one encounters in everyday reality are particular, determinate individuals. The subject is never fully determinate according to psychoanalysis, which treats this indeterminateness as a real feature of the subject. This is why the historicist response to the psychoanalytic concept of the subject is so misguided. The response—which characterizes much of contemporary theory—approaches the universal subject as a vague concept that can, with more or less effort and a better knowledge of history, be given more precise attributes. This hasty historicism fails to understand that the universal subject is not a *vague* concept but, in Charles S. Peirce's sense of the term, a *general* one. That is, the concept does not poorly or wrongly describe a subject whose structure is actually determinate but precisely indicates a subject that is in some sense *objectively indeterminate*. Against the faddish critique of the universal subject, psychoanalysis insists on this concept's political importance.

But even while admitting the similarity between the psychoanalytic and Cartesian notions of the subject, we have already begun to underline their differences. For if both subjects proclaim themselves to be devoid of substantial, determinate existence, only the psychoanalytic subject can properly be described as *in*determinate. The cogito, on the contrary, is an instance of certainty. What is it that accounts for this difference? The love of the Other. The cogito is the object *a* under the aspect of love.

Let us cite the Lacanian formula once again: love is giving what one does not have. But let us this time put the formula in perspective by reviewing the distinctions between need, demand, and desire. On the level of need the subject can be satisfied by some *thing* that is in the possession of the Other. A hungry child will be satisfied by food—but only by food. If the mother, mistaking the meaning of her child's cry, proffers, instead, a blanket, she will, of course, fail to satisfy the child. Need requires for its satisfaction a *particular* object, nourishment, for example, *or* warmth. It is not a matter of indifference which; one cannot be substituted for another. It is on the next level, that of demand, that love is situated. Whether one gives a child whose cry expresses a demand for love a blanket, or food, or even a scolding, matters little. The particularity of the object is here annulled; almost any will satisfy—as long as it comes from the one to whom the demand is addressed. Unlike need, which is particular, demand is, in other words, absolute, universalizing. The indifferent objects are all received as signs of the Other's love. But what does this mean? It means that the objects come to represent something more than themselves, that the Other now appears to give something more than just these objects. What is this "something more," and what, then, is love? The something more is the indeterminate part of its being (in Lacanian terms the object *a*), which the Other (or subject) *is* but does not *have,* and therefore cannot give. Love's deception, however, is that the object *a* can be given, that the Other can surrender the indeterminate part of its being to the subject who thus becomes the Other's sole satisfaction, its reason to be. This relation is reciprocal, with the subject also surrendering that which *it* lacks to the Other. Finally, there is desire. On this level the Other retains what it does not have and does not surrender it to the subject. The subject's desire is aimed, then, at a *particular absolute, absolute* in the sense that, like demand, it aims beyond particular objects to that "something more" that exceeds them, *particular* in that the refusal to surrender it means that it remains unique to the Other—it is nontransferable.

Let us return to our discussion: the cogito's certainty derives from the love of the Other. In addition to the cogito's certainty, this logic of love explains the curious fact that while Descartes began by placing his certainty with the cogito and doubting all the cogito's thoughts, he (and the historicism he enabled) ended up by allowing the cogito to disappear beneath the truth of its thoughts and statements. As long as these indifferent, doubtable objects come from the cogito, they are received as the signifiers of the Other's love, of the communicability and truth that unites one cogito with another.

The situation in America is somewhat altered. Here we make a point of resisting the universalizing that belongs to the order of the cogito in order to celebrate difference, particularity. This does not mean that we have given up loving our leaders; unfortunately we still continue to participate in love's deception that the Other will give us what it cannot possibly give. We continue, in short, to demand a master, but one that is significantly different from the Other that sustains the cogito, since we require *this* master to accredit our singularity rather than our commonality. Yet in posing this demand to its elected leaders, Americans are confronted by a dilemma: every sign of accreditation cancels the difference to which it is supposed to bear witness, for it is precisely by bearing witness, by making difference communicable to another, that any sign automatically universalizes what it represents and thereby abolishes its singularity; how, then, to maintain simultaneously one's relation to a master and one's uniqueness?

America's solution is, in analytic terms, hysterical: one elects a master who is demonstrably fallible—even, in some cases, incompetent. What may first appear to be a stumbling block turns out on closer inspection to be a solution: Americans love their masters not simply in spite of their frailties but because of them. We can put it this way: the pluralism that characterizes American democracy depends on our devotion to an *unvermögender* Other.[8] If everything this Other says or does *fails* to deliver the accreditation we seek, if all the Other's responses prove inadequate, then our difference is saved, it survives intact, as undiminished as our devotion—which is lodged, like our demands, with the Other and not with the Other's responses. It is, in fact, the differential between demand and response, the very vanity of our hopes, that sustains them. Unlike the relation to the cogito, in which all its statements are taken for truths, the relation to the *unvermögender* Other ensures that its statements will be taken for lies.

Television news, then—to conclude our consideration of the teflon totem—by pointing out the errors in Reagan's statements was not, as we originally assumed, simply attempting to discredit the president. Rather, by discrediting him, it sought to sustain our appeals to him. Like Dora, who dedicated herself to procuring for her invalid father, the news dedicated itself to hysterical, televisual displays designed to keep the American demand for a master alive.

It must be made clear, however, that the paradox that supports the peculiarly American relation to its masters is, in some sense, specific to democracy *as such*. Democracy hystericizes the subject. This observation can be sustained by reference to a number of ineliminable paradoxes, but we will cite only one, that provided by the practice of universal suffrage. According to the terms of this stated right, every citizen is given the opportunity to express his or her individual will; every citizen is given a vote that counts. The paradox is that it only counts as one, as an abstract statistic. The individual's particularity is thus annulled by the very act of its expression.[9] If one's difference is, by definition, that which escapes recognition, then any recognition of it will always seem to miss the mark, to leave something unremarked. The subject of democracy is thus constantly hystericized, divided between the signifiers that seek to name it and the enigma that refuses to be named.

The problem with the American *form* of democracy is that however visibly it decries the actions of the Other, it still continues to believe in the Other's power to sanction the vast array of differences to which its citizens lay claim. This belief encourages that "narcissism of small differences" against which Freud and all the other critics of "bourgeois individualism" have for so long warned us. This narcissism fuels that single-minded and dangerous defense of difference that so totally isolates us from our neighbors. And yet this belief in the Other-who-authorizes convinces us (despite every indication to the contrary) that this isolation can, in principle, be peacefully maintained, that the Other presides over a nonconflictual space in which all differences can harmoniously coexist.

Lacan's systematic assault on American ego psychology and, beyond this, the "American way of life" is mounted in defense of a different notion of difference. Not one that demands to be attended to *now,* recognized *now,* but one that waits to be exfoliated in time and through a relation to others. This other difference will emerge only once our appeals to the Other have been abandoned, once we accept the fact that there is "no Other of the Other." Nothing guarantees the Other's certainty, consistency, or completeness. The Other possesses nothing that we want, nothing to validate our existence.

That the time for understanding this notion of difference has not arrived in America is everywhere apparent, from local phenomena like that of the Reagan/news relation to our basic conception of the role of the law. In America it is assumed that the law of democracy is one that withdraws, that recedes as far as possible, intervenes as little as possible in order to allow the individuality of each subject to flourish unhampered. Big government is urged to retreat, to assert itself merely as the neutral agent overseeing the protection of the individual. To illustrate this principle, let me recall for you the way America has been, to a large extent, spatially disposed. With the Land Ordinance of 1785, Thomas Jefferson (another "father of democracy") decreed that the western territories would be laid out according to a grid plan adapted from several important eastern cities. This was a Cartesian gesture if ever there was one, for the grid disregarded all characteristics of topography and submitted America to an abstract law. The argument made to defend the plan, and the reason it was so widely accepted, was that it was thought to be the least obtrusive, most neutral way of legislating the carving out of space. The grid does not rule in advance the sort of building, city, or whatever will come to occupy any particular quadrant; it was perceived to be a plan without a program.

Supporting this conception of the law is a belief in a protective (against what, we shall soon see), consistent Other that can, in principle, accommodate all the demands of its citizens. The psychoanalytic notion of the law is not like this; rather than being merely "neutral," this law comports a certain exceptional violence. There is within the law itself something lawless—let us call it, with reference to our image of the grid, Broadway. Lacan's critique of the "American way of life" is directed, we might say, at our suppression of "Broadway." As opposed to the American conception, which believes that justice has only to be distributed, this psychoanalytic conception believes justice must be created.

The Modern Forms of Power

> Above the race of men stands an immense and tutelary power . . . that power is absolute, minute, regular, provident and mild . . . it provides for [the] security [of its citizens], forsees and supplies their necessities, manages their principal concerns, directs their industry. . . . I have always thought that the servitude of the regular, quiet and gentle kind which I have just described might be combined more easily than is commonly believed with some outward forms of freedom and that it might even establish itself under the wing of the sovereignty of the people.[10]

It is de Tocqueville who is the author of this, one of the best-known passages from *Democracy in America.* It may, nevertheless, strike some of us as a bit uncanny. For since the dramatic opening of *Discipline and Punish,* in which we witnessed the whole-scale displacement of a repressive form of power by one that sought to provide for the welfare of its subjects, we have become more familiar with Foucault's analysis of the paradoxical effects of this brand new "mild and provident" form of law. But this comparison obliges us to observe an important and unsettling difference: when de Toqueville wrote his book, in 1835, the new form of despotism whose emergence he feared had not yet come into existence; when Foucault wrote, however, fascism and a whole list of other despotic horrors had already been unleashed by totalitarian regimes. How is it, then, that Foucault continued to speak of *the* modern form of power, as though there were only one? What I wish to criticize is not only his historical blindness but (since it is more fundamental, the very source of this blindness) his conception of disciplinary power itself. Foucault presents it as though it were a permanently viable form of power, as though its prolonged continuance did not lead inexorably to its own subversion by totalitarianism. The strength of the argument advanced by de Toqueville is that it understands the tutelary form of democracy as an unstable form that must be either overthrown in favor of new freedoms or taken over entirely by a new despotism.

What is the basic argument—shared not only by de Tocqueville and Foucault but by others as well—regarding this modern form of power? It is a power enabled by the historic overthrow of monarchy. At this point power ceases to be incorporated in the body of the king or in any other source. All connections to the old order of society—to its traditions, knowledge, heirlooms, as well as its fathers—are radically severed; the new order is structured around their disappearance. But if it is no longer incorporated in a source, if no authority wields it, what is it that legitimates the modern exercise of power? With no external support, it appears that it legitimates itself. Power is simultaneously that which society produces and that which produces society—we encounter here that circularity which characterizes the performative utterance. Modern power is immanent in the very relations that structure the social order. It is this aspect of modern power—its impersonal and omnipresent nature—that is most disturbing, since it threatens to enmesh the subject in a network of domination. Yet Foucault's theory seems to offer an escape from the totality of this domination by maintaining that the social field cannot be totalized, that it is crossed by an array of different and even competing discourses. In the ruptures sparked by this competition, in the interstices of the network, pockets of resistance form.

I don't think anyone has ever stopped to wonder if these contradictory discourses would, in fact, necessarily enable resistance; perhaps this is because Foucault banished all the psychoanalysts from his republic. For, while it seems logical to expect that the different subject positions one is summoned to occupy would come into conflict with each other, psychoanalysis has developed a logic that allows us to understand how one might simultaneously hold two contradictory positions; how one might hold to one term and repress its contrary; how a society could be founded on a nonrecognition of the contradictions it contains.

It is this last possibility that interests us at the moment, and so we turn to *Totem and Taboo,* where the conditions of this possibility are elaborated by Freud in his description of the totemic form of society. How is this society formed? The primal father—the father who kept all the power and all the enjoyment to himself—is slain by the brothers.[11] In order to inscribe the parricide as a fait accompli, in order for the brothers to assure themselves that they will all be equal henceforth, that no one will take the place of the dead father, society is installed under the banner of the son who signifies the father's absence. Since the primal father is the principle of *jouissance,* of excess enjoyment, the signifier of his absence will be the son who promises to protect society from the trauma of *jouissance*'s return. The son stands for the evacuation, or drying up, of excess enjoyment and thus for the possibility of pleasure's even apportionment. In Lacanian terms, it is the object *a* that the son evicts, for if you recall, it is that object which is the excess in the subject, which causes the subject to be excentric to, or other than, itself. This eviction of excess pleasure forms the son as an ideal father, "mild and provident" in de Tocqueville's words, "kinder and gentler" in Peggy Noonan's.[12] He is the place to which all our questions are addressed, the place of knowledge; he is therefore often imagined under the traits of the educator (think for example of Noonan's ideal: America's new "education president"). The ideal father installs a badly needed certainty in the place of the devastating uncertainty, the crisis of legitimation, that follows in the wake of the primal father's murder.

Now, it seems to me that Foucault's description of modern power resembles this description by Freud. *Discipline and Punish* begins with the spectacle *not* of monarchical power, as Foucault claims—he has isolated only a moment and not the structure of this earlier form of power—but with the spectacle of the obscene, traumatizing *jouissance* of the primal father constructed *retroactively* by the society of brothers. The body of Damiens is ripped apart, totally shattered in order to feed his enjoyment. His parricide is then marked in Foucault's text by a recitation of some of the rules "for the House of young prisoners in Paris." Reading these rules, we can see that the law has now assumed a tutelary form: it instructs, it guards, it protects, and it guides the prisoner throughout his day. Not only that, it *constructs* the day and the prisoner along with it. The law comports the affirmative, positive force of the symbolic; it causes the world to come into being by naming it. Lacan called this form of the law the paternal metaphor, or the Name-of-the-Father. A symbolic coalescence of knowledge and power, it bathes the prisoner in the bright light of intelligibility. As we have said, it subjects the prisoner totally, since it is the cause of its existence as well as its visibility. And yet the hope of transgression is never distant from the disciplinary society Foucault analyzes. The possibility of the overthrow of power haunts the structure like a phantom. Why is this?

Again, Foucault's point is that it is because there is a multiplicity of discourses that this promise is held out. But Freud's analysis of the totemic form of society offers a different answer. The ideal father—the number-one son in the society of brothers—only affirms, only becomes the principle of the regulation of alliances, *by forbidding excess enjoyment,* only becomes the principle of knowledge and intelligibility by casting out the object *a* that marks the point at which the order of intelligibility collapses. Foucault wanted to found his analysis of disciplinary power on the expulsion of the notion of the repressive father. He thought he accomplished this by describing a mild and provident form of law—an ideal father, in psychoanalytic terms. The problem is that in expunging the primal father, the one who commands *jouissance,* and replacing him with the ideal father (the law of power/knowledge), Foucault installed the very principle he meant to eject: the principle of interdiction. For the ideal father *is* the father who interdicts—*jouissance.* He is able to shelter and protect only because he interdicts excess pleasure. According to Freud, it is his interdictions—therefore not the other contradictory discourses or subject positions—his *interdictions* that give the subject a whiff of hope; it is they that suggest the possibility of transgression. In forbidding excess enjoyment, they appear to be its only obstacle; the subject/prisoner is thus free to dream of their removal and of the bounty of pleasure that will then be his.

But how can we be so sure that Foucault is incorrect, that it is not the potential collision of different discourses that provides the possibility of transgression? Because in a totemic society, a society ruled by a tutelary power, the contradictions among discourses are largely unacknowledged and conscientiously guarded against. The totemic is a pluralistic society. America is a good example. The scrupulous autonomy and independence of the brothers are assured in this fraternity. The field may be glutted with contradictions without disturbing the society in the least. This is not to say that the social order remains stable; we claimed earlier that it is not. As Freud makes clear in *Civilization and Its Discontents,* the more one renounces enjoyment, the more one is obliged to renounce it. Every sacrifice of pleasure strengthens the demand for sacrifice. In a society ruled by a provident power—an ideal father—interdictions grow more and more numerous. Witness the fresh lot of interdictions that besiege us daily: barriers—from gates, to moats, to attack dogs—have begun to encircle our homes and to forbid entry to any strangers; injunctions are posted on everything from walls to milk cartons—don't smoke here, don't smoke there, don't eat this, don't eat that, and above all don't abuse your children. If you need any proof that a tutelary power is fundamentally the signifier of the death of the primal father (the one who enjoys), you will find none better than this current obsession with child abuse. The primal father is primarily the father who seduces the child—at least this is the guise under which he appears most often to psycho-analysis, in the complaints of the hysterics. More generally we could say that the campaign against the primal father is visible in the increasing abhorence of the pleasure of others. In fact, the intolerable Other *is* pleasure in today's society. What have increased as of late are interdictions. These are the mechanisms that construct the phenomenon that Foucault calls surveillance.

You may have recognized here what we earlier called the *unvermögender* Other; the ideal father is "a man without means." The only way to be master of desire—which is what the ideal father is supposed to be—is to be either impotent or dead. The fraternity this father constructs is equally impotent, paralyzed by the interdictions that are required to stave off the conflict between the brothers. The best literary illustration of this is James Joyce's *Dubliners*. Language, country, religion. Three ideal fathers and a slough of interdictions. Such a society cannot continue indefinitely. The law of the ideal father is eventually repealed, and the despotic primal father returns. A totalitarian regime takes over.

It is essential to recognize that totalitarianism is not simply the reinstatement of some earlier form of despotism, a reversion to an especially brutal monarchical order, for example. If, as we stated at the start, totalitarianism is a specifically *modern* form of power, this is because it is dependent on the democratic revolution's privileging of the individual, of the *people* rather than the king, or some other leader. The totalitarian leader's power "comes from below," as Foucault would say; his is only the power that the people confer on him—by placing him in the position of their ego ideal, as Freud says in *Group Psychology and the Analysis of the Ego*. This is so clearly the case that Gustav Le Bon does not bother to say very much at all about the leader of the totalitarian group, and, though Freud notes this as a criticism, neither does he. Yet where Le Bon had focused on the relations among the members of the group, Freud insisted that it was their common, preexisting relation to the leader that determined the totalitarian formation of the group.

Psychoanalysis does not, however, as is sometimes proposed, argue that all groups are basically totalitarian in nature. Instead it provides an analysis that allows us to see how totalitarianism follows—but not inevitably—from democracy. But under what conditions can democracy be maintained and totalitarianism forestalled? Lefort's formula is still the best: "Power is and remains democratic [only] when it proves to belong to no one." ". . . *when it proves to belong to no one.*"[13] The phrasing is exact, but in need of elaboration, for by itself it admits of more than one interpretation. Have we not argued that a totemic society is founded on this very same principle, that of the *exclusion* of the primal father from the community of brothers? And hasn't Foucault made the same argument about the modern, disciplinary society: that no one need occupy the central tower in the panopticon, no one need possess power, for power to exert itself? And yet we have also argued that a totemic society initiates the *subversion* of democracy and have criticized Foucault for collapsing different forms of modern power, for failing to distinguish democracy from its subversion in totalitarianism. Isn't it precisely this notion of "no one" that justifies the collapse? Justifies, no, but facilitates, certainly—by lending to Foucault's theory just that quiver of paradox that has so far proved seductive: at the very moment when power began to be wielded

by no one, everyone became subjected to it. We may as well state at the
outset that the "no one" of Foucault's theory does not seem to be quite
the same as the "no one" of Lefort's.

What exactly does Foucault say about this "no one" who occupies
the place of power?

> It does not matter who exercises power. Any individual, taken
> at random, can operate the machine. . . . Similarly, it does not
> matter what motivates him: the curiosity of the indiscreet, the
> malice of a child, the thirst for knowledge of a philosopher, or
> the perversity of those who take pleasure in spying or
> punishing.[14]

In other words, this no one is, more properly, *no one in particular,* anyone.
It may seem unfair to put too much emphasis on a statement made with
reference to Bentham's panopticon, since this architectural device may be
insufficient to support the complex theory of Foucault. But the essential
point remains that in his theory the notion that power "belongs to no
one" is attached, as here, to the observation that since the modern form
of power—or law—has no external guarantees, it may be seen to guarantee itself. This means that the discourse of power or the statement of
law does not derive its power from the person who speaks it; it is not by
virtue of any quality, power, or interest of the enunciator that the discourse possesses its force. In fact, the discourse or statement annuls all
qualities, powers, or interests of the enunciator; it effaces all contingent
characteristics in order to fill this empty, anonymous space with its own
tautological truth. The enunciator coincides with his function, that of
enunciator; the bureaucracy "automatizes and disindividualizes power,"
creating as its product the anonymous, impersonal bureaucrat.

From this angle the paradox of the modern form of power begins
to look more familiar. Is this not the same paradox that is manifest in
scientific statements, historical narratives, maxims, that nineteenth-cen-

tury class of utterances whose badge of truth was their erasure of all the traces of their enunciation? If Foucault's work was so easily accepted as a theory of the nineteenth-century novel, this is because the realist novel had already been theorized in his terms. It had already been argued that the narrator was nobody in particular, nobody but a generalized consciousness. And if, despite all the well-meaning and careful attempts, by Foucault and others, to dispel the "paranoid" interpretations of his theory, power, as he described it, still seems inescapable, then this is surely the result of the fact that by announcing themselves in such a neutral, general form (that is, as coming from nowhere), the discourses of power seem to embrace everyone in their address.

When Lefort says that power belongs to no one, he means something different from this. His "no one" is attached not to the fact that the law guarantees itself but to the fact that *there are no guarantees*. Democracy, Lefort argues, is "the dissolution of the ultimate markers of certainty." The discourse of power—the law—that gives birth to the modern subject can guarantee neither its own nor the subject's legitimacy. There where the subject looks for justification, for approval, it finds no one who can certify it. The modern subject encounters a certain blind spot in the Other, a certain lack of knowledge—an ignorance—in the powerful Other.

Historians are undoubtedly correct to point out that a great gathering of information was begun in the nineteenth century. The moment the individual subject became visible as a social value, it also became the object of an intense scrutiny. But it must also be remembered that this information proliferated as verificationism collapsed. Which resulted in what? A mass of information that could not be verified. It was the combination of these two conditions—and not simply the fact that the individual subject became the object of several new "human sciences"—that produced the modern democratic subject. It is to the fact that power is *disjoined* from knowledge, that the force which produces the subject is blind, that the subject owes its precious singularity. For, if there is a *lack of knowledge* in the Other, then there is necessarily a *surplus of meaning* in the subject, an excess for which the Other cannot account, that is to say, there is something in the subject that escapes social recognition.

How to conclude? The space inhabited by indeterminate subjects will never be harmonious; a democracy is not a utopia. First of all, the attendant paradoxes that we referred to earlier through the example of universal suffrage contribute to a great deal of neurotic insatisfaction. It seems that the preeminent form of modern power is the source of "modern nervousness." Additionally, since there where the "markers of certainty" are erased, enjoyment breaks out, democracy seems designed, if not to brew up more dissatisfaction, at least to acknowledge the impossibility of its alleviation. For, as Freud says in *Totem and Taboo,* "sexual needs are not capable of uniting men"; they separate them.[15] In other words, once you admit enjoyment into the system, you have, unavoidably, a conflictual space, one that will not lie down flat, as on a grid. Yet it is just this conflict that preserves democracy. It is only this dissatisfaction and this struggle over the definition of the subject and of its relations to other subjects that prevent us from surrendering these definitions to the Other. It is only because I doubt that I am therefore a democratic citizen.

The Actuarial Origins of Detective Fiction

Barton Keyes is a first-rate detective, or so we learn from Walter Neff whose voice-over narration, addressed to Keyes, is dense with praise for him and with recollections of his remarkable talent for detection. Of these recollections, one stands out particularly, and not only because the case on which it bears is the very one in which Neff is himself guiltily entangled. This scene of Keyes's magisterial display of reason is clearly invested with all the emotions of fear and relief that stem from Neff's involvement in the insurance scam under investigation, but it is also invested with the emotions of admiration and pride that characterize Neff's involvement with Keyes. Dramatizing, then, the full ambivalence of Neff's relation to the mentor whom he will not choose to follow, the scene is nevertheless *unam*bivalent with respect to its evaluation of this mentor's logic.

Keyes's superior, the man with the biggest "office" at the Pacific All-Risk Insurance Company, is Mr. Norton. An extremely foolish man, he has just pompously and precipitously announced to Keyes, Neff, and the newly widowed Mrs. Dietrichson his ill-founded conclusion: Mrs. Dietrichson is not entitled to collect any insurance money from her husband's death since it was obviously a suicide and a clear attempt to defraud his company. It is precisely by exposing the foolishness and ill-foundedness of this conclusion that Keyes's performance derives its power. Delivered with great rhetorical flair and punctuated by the frenetic gestures of a man impatient with, even contemptuous of, his opponent, Keyes's counterargument begins with what is meant to be an outright dismissal of his opponent's reasoning. The devastating charge? He is ignorant of statistics:

You've never read an actuarial table in your life, have you? Why there are ten volumes on suicide alone. Suicide: by race, by color, by occupation, by sex, by season of the year, by time of day. Suicide, how committed: by poison, by firearms, by drowning, by leaps. Suicide by poison, subdivided by types of poison, such as corrosives, irritants, systemic gases, narcotics, alkaloids, proteins, and so forth. Suicide by leaps, subdivided by leaps from high places, under the wheels of trains, under the wheels of trucks, under the feet of horses, under steamboats. But, Mr. Norton, of all the cases on record, there's not one single case of suicide by someone jumping off the back end of a moving train.

Appearing in what is arguably the climactic scene of the film *Double Indemnity* (Billy Wilder, 1944), this speech by Keyes is presented as decisive. But all the rhetorical force and narrative consequence of this argument should not prevent us from observing that there is, nevertheless, something unsatisfying about it. How is it that an appeal to statistics can come to be taken as a devastating argument? What power can possibly issue from a recourse to mathematical probability? Every investigation begins when we cease to be able to take something for granted. Mine begins here with this scene and with this question: what, in the final analysis, do numbers have to do with detection?

It would seem at first that we could begin answering these questions by linking detective fiction to the advent of rationalism. Marjorie Nicolson, for example, makes this link in her description of the detective, who, she says, "ignores . . . clues in order to devote himself to thought. Having like his great predecessor [Descartes] thought away all the universe, nothing remains but the culprit. By the strength of logic alone, he has reconstructed the universe, and in his proper place has set the villain of the piece."[1] While she is referring specifically to the French tradition of detectives as opposed to the English, whose prime exemplar, Sherlock Holmes, "laboriously and carefully accumulate[s] all possible clues, passing over nothing as too insignificant, filling his little boxes and envelopes with everything that comes his way," it has often been argued that even Holmes, who always looks a little out of place at the scene of the crime, is not primarily a man of experience. If he sees things that others miss, this is because his investigation takes off from rational categories that they do not seem to possess. From C. Auguste Dupin to Ironside, then, the tradition of detectives is that of the armchair rationalist, known less for his perceptiveness than for his skepticism; the detective is one who withdraws from the world of the senses, of which he remains infinitely suspicious, in order to become more attentive to the clear and distinct prescriptions of a priori ideas.

Keyes is a detective in this mode: suspicious of everything and everyone, including the one woman he ever got close to, unwilling even to state what day of the week it is until he consults his calendar and then checks to see if the calendar is this year's, he trusts only the feeling he gets in the pit of his stomach that tells him when something is wrong. This feeling—his "little man," he calls it—that never errs, how are we to understand it if not as a remnant of the Cartesian tradition, a somewhat hypochondriacal version of the cogito? If Keyes's recitation of a list of statistics from an actuarial table leaves us somewhat unsatisfied, we might attribute this to nothing more than the fact that the rationalist, as compared to the man of experience, is always less exciting, more colorless. Detectives, insofar as they are rationalists, are never far from insurance men, claims adjustors. This seems to have been the insight of James M. Cain, who equated detection with insurance in *The Postman Always Rings Twice* as well as in *Double Indemnity*.

But this insight overruns the work of Cain, for the connection between detection and insurance can be established historically. The origins of detective fiction coincide, it turns out, with what Ian Hacking has termed "the avalanche of numbers." According to Hacking, there was an exponential increase in the printing of numbers between 1830 and 1848 (the precise moment at which the detective story emerges) as a passion for counting—both things and people—incited the Western nations.[2] This new numberlust was an immediate response to the various democratic revolutions demanding that people be counted. The increased interest in numbers had a double-edged effect. The first was *corrosive:* statistics had a mordant effect on the image of the monarchical body that had held the old, premodern nations together.[3] The second was *constitutive:* statistics served to individualize the bodies of the citizens, to create more and more kinds of people. As Keyes's speech illustrates, after the avalanche of numbers, there were no longer simply people who attempted suicide and others who did not. Instead there were those who attempted suicide by poison, subdivided by types of poison and subdivided again by race, by color, by occupation, and so on—and all sorts of others who did not.

Entire bureaucracies grew up around these numbers, to count, cross-reference, and analyze them. But it was not merely numbers that were being manipulated by these bureaucracies; it was people, their happiness and well-being, that were primarily at issue. The interest in numbers was part of the modern nation-state's concern for the welfare of its population, with whose well-being the state's own was now intimately linked. What statistics calculated was the "felicity"[4] of citizens, and what they aimed at was indemnification against every sort of infelicity, every accident and misfortune. Statistics structured the modern nations as large insurance companies that strove, through the law of large numbers, to profit from the proliferation of categories of people, the very diversity of its citizens, by collectivizing and calculating risk.[5]

Murder is one of the risks that increased at an alarming rate as modern cities grew ever more populous. It would seem that one could never protect oneself from the randomness of a violence such as this; "Nothing would seem more to escape foreknowledge than murder," Quetelet once observed, but as a statistician he demonstrated that there was more stability in the area of "moral deviancy" than in that of procreation or mortality.[6] "The terrifying exactness with which crimes reproduce themselves" was a matter of enormous fascination to populations who were made aware for the first time of the statistical regularities of crime. The frequency distribution of kinds of murder, murderers, and instruments used were all charted to reveal amazing uniformities when correlated with variables such as sex, class, nationality, and so on. Statistics, then, created a mathematical expectation within which we could come to believe in the calculability of risk. Before statistics, this sort of expectation was strictly impossible, and so, I would argue, was detective fiction. For it was statistics that formed the basis of classical detective fiction's narrative contract with its reader; the nineteenth century's fictional belief in the solvability of crime was specifically a *mathematical expectation*.

The thesis that modern bureaucracies and detective fiction spring from the same source lends itself to a Foucauldian interpretation. It could be argued that statistics and the bureaucracies that are sustained by them are, like detective fiction, techniques of surveillance, mechanisms of a disciplinary form of power. Each of these techniques isolates minute, differentiating and therefore incriminating details that give access to the most intimate secrets of the individuals they investigate. It is, in fact, the very passion for counting, recording, and tabulating that deposits many of the clues used by detectives to track their suspects. Laundry lists, insurance records, telephone bills, parking tickets, the criminal and the criminal act always turn up as figures in some bureaucracy's accounting. When Walter Neff attempts to avoid detection, he establishes his alibi by making a long distance call that he knows will be recorded and thus help to place him at home at the hour of the crime. Keyes begins to unravel the case when he notes that Mr. Dietrichson did not put in a claim for his broken leg, though he was insured against such an accident. In detective fiction, to be is not to be perceived, it is to be recorded. This is one of the fundamental differences between the realist novel (with its emphasis on the intersubjective network of perceptions) and detective fiction.

In *The Novel and the Police,* D. A. Miller emphasizes not the differences between the detective and the realist novel so much as their "radical entanglement."[7] Taking the detective novel as a special case of the novel in general, Miller sees them as the bad cop and the good cop of modern surveillance. Because the detective novel is set in a bounded space and deals with a limited and, by convention, closed set of characters, it passes off its deployment of investigative techniques as extraordinary, that is, as special and temporary. The ordinary novel, or the novel as such, thus appears as a space vacated by detectives, a space that no longer requires or is exempted from the intervention of any special policing power. Detective novels, then, fill an ideological function by lulling us into the belief that everyday life—the one we ordinarily live and the one we read about in realist novels—is free of surveillance. This blinds us to the fact that our ordinary life is structured by the very diffusion or dispersal of the same techniques found in detective novels. In this more subtle, discreet form the detective function is permitted to go undetected.

But what is meant here by the "detective function"? What actions does it perform? It scrutinizes, it invades, but above all, it constitutes the very people with whom it comes into contact. It "makes up people."[8] The function of the nineteenth-century novel, detective and otherwise, is the invention of character, not simply as a literary category, but character as such. Here we may stop to note a certain similarity between the rationalist project and that of new historicism. Both believe that categories of being subsume being itself. As the Cartesian "I think" is supposed to subsume the "I am," so the categories of people invented in the nineteenth century are supposed to subsume the actual people who came to be numbered in them. It is this new historicist conviction that Hacking wants to reinforce through his reference to Frege's work on numeration: "As Frege taught us, you can't just print numbers. You must print numbers of objects falling under some category or other."[9] Hacking's point is that statistics did not simply count varieties of people, it accounted for them, that is to say, it created them. Beneath the categories actual people came into being.

Making a similar point (e.g., "It is not just that, strictly private subjects, we read about violated, objectified subjects, but that, in the very act of reading about them, we contribute largely to constituting them as such"[10]), Miller refines this argument by rendering an account of the subtlety of this constitutive panoptic power. For this power to function properly, it must make itself invisible; it must conceal its own operation. The function of detection, then, is not only to construct various categories of the self, of character, but to construct character *as* quirky, *as* resistant to categorization, to construct the self, finally, *as* private. In this way, the knowledge in which he is held is concealed from the subject. Secrecy is here conceived as a necessary ruse of modern power, simply that; for there can in fact be no secret that keeps itself from power, no self that is not always already known. Keyes's argument is a corollary of this principle: Mr. Dietrichson cannot have attempted suicide by jumping off the back end of a train since there exists no such statistical category. If there is no secret self, no hidden or private domain that is not always already public, then there is no deception, no ignominy other than that which attaches itself to the law. How then is crime possible? How is it possible to transgress territories that have no private boundaries, to steal something that belongs to no one?

The Locked-Room Paradox and the Group

In his famous interview with François Truffaut, Alfred Hitchcock describes a scene he planned to include in *North by Northwest* but never actually shot:

> I wanted to have a long dialogue scene between Cary Grant and one of the factory workers [at a Ford automobile plant] as they walk along the assembly line. They might, for instance, be talking about one of the foremen. Behind them a car is being assembled, piece by piece. Finally, the car they've seen being put together

from a single nut and bolt is complete, with gas and oil, and all ready to drive off the line. The two men look at each other and say, "Isn't it wonderful!" Then they open the door to the car and out drops a corpse.[11]

What we have here is one of the defining elements of classical detective fiction: the locked-room paradox. The question is, Where has the body come from? Once the complete process of the car's production has been witnessed, "once the measures of the real are made tight, once a perimeter, a volume, is defined once and for all, there is nothing to lead one to suspect that when all is said and done,"[12] some object will have completely escaped attention only later to be extracted from this space. So, if no hand on the assembly line has placed the corpse in the car, how is it possible for another hand to pull it out? The Foucauldian solution would be to consider this paradox a deception of panoptic power, to treat the corpse as a fiction necessary to the discreet functioning of the law. One merely subscribes to the illusion of depth created by this fiction when one believes that something can escape power's meticulous inspection.

Lacan devotes his "Seminar on 'The Purloined Letter'" to a completely different treatment of the locked-room paradox. He argues that those who consider concealment simply a matter of depth, those who think that that which lies hidden must lie *underneath* something else, subscribe to "too immutable a notion of the real,"[13] since what is concealed may just as easily lie on the surface. Lacan, then, like Foucault, believes there is nothing but surface, but he maintains, nevertheless, that the corpse, the private "self," the purloined letter are not simply fictions; they are real.

To understand this position, let us return to our original observation that detective fiction arises in tandem with a passion for counting. We have so far left unchallenged the lesson Hacking derives from Frege, that counting registers more than numbers, it registers objects—in this case, people—falling under categories. If Lacan argues, on the contrary, that there are real objects that are not reducible to any category, this is because he seems to draw a different, more basic lesson from Frege: in order for counting to be possible in the first place, the set of numbers must register one category under which *no* objects fall. The category is that of the "not-identical-to-itself"; the number of objects subsumed by it is zero. Our argument will be that it is precisely *this* principle that establishes the link between detective fiction and statistics. The group of suspects that forms around the murdered corpse and the paradox of the locked room are two different phenomena that emerge simultaneously in detective fiction to confirm this hypothesis.

The implications of Frege's theory of numeration for Lacanian psychoanalysis have already been clearly spelled out by Jacques-Alain Miller in his influential article "Suture (elements of the logic of the signifier)." But since this article has been so often misinterpreted, it will be necessary to repeat its main points here. Miller begins by noting that Frege initiated his theory by rigorously *excluding* from consideration the subject who counts; more precisely, Frege began by excluding the *empirical* subject, "defined by attributes whose other side is political, disposing . . . of a faculty of memory necessary to close the set without the loss of any of the interchangeable elements."[14] From this exclusion two interrelated consequences follow:

1. Numbers can no longer be considered the neutral tool of a subject who wants to designate empirical things.

2. The question of how the no-longer-closed set of numbers, a pure and infinite series of numbers, can come to subsume objects is raised. How does the series close *itself,* in other words?

From the first point to the second it is clear that a distinction between things and objects is being made: objects are defined as logical entities as opposed to things, which are empirical; but what is it that allows the abolition of the thing, the suppression of all its attributes, to give rise to a logical object—to something that can be substituted for another without loss of truth?

Do not let the reference to the suppression of attributes ("whose other side is political") fool you; this question is not at all apolitical. It is, on the contrary, one of the most fundamental questions of political modernism. How, after destroying the body of the king, which had formerly defined the boundaries of nations and thus closed the set of subjects belonging to them, how does one then constitute a *modern* nation? What is it that allows the nation to collect a vast array of people, discount all their positive differences, and count them as citizens, as members of the same set, in logical terms, as *identical*? This question poses itself within detective fiction, which, classically, begins with an amorphous and diverse collection of characters and ends with a fully constituted group. What we want to know is, What happens to produce this entity, the group? What is the operation that renders these diverse entities—*countable*?

As Miller tells us, this reduction to a purely logical object, that is, to a countable entity, requires us to conceive the concept that subsumes objects as a redoubled concept, as a concept of identity-to-a-concept. Thus, members of a modern nation do not fall under the concept "citizens of X" but under the concept "identical to the concept 'citizens of X.'" While the simple concept "citizens of X" seeks to gather the individuals it subsumes by "picking out" the common attribute that qualifies them for inclusion in the set, the redoubled concept gathers by reducing individuals to their identity to themselves. The circularity of this definition should alert us to the fact that we have entered the dimension of the performative. The attribute that distinguishes the objects of a numbered set does not preexist, but subsists in the very act of numeration. And since this attribute is simply tautological, their retroactive belonging to the nation confers on its citizens no other substantial identity or representational value.

So far this theory of numeration may not seem incompatible with the one Hacking presents. In both cases an object's existence is made to depend on its falling under a concept. The difference stems, as we have said, from the introduction of the concept "not-identical-to-the-concept." With this addition, (1) the performative operation of subsumption that appears to close the set is made visible as an *effect* of this closure, and (2) numbers or signifiers can no longer be thought to subsume the entire universe of objects. For the performative does not, in fact, resolve the problem we cited; that is, with the expulsion of the empirical subject, the set of numbers remains open. To any number appearing at the end of the series it is always possible to add one more. If we can detect a performative dimension in numeration, this must mean that some limit has been applied to the series of numbers. And since no exterior limit is conceivable (this is, after all, the point of the exile of the empirical subject), only one possibility remains: the limit has to be conceived as *interior* to the series. This is what the concept "not-identical-to-itself" is: *the interior limit of the series of numbers.* That which is unthinkable within the logical functioning of numbers has to be conceived *as* unthinkable for the set of numbers to be closed or, as Miller says, *sutured.* The fact that this suturing concept does not subsume any objects should clarify any ambiguity that may persist. What is thought is not the unthinkable but the impossibility of thinking it. The suturing concept is empty of content. In marking the limit of the series of numbers, this concept at the same time severs the numbers from empirical reality and solders them to each other; in a phrase, it establishes the autonomy of the numerical field. Henceforth, the value of the numbered objects will not be determined empirically but differentially, through their relation to other numbered objects.

As we have stated, Frege's theory reveals the logic not only of the foundation and operation of the series of numbers but also of the modern state, which was, from the moment of its emergence in the nineteenth century, conceived in actuarial terms. The statistical accounting of citizens resulted in their normalization by assigning to each citizen a value that was merely the translation of its relation to the others. The modern social bond is, then, differential rather than affective; it is based not on some oceanic feeling of charity or resemblance but on a system of formal differences.

The group forming around the corpse in detective fiction is of this modern sort; it is logically "sustained through nothing but itself." The best proof of this, the most telling sign that the social world of the detective is in this sense a sutured space, is the fiction's foregrounding display of the performative: in classical detective fiction it is the narrative of the investigation that produces the narrative of the crime. On this basis we will want to claim that the relations of the suspects to each other are *not* emotional, familial, or economic; they are *not* "the molecular affinites which structure bourgeois society, the ones that reveal themselves to be the last sociological cement between individual persons in a situation in which class divisions no longer exist and despotic methods are not yet binding."[15]

But if the relations among the suspects are, as we are arguing, differential, what then is their relation to the corpse? It is here that detective fiction appears to offer a more sophisticated explanation of these differential relations than that offered by historicists. For by producing a corpse at the very center of the group, detective fiction acknowledges that the differential relations that sustain the group depend on an internal limit to the series of suspects. Representing this limit, the corpse becomes, in Helmut Heissenbuttel's words, "the trace of the unnarrated," that without which the narrated world and the groups of suspects would cease to exist.[16]

Suture, in brief, supplies the logic of a paradoxical function whereby a supplementary element is *added* to the series of signifiers in order to mark the *lack* of a signifier that could close the set. The endless slide of signifiers (hence deferral of sense) is brought to a halt and allowed to function "as if" it were a closed set through the inclusion of an element that acknowledges the impossibility of closure. The very designation of the limit is constitutive of the group, the reality the signifiers come to represent, though the group, or the reality, can no longer be thought to be entirely representable. At the risk of repetition, I would like to underline the point that must not be missed in all this argumentation: *the modern phenomenon of statistics, of counting people, would be impossible (i.e., one could never convert a disparate array of persons within the empirical field into categories of persons) without the addition of a nonempirical object* (Lacan calls this the object *a*) *that closes the field. Within detective fiction the strongest evidence of the obligatory addition of this object by statistics is the paradox of the locked room.*

We may now return to the assembly-line scene that Hitchcock planned for *North by Northwest* to observe this paradox at work. Although the corpse that tumbles out of the car—whose assembly we witness, piece by piece, whose elements are joined before our very eyes—appears to be the very surplus element that haunts every symbolic structure and thus allows the articulation of its parts, this corpse does not function in the same way as the one that organizes the group of suspects. For the locked-room paradox is only comprehensible if we view the surplus element *not* as the corpse itself but as that which allows the corpse to be pulled out of an apparently sealed space. The logic which says that an element is added to the structure in order to mark what is lacking in it should not lead us to imagine this element as an isolatable excess hidden beneath the structure. The excess element is, instead, located on the same surface as the structure, that is, it is manifest in the latter's very functioning. It is under the species of default that the excess marker of lack appears, in the internal limitation that prevents the signifier from coinciding with itself. It is in the fact that a signifier is unable to signify itself but must always call on another in an infinite appeal to one signifier more, that language's internal limit is located.

This means what in terms of the paradox of the locked room, which structures *all* of detective fiction, all its carefully limited spaces? The locked room is a space that contains *an excess element, its own limit,* and this limit alone is what guarantees the infinity of its contents, guarantees that an unlimited number of objects may be pulled out of it. Or: the space of detective fiction is a *deep space,* an infinite space, not because it has trap doors or hidden passageways but precisely because it does not. This renders the locked room the equivalent of the set of numbers, whose limit is the condition of numeration, that is, the infinity of the elements of the set of numbers. This paradoxical notion of space is incomprehensible to the dimwitted police, whose realist imbecility consists in their failure to count the limit as an element of the space, as internal to it.

The limit internal to language—and thus to the locked room—makes it impossible ever to complete the description of this space once and for all. The full details of this bounded yet abyssal space can never be enumerated; their list will never be countable as long as language depends for its meaning on the interpretation of language, on a supplement of meaning. The corpse that tumbles out of the car at the Ford assembly plant is just to suggest a supplement. If the locked room is always breached, this is not because every private space has always already been intruded upon by the public power of the symbolic, but because within the symbolic the real always intrudes, limiting the symbolic from within and producing its infinite commodiousness. As the one who extracts a letter, a clue, a corpse that was literally undetectable before he arrived on the scene, as the representative of the always open possibility of one signifier more, the detective is the upholder of a particular law, the law of the limit, specifically, the limit of knowledge. The law that governs detective fiction is, then, one that remains hidden, that supports itself on no external guarantees, operates by not revealing itself in any positive form.

We might even argue that the detective distinguishes himself from the police by virtue of his passion for ignorance, not for eliminating it. For while the police search for the telling clue, the index in the belief that at this point reality "impresses" itself on the symbolic, "brushes up against" and thereby disambiguates it, the detective approaches the index as the point where the *real* makes itself felt in the symbolic, that is, the point at which the symbolic visibly *fails* to disambiguate itself. Dashiell Hammett's "Bodies Piled Up" contains an excellent illustration of this point; here the modus operandi of detection is explicitly described thus: "From any crime to its author there is a trail. It may be . . . obscure; but since matter cannot move without disturbing other matter along its path, there always is—there must be—a trail of some sort. And finding such trails is what a detective is paid to do."[17] While this description sounds as though it belongs more readily to the genre of the police procedural, the clue upon which the solution pivots belies this assumption. As long as it is believed that it was these bodies piled up in room 906 that were the murderer's targets, the investigation remains stalled. In order to solve the crime, someone must first realize that the murderer *mistook* room 906 for the room of his intended victim, who was actually registered in room 609. How does the investigation arrive at this realization? By noting that the murderer would, when he glanced at the hotel register, be looking at it upside down. But 609 read upside down still reads 609. Yes, the reasoning goes, but the murderer in his furtive haste would have forgotten this and would have automatically made an adjustment for the error that, in fact, did not exist.

The detective, like the police, believes that the criminal leaves traces in endless incriminating details; what he denies—and what is denied by the previous example—is the possibility of *deducing* the criminal from his traces. The detective does not refute the belief that the criminal author reveals himself completely and exclusively in his criminal works; he simply, but critically, denies that the evidence itself can account for the way it gives evidence. There is a gap, a distance, between the evidence and that which the evidence establishes, which means that there is something that is *not* visible in the evidence: the principle by which the trail attaches itself to the criminal. The registration of the room number 906 does provide a clue essential to the solution of the crime, but however exhaustively we examine this piece of evidence, we will never arrive at the principle of how it leads us to the criminal perpetrator.

Here interpretation must intervene—interpretation that, Lacan says, *is* desire. All of a sudden it becomes possible to understand what he means. To say that the detective manifests his *desire* in interpreting the clues is not to say that in the absence of complete knowledge a historical or personal bias directs the interpretation. Desire is not an impurity that threatens the "objectivity" of the detective, but the quasi-transcendental principle that guarantees it. In other words, desire does not impose a bias but supposes a gap: the detective reads the evidence by *positing an empty beyond, a residue that is irreducible to the evidence while being, at the same time, completely demonstrated in it*. Interpretation means that evidence tells us everything but how to read it. Beyond the evidence, in other words, there is no other reality, nothing—except the principle that guides our reading of it. One of the primary imperatives of detective fiction may be stated in the following way: *desire must be taken literally*. This imperative is a positive and more complete restatement of the well-known stricture against the introduction in detective fiction of some new reality—a trap door or a suspect who is not already known to the reader—for the the purpose of solving the crime. This stricture does not mean simply that the culprit must be one from the known gallery of suspects, it also means that he is himself not to be reintroduced as another reality, a substantial entity beyond the trail of evidence he leaves. The culprit is consubstantial if not with the evidence per se, then with a reading of it; he is no more nor less than this. The desiring detective, then, concludes by taking the culprit's desire literally, seeing the way it manifests itself in the clues. In this way does the detective make buffoons of the police, who busy themselves with the senseless task of ignoring desire and taking the *evidence* literally, conflating signifiers and signifieds.

The gap that necessitates interpretation, that prevents the signifier from signifying itself, is caused, as we've argued, by the absence of one signifier, a *final* signifier that would establish an end to the chain. It is because this final signifier (or number) *is* missing that detective fiction and statistics are, as we have been arguing, possible. On the other hand, the absence of this signifier makes the sexual relation impossible. This signifier, if it existed, would be the signifier for woman. As anyone with even a passing acquaintance with the genre knows, the absence of this signifier is evident in detective fiction not only in the nontotalizable space that produces the paradox of the locked room but also in the unfailing exclusion of the sexual relation. The detective is structurally forbidden any involvement with a woman.

In the middle of writing this, I take a break to watch *Columbo* on T.V. He is badgering, patronizing one of the characters, which means, according to the formula, that this character is the guilty suspect. Columbo asks this man, who is running for Congress, for an autograph for his wife. As everyone knows, the wife of this most uxurious of detectives is simply the condition of the impossibility of his involvement in any sexual relation; she never appears, must never appear, in the diegetic space. The congressman agrees to the autograph. Taking a piece of paper from his drawer and beginning to write on it, he asks Columbo, "What is your wife's name?" "Mrs. Columbo," is the only, and from the matter-of-fact look on the detective's face, the only possible, reply.

Detour through the Drive

Whereas this elision of the signifier for woman can be shown to define the fictional space of classical detective fiction, the very presence of Phyllis Dietrichson, the film's femme fatale, reminds us that *Double Indemnity* constructs a different sort of fictional world. Although it is inconceivable for Keyes, as a classical detective, to have any involvement with a woman, it is equally inconceivable for Neff, as a noir hero, to escape such involvement. One of the most theoretically compelling aspects of *Double Indemnity* is its inscription not only of this difference but of the very topological incompatability of classical detective fiction and film noir. In one scene Neff receives a call from Phyllis while Keyes is in his office. Since Keyes seems disinclined to leave, Neff must conduct the entire conversation in his mentor's presence. The uncomfortableness of this situation, combined with the shot/reverse shot cutting between Phyllis on one end of the line and Neff (together with Keyes) on the other, serves to underlie this incompatibility. In another scene, as Neff awaits a visit from Phyllis, Keyes drops by his apartment unexpectedly. While Neff attempts to usher Keyes out, Phyllis arrives and has to wait behind the door until Keyes walks down the corridor toward the elevator before she can slip, unseen, into Neff's apartment. Throughout the film, Phyllis and Keyes have a "revolving door" relationship; they do not and cannot occupy the same space. But this relationship is trivialized, its real stakes obscured, if one interprets its either/or dimension in strictly narrative terms. The choice that Neff faces is not one between two people, a mentor and a lover, but between the space of classical detection and that of film noir.

One of the most common descriptions of the historical shift between these two worlds makes identification the pivotal term; that is, it is argued that the detective comes to identify more and more closely with his criminal adversary until, at the end of the noir cycle, he has become the criminal himself, as here in *Double Indemnity,* where Neff is both investigator and murderer. The moment Neff stops "watching the customers to make sure that they don't crook the house" and gets to thinking how he could crook the house himself "and do it smart," Neff enters the noir world. But if the reversal were that simple, the choices that symmetrical, if noir depended merely on the hero's rejection of a lofty goal for a base one, one would be forced to wonder why the hero always ends up not getting the money and not getting the woman.

I would like, then, to offer a different explanation of Neff's choice to try to "crook the house." This explanation is derived from the fort/da game that Freud describes in *Beyond the Pleasure Principle.* I propose that we consider this little game of hide and seek as the elementary cell of detective fiction—in both its incarnations. A few pages after his original analysis of it, Freud adds that his grandson later developed a variant of

Double Indemnity, Billy Wilder, 1944 (courtesy Jerry Ohlinger).

the game. In this later version the child himself functioned as the cotton reel; hiding beneath the mirror for a time, he suddenly jumps up to observe the emergence of his mirror reflection. Now there is, it would seem, a fundamental distinction to be made between the two versions of the game. For when the child throws the cotton reel, he throws that part of himself that is lost with his entry into language. The child thus situates himself in the field of language; he chooses *sense* rather than the being that sense continually fails to secure. He thus becomes a subject of desire, lacking-in-being. But when the child takes up the position of the cotton reel, he situates himself in the field of being; he chooses being, *jouissance,* rather than sense.

This distinction causes us to note a difference in the two forms of repetition that the games instantiate. In the first game it is failure, or desire, that propels the repetition. Something escapes, or to use one of Lacan's phrases, something "does not stop *not* writing itself," in the field of representation structured by the game, and so the game is repeated endlessly with the hope, but without the possibility, of capturing that which escapes it. In the second game repetition is driven not by desire but by satisfaction; some satisfaction is repeated, "does not stop *writing* itself," in the game.

I am proposing that the inversion that defines the shift from classical detection to film noir is to be understood not in terms of identification but in terms of the choice between sense and being, or—in the dialect of psychoanalysis—between desire and drive.[18] Lacan has argued that this shift describes a general historical transition whose process we are still witnessing: the old modern order of desire, ruled over by an Oedipal father, has begun to be replaced by a new order of the drive, in which we no longer have recourse to the protections against *jouissance* that the Oedipal father once offered. These protections have been eroded by our society's fetishization of being, that is, of *jouissance*. Which is to say we have ceased being a society that attempts to preserve the individual right to *jouissance* to become a society that commands *jouissance* as a "civic" duty. *Civic* is, strictly speaking, an inappropriate adjective in this context, since these obscene importunings of contemporary society entail the destruction of the *civitas* itself, of increasingly larger portions of our public space. We no longer attempt to safeguard the empty "private" space that counting produced as a residue, but to dwell within this space *exclusively*. The ambition of film noir seems to have been monitory: it sought to warn us that this fetishization of private *jouissance* would have mortal consequences for society, would result in a "rise of racism,"[19] in ever-smaller factions of people proclaiming their duty-bound devotion to their own special brand of enjoyment, unless we attempted to reintroduce some notion of community, of sutured totality to which we could partially, performatively belong. Thus, of all the admonitory ploys in the noir arsenal, surely the most characteristic was its insistence that from the moment the choice of private enjoyment *over* community is made, one's privacy ceases to be something one supposes as veiled from prying eyes (so that, as in the case with Keyes, no one can be sure that one even has a private life) and becomes instead something one visibly endures—like an unending, discomfiting rain. In film noir privacy establishes itself as the rule, not as a clandestine exception. This changes the very character of privacy and, indeed, of "society" in general—which begins with the introduction of this new mode of being to shatter into incommensurable fragments.

The Voice and the Voice-Over

If there is one feature of film noir that seems to stand in the way of the acceptance of our thesis, it is the voice-over narration, which definitively links the hero to speech and hence, we would suppose, to community, to sense. Speech, as we know—language—is the death of the thing, it contributes to the drying up of *jouissance*. And nothing has seemed more obvious in the criticism of film noir than this association of death with speech, for the voice-over is regularly attached to a dead narrator, whether literally as in *Sunset Boulevard* and *Laura,* metaphorically as in *Detour,* or virtually as in *Double Indemnity.*

But before we can contest this reading of the voice-over in noir, we must first confront a certain theorization of the voice in cinema. In an excellent article entitled "The Silences of the Voice," Pascal Bonitzer makes a distinction, which will form the basis of a great deal of subsequent theorizing, between the disembodied voice of the documentary voice-over—a voice that remains offscreen throughout the film and thus never becomes anchored to a body imaged on screen—and the voice-over that at some point becomes attached to a visible body. Neff's voice, and that of other noir narrators, belongs to the latter category, and, in fact, Bonitzer uses the example of a late film noir, *Kiss Me Deadly* (Robert Aldrich, 1955), to great advantage in furthering his argument. Throughout most of the film, Dr. Soberin, the arch criminal, is absent from the screen; we hear only his offscreen voice and see only his blue suede shoes. At the end of the film, however, he appears bodily in the space for the first time and, almost immediately, is shot and falls, dead, to the bottom of the frame. That is to say, at the moment the voice is anchored to a body, it relinquishes its apparent omnipotence and is instead "submitted to the destiny of the body"; corporealized, it is rendered "decrepit and mortal."[20] The voice, we could say, dies in the body. In opposition to this, the noncorporealized voice of the classical documentary issues from a space other than that on the screen, an unrepresented, undetermined space; thus transcending the visible, determined field, the voice maintains its absolute power over the image, its knowledge remains unimpugned.

This distinction between the disembodied voice, which conveys knowledge and power, and the embodied voice, which conveys the limitation of both, is underwritten by a simple opposition between the universal and the particular, the latter being conceived as that which ruins the possibility of the former. The embodied voice, particularity, and lack of knowledge line up on one side against the disembodied voice, universality, and knowledge on the other. Within this framework of nestled oppositions, another notion is introduced toward the end of the article, that of the "body of the voice." Bonitzer effortlessly sweeps this notion beneath the "particular" flank of his oppositions, using it to argue that any voice at all, any commentary, threatens the assumption of universality upon which documentary realism depends. For though the voice may never become visibly anchored in a place, place may be audibly anchored in the voice, thus betraying it through accents that indicate its regional, class, sexual, or some other rootedness. By "the body of the voice" Bonitzer means any accent that particularizes the voice, spoiling its ideal atony, hence the omniscience and authority that are assumed to define the neutral, unaccented voice-over. Once the body of the voice becomes audible, it betrays "a subject fallen to the rank of an object and unmasked. . . . [The body of this voice is] its death to meaning. . . . The voice . . . 'labors.' It is perceived as an accent . . . and this accent neutralizes meaning."[21]

But the films of Marguerite Duras, which Bonitizer mentions in his article, manage to perturb his argument more than they bear it out. Consider *India Song*. In this film the images are almost completely silent. The voices all issue from offscreen (as in a documentary), though they are all heavily "accented." We can speak properly here of the "laboring" of the voices, their grain. Distinctly female, except for one at the end, they seem to suffer throughout the film. One could say that they are the very embodiment of everything the documentary voice is *not* supposed to be: they are "burning" voices, seemingly "ephemeral, fragile, troubled." But while they appear to comment on the images on the screen, there is in what they say a constant ambiguity of reference, since they may also be commenting on their own situation. "The heat!" "Can't bear it. No, can't bear it!" We begin to be unsure whether it is the heat that suffuses the diegetic space or that which warms the offscreen space which these voices find insupportable. Sometimes they dispense altogether with any pretense of commenting on what we see on screen and speak to each other of their own situation.

What are we to make of the fact that these voices are situated permanently offscreen? that they are so painfully, burningly "grainy"? The standard argument would probably try to convince us that they were "desiring" rather than omniscient voices; that they express a yearning and loss rather than power; that they reduce their bearers to a merely mortal, corporeal existence. Yet this description clearly misses its mark, for these offscreen voices cannot be construed as mortal. They are, as Duras defines them, *intemporal voices;* they cannot be situated in—nor submitted to the ravages of—time or place. This is not to deny that the voices are associated with death but to note that this death brings no expiry; rather, in them, death persists. The voices bear the burden of a living death, a kind of inexhaustible painful/pleasurable suffering.

Though film noir does not, like Duras, acoustically mark the break between image and voice, it does, I would argue, similarly tear the voice from the image in a way that remains unexplained—is effaced even—by the commonplace observation that the noir hero's voice-over narration simply diverges from the *truth* of the image. Seeing in film noir the evidence of a postwar waning of masculine self-certainty and power, this observation reads the grain or laboring of the voice-over as well as its periodic diegeticization as proof of the faltering of the hero's knowledge, his inability to control or comprehend the image, which then often seems to belie what he says. It is the pertinence for film noir of this definition of the voice-image relation that must be challenged, together with the pop-psychological diagnosis of postwar male malaise that has lent it credibility. We will continue to argue instead that the aspect of this period that most concerns the development of noir is the perceptible ascendancy of drive over desire. To this shift a whole range of "social" policies encouraging suburban expansion and ethnic and racial segregation (mandated most notably, but not exclusively, by the Federal Housing Administration, which was founded in 1934 and gained momentum only after the war) clearly bear witness.

There is no need, however, to limit our observation to these official state policies, for a number of other cultural and intellectual phenomena will just as readily attest to this shift, including the vogue for existentialism, which also reached its peak after the war. From the moment the first hard-boiled novels were translated into French in the *Série Noire,* the existentialists recognized in this new type of detective novel something of their own philosophy. What they must have seen in these novels was a commitment, similar to their own, to the priority of being—or, in existentialist parlance, the in-itself—over sense. For both the philosophy and the novels isolate an instance, thought to be outside and before all social relations, from which these relations are supposed to be forged by the ethical hero. The problematic of duty or responsibility that obliges the hero to make sense of his world is, as has often been noted, as central to film noir as it is to existentialism, from Sam Spade's moral code—his ultimate refusal, for example of Brigid O'Shaunessy: "I won't because all of me wants to"—to the extravagant, delirious form it takes in Mike Hammer's contempt for death itself, his mad vengeance against injustice. What has not yet been noted is that the treachery that besets all these ethical vocations (from existentialist to noir), causing them more often than not to fail, to revolve in an endless loop around the very enjoyment of their failures, is a direct consequence of the initial, fateful choice of being. For to *begin* with *jouissance,* rather than the other way around, with community, is automatically to problematize community as such, to make the link between enjoyment and society nearly unfathomable.

How does this diagnosis of the postwar period bear on our understanding of the voice in noir? It supports our perception that however contiguous it is with the diegetic space, the space of the voice-over is nevertheless radically heterogeneous to it. It is to this fact—and not to the limited knowledge of the bearer of the voice—that we ascribe the apparent incompatibilities between image and voice. What is most questionable about standard interpretations of film noir is their insistence on subsuming the function of the voice under the category of commentary, since what seems to us distinctive about this voice-over narration is the way it refuses to spend itself as commentary. Certainly this narration performs the same function that every speech does: it vehicles a message addressed to another. In *Double Indemnity,* for example, the voice-over is explicitly addressed to Keyes. But the film also deliberately severs this speech from its addressee in order to return us repeatedly to the image of a solitary Neff, seated in an empty office at night, speaking into a dictaphone. In these scenes the destiny of the voice-over seems not to be exhausted by its function as message. An excess of pleasure, a private enjoyment, seems to adhere in the act of speaking as such, as Neff contents himself, beyond the content of the message, with the act itself. This is to say that the voice-over narration serves less to describe or attempt to describe the world that the narrator inhabited than to present that world at the point where he is abstracted from it. Neff clings not to the community with which speech puts him in touch but to the enjoyment that separates him from that community.

We can begin to grasp what is at stake here by returning to our discussion of the "body of the voice." Though Bonitzer offers this notion as the equivalent of Roland Barthes's "grain of the voice," the two notions are, in fact, quite different. The body of which Barthes speaks "has no civil identity, no 'personality.'"[22] In no way, then, can it be considered the "accent of an era, a class, a regime";[23] in no way can it be imagined to betray anything like the caricatured types appropriately indicated by Bonitzer in quotation marks: "the paranoid anticommunist," "the jovial Stalinist."[24] The grain is not the index of a particularity with any content, social or otherwise, it is the index of an *particular absolute.* This means that it marks the voice as belonging to *this* speaker, uniquely, even though the grain must not be considered "personal: it expresses nothing" of the speaker.[25]

The grain of the voice has no content; it appears only as the "friction" (Barthes's word) one hears when one perceives the materiality of language, its resistance to meaning. The grain works in the voice as index in the same way as the index works in detective fiction: to register a resistance to or failure of meaning. It is this friction that prompts interpretation. *Don't read my words; read my desire!* This is what the grain of the voice urges. That is, don't take me literally (i.e., universally), but realize that these words are the unique bearers of my desire. Functioning as limit, the grain of the voice does spell the collapse of the universal, of the universality of sense; some excess of being over sense suggests itself and begins to undermine knowledge. But it is the knowledge of the listener that is in question here, not that of the enunciator. The enunciator becomes all at once not unknowing (as in Bonitzer's account), but unknown, voluptuously an X. The phenomenon just described, and fully exhibited in Barthes's essay, is that of transference. Confronted with the limits of our knowledge, we fictively add to the field of the Other, to the voice, an X, the mark of our nonknowledge. This simple addition is enough to eroticize the voice, to transform our relation to it to one of desire, of interpretation. As Barthes attempts to elucidate the difference between two singers, Panzera and Fischer-Dieskau, we cannot help suspecting at first that his distinction is completely arbitrary, subjective. For he isolates in the voices no positive features that would help us to understand his preference for Panzera, in whose voice he hears "the tongue, the glottis, the teeth, the mucous membranes, the nose." One cannot be trained to hear vocal "features" such as this; we learn nothing, in short, about "music appreciation" from Barthes's essay. And yet there is clearly a difference between the two voices, and it amounts basically to this: the addition of an X to Panzera's voice, which turns Barthes's relation to it into one of desire. One must be careful, however, not to dismiss this relation as simply subjective: because the X is the cause of desire and not its consequence, we cannot claim that Barthes imposes something of himself onto the voice. He merely "set[s] up a new scheme of evaluation which . . . certainly . . . is individual."[26] Thus do relations of desire preserve particularity, difference, by supposing, via the grain of the voice, a private beyond, a being that does not surrender itself in speech.

When desire gives way to drive, this private beyond no longer remains hidden. What's involved in the drive, Lacan tells us, is a *making oneself heard* or *making oneself seen;*[27] that is to say, the intimate core of our being, no longer sheltered by sense, ceases to be supposed and suddenly becomes exposed. It thrusts itself forward, pushing through the surface of speech to take up a position alongside it. This does not mean that the merely supposed, hence empty, domain of private being emerges unveiled, its contents finally visible for anyone to see. In shifting its topological position, being does not lose its essential nature as resistance to sense: what is made audible—or visible—is the void as such, contentless and nonsensical. The "making oneself heard" or "making oneself seen" of the drive must not be confused with a desire to hear/be heard or a desire to see/be seen, since the very reciprocity that is implied by desire is denied in drive. The intimate kernel of our being is susceptible neither in its hidden nor in its exposed form to "objective" knowledge; in exposing itself, it does not seek to communicate itself. Or, we might put it this way: surfacing within the phenomenal field, private being, *jouissance,* nevertheless does not take on a phenomenal form. Phenomenal/nonphenomenal, *this* (more accurately, perhaps, than inside/outside) names the division troubled by drive. It does not communicate itself by exposing itself.

In film noir the grain of the voice surfaces alongside the diegetic reality. Issuing from the point of death, it marks not some ideal point where the subject would finally be absorbed into his narrative, used up; it materializes rather that which can never be incorporated into the narrative. Death becomes in noir the positivization of the narrator's absence from the very diegetic reality his speech describes.

Locked Room/Lonely Room

Neff's absence from the narrative—that is, from the social space—is imaged as we've said in the repeated scene of a confession that we are refusing to take purely as such. The clue that allows Keyes to begin to unravel the Dietrichson case should not be lost on us; Keyes realizes that the fact that Mr. Dietrichson did not put in a claim when he broke his leg is clear proof that the man who boarded the train on crutches must have been someone else. The one detail that trips Neff up, his "blind spot," is the one that ultimately distinguishes him as a noir hero: he cannot think of claiming the protection of the law. For Neff, and his like, the benevolent-impotent Other no longer exists, and Neff can, then, no longer seek from it what it is able to provide: protection from *jouissance*. Neff is thus a man who enjoys too much—too much to surrender his words to another, when they hold for him such exquisite pleasure. The difference between the crime film and film noir amounts to this question of enjoyment: in the crime film, despite their transgressions of the law, the criminals are still ruled by the impotent Other whom they, understandably, try to cheat; in film noir the reign of the Other has been superseded; its law is not so much transgressed as disbanded. The emergence of the enunciation on a level with the narrative statement constitutes our proof of this.

But there exists further evidence. Since it is the cloaking of the enunciative instance, its marked retreat from the phenomenal field, that defines the very space of classical detection, we would expect the surfacing of the enunciation to produce within noir a wholly different sort of space. This is exactly what happens; the infinite, inexhaustible space of the older model—exemplarily realized in the paradox of the locked room—gives way in noir to its inverse: the lonely room, such as the one in which Neff utters his confession. For Neff sits in one of those vacant office buildings, those plain and, for the moment, uninhabited spaces that constitute the characteristic architecture of film noir. Office buildings late at night, in the early hours of the morning; abandoned warehouses; hotels mysteriously untrafficked; eerily empty corridors; these are the spaces that supplant the locked room. One is struck first of all by the curious depopulation of these spaces, and then by their spareness. In *The Big Heat*

(Fritz Lang, 1953), Debbie Marsh, looking around the woefully under-decorated hotel room in which Dave Bannion temporarily resides, delivers an accurate appraisal of this typically noir interior: "Oh, early nothing!" she quips. But it would be wrong to stop at the observation that these lonely rooms are simply empty of people and decoration. More fundamentally, what noir presents to us are spaces that have been emptied of desire. Or, the emptiness of the room indicates less that there is nothing in them than that nothing more can be gotten out of them. They are no longer interpretable, in the strict sense: that is, they will never yield anything new and cannot, therefore, hide anything.

Primarily, it is the hero himself who suffers the loss of a hiding place. Think, for example, of Al Roberts in *Detour* (Edgar Ulmer, 1946), who at the end of the film walks resignedly, without wondering how he's been found, toward the police car that stops to pick him up; or Vincent Parry in *Dark Passage* (Delmar Daves, 1947), who is recognized wherever he goes, no matter how late at night or that he has been totally transformed by plastic surgery. Or, think of an earlier moment in *Detour* when Roberts's private voice-over contemplation of the events leading up to his current desperate situation is cut short by this venomously delivered question from the hitchhiker he has recently picked up: "Where did you put the body?" All of a sudden the voice-over no longer contains his privacy; the seam separating it and him from this cruel passenger melts as the hiss of her viciousness marks the edges of their beings coming into contact. It is almost as if she has read his thoughts, and yet she doesn't really respond directly to his words on the soundtrack. Here we find ourselves in that paranoid universe that noir is so often taken to be. But while this paranoia is usually assumed to indicate an erosion of privacy that permits the Other to penetrate, to read one's innermost thoughts, noir helps us to see that the opposite is true. It is on the public level that the erosion has taken place. No social distance separates individuals; no social "clothing" protects their innermost being. But since there is no distance to traverse, no layers of disguise to penetrate, the exposure of being is not preceded by any ignorance or curiosity. Noir heroes may never successfully hide out in their urban spaces, but neither are they seriously pursued. Nor does their being become readable, in the proper sense, that is, no *discursive* knowledge is gained by its exposure. It is not Roberts's words, his thoughts that are revealed to Vera, but rather that which his thinking ordinarily preserves: his being.

In *Double Indemnity* Neff's decision to try to "crook the house" issues in a situation that is not comprehensible in strictly narrative terms. Henceforth Neff and Phyllis will refrain from meeting in private and will be forced to rendezvous only in public places. Jerry's Market becomes their meeting place. This narrativized description of what takes place doesn't quite make sense. Wouldn't there be more rather than less risk in their public encounters? Wouldn't the hatching of the plan require private consultation? What this description fails to grasp, however, is that within the terms of the noir universe Jerry's Market *is* a private space. Empty except for a few shoppers who take no interest in their existence, Neff and Phyllis are in little danger of discovery here, though they are equally incapable of concealing themselves. Phyllis's dark glasses are as humorously ineffectual, and unnecessary, as Vincent Parry's plastic surgery. This seems, in fact, to be the point of both the glasses and the surgical bandages. Every disguise turns out to be futile within a space defined by the drive, where what is at stake is making one's private being seen.

But how does film noir exhibit the workings of drive, the exposure of being, when, as we've noted, this being has no phenomenal form, when it is and remains essentially contentless? How is the intrusion of the nonphenomenal private realm into the public, that is, phenomenal, world made apparent in noir? As Neff's crepuscular office, Jerry's Market, and the many abandoned sites in these films demonstrate, this is accomplished by adding to public spaces the very emptiness we have already described. The intrusion of the private—the object *a,* the grain of the voice—into phenomenal reality, its *addition,* is registered in the *depletion* of this reality. Lost, thereby, is the sense of solidity that ordinarily attaches

Double Indemnity (courtesy Photofest).

Dark Passage, Delmar Daves, 1947 (courtesy Jerry Ohlinger).

to the social field, as well as the illusion of depth that underwrites this solidity. This illusion is simply the perception—unnegatable by any counterperception—that we have never gotten to the bottom of our reality. It is film noir's suspension of this illusion that renders it incapable of concealing anything, least of all its heroes. This is the logic that leads us to argue that Jerry's Market is a private space, that film noir continually exposes the landscape of privacy. In such a landscape, where private being exhibits itself as complete, as independent of the desire of others, the hero's encounters with other people will be jarring, at least (the series of women with whom Marlowe meets up in *The Big Sleep*), threatening at most. This is why the palpable claustrophobia of noir spaces is not at all inconsistent with their visible emptiness.

Jerry's Market is the result, then, of Neff's choice of private being, *jouissance,* rather than the signifying network that structures social reality. What he gets is being, but deprived of the inaccessibility that gave it its value; in short, he gets nothing. It would be an error, however, to think that the consequences of this choice stir in the hero a kind of "disappointment," for it is precisely this nothing that satisfies. And therein lies the problem, the potential fatality of this choice. Despite some attempts by Hollywood—for example, the revised ending of *Double Indemnity,* which eliminates Neff's ultimate isolation in a gas chamber and substitutes instead the reciprocity of the cigarette-lighting ritual between Neff and Keyes—to disguise the unabatedness of this satisfaction, there is still evidence enough that the heroes in these films often cling to the satisfaction of this nothing to the bitter end.

Lethal Jouissance and the Femme Fatale

This is not to say that there are no defenses against the drive, no means of curbing its satisfactions. Drive is, of course, not instinct, and just as in the symbolic realm some real is manifest (in the *failures* of the signifier), so in the realm of the real some symbolic makes itself felt (in the very repetitions of the drive's circuits). That is, the drive is not indifferent to symbolic intervention, which is available in film noir on two different levels. The first level is that of the filmic system. Here we encounter the deep-focus photography and the chiaroscuro, "expressionist" lighting that pervade this cycle of films. The function of these devices only becomes clear when we consider them in relation to the empty, private spaces that compose the primary territory of noir.[28] Through the use of wide angle lenses and low-key lighting, these spaces are represented as deep and deceptive, as spaces in which all sorts of unknown entities may hide. One must distinguish between the genuine illusion of depth—which is a matter of *desire,* of not knowing something and wanting, therefore, to know more—and the ersatz representation of depth—which is simply a matter of a technical skill in rendering, of verisimilitude—if one wants to avoid being misled by the shadows and depth of field that so famously characterize the noir image. The visual techniques of film noir are placed in the service of creating an artificial replication of depth *in the image* in order to make up for, to compensate for, the absence of depth *in the diegetic spaces;* that is, these techniques are placed in the service of a defense against the drive. The makeshift domain of illusion that they create erects a facade of nonknowledge and thus of depth, as a substitute for and protection against their dangerous, and potentially lethal, lack in the noir universe itself. These techniques of deception install a kind of ersatz symbolic as bulwark against its diegetic collapse. It is only because this distinction between the technical replication or representation of depth (verisimilitude) and the illusion of depth that depends on the signifier's failure (a structural illusion) has not been taken into account in the analysis of these films that the noir universe has been perceived as essentially deceptive, though it is, in fact, a world in which nothing can lie hidden, everything must come to light. This is really the dark truth of noir.

On the narrative level the defense against the drive takes another, but no less genre-defining, form: that of the femme fatale. The femme fatale is in everyone's estimation one of the most fascinating elements of the noir world. As such, she has provoked a great deal of critical attention, especially from feminists who have wanted to see in this powerful female figure some proof that Hollywood's tendency toward a "minorization" of women was not absolute. These women had a kind of strength, a kind of privilege and command over the diegetic space that most of their cinematic sisters did not. And yet they seemed always to be presented from the point of view of the male protagonists. Christine Gledhill was able to see in their strength a sort of rebellion against the point of view that could only barely contain them: "Thus, though the heroines of film noir, by virtue of male control of the voice-over, flash-back structure, are rarely accorded the full subjectivity and fully expressed point of view of psychologically realist fiction . . . their *performance* of the roles accorded them . . . foregrounds the fact of their image as an artifice and suggests another place behind the image where the woman might be."[29] The quasi-Brechtian interpretation of the women's tenuous habitation of their roles is questionable, but an important perception underlies this interpretation: the femme fatale does have an initially dependent and visibly artificial existence within this nightmarish world.

Consider the scene of Neff's second visit to the Dietrichson home, arranged by Phyllis so that her husband can hear Neff's sales pitch. Her husband is not in, of course, nor is the maid, though Phyllis plays it—unconvincingly—as if she had forgotten that it is Nettie's day off. She has not forgotten at all; her deceit is transparent to us and to Neff. If the femme fatale is the embodiment of deceit, it is always a deceit of this order: transparent, painted on—a deceit that does not disguise itself. Theoretically, nothing precludes this visible deceit from hiding another, but in the world of noir this second-order deception never takes hold. The femme fatale remains a two-dimensional figure with no hidden sides; the deception is *only* up front. In other words, although she, too, seems to function, for the hero this time, as a sort of proto-illusionistic element in noir's nonillusionist field, she usually fails to become a proper barrier, to protect him in the way real illusion does. Rather than screening *jouissance,* she hoards it.

For, the femme fatale also functions in another strategy of defense. Having chosen *jouissance,* the noir hero risks its shattering, annihilating effects, which threaten his very status as subject. In order to *indemnify* himself against these dangers, he creates in the femme fatale a *double* to which he surrenders the *jouissance* he cannot himself sustain. That is, he tries to take some distance from himself, to initiate some alterity in his relation to himself—to split himself, we could say, not as the desiring subject between sense and being, but between knowledge and *jouissance.* Giving up his right to enjoyment, the hero contracts with the femme fatale that she will henceforth command it from him, as levy.

In *Double Indemnity* we are not left simply to surmise the existence of this contract, we actually witness its drawing up in the scene in which Mr. Dietrichson is tricked into signing a document other than the one he thinks he is signing. The document he in fact signs is the contract that binds Neff to the will of Phyllis. Initially entered into through an act of the hero's own volition and in order to forestall his ruin (i.e., to impose restrictions on the drive's satisfactions), this document nevertheless fails to secure the hoped-for stability and instead leads Neff to his absolute destruction.

The problem stems from the greediness of the femme fatale. In *Double Indemnity* as well as in *Detour, Gilda, Kiss Me Deadly, The Maltese Falcon* (to name only those films that come immediately to mind), explicit reference is made to the femme fatale's greed, her constant demand for more and more satisfaction. The more the hero devotes himself to procuring it for her, the more she delights in hoarding it. The contract thus binds the hero to a lethal relation, one that goes from bad to worse. Neff's turning down of his promotion is only the first step toward his eventual abdication of life itself. It is this progressive instability—which is enabled, but not necessitated, by the contract—that accounts not only for the regularity of the final, mutually destructive encounter between hero and femme fatale but for the escalation of violence in the film noir cycle as a whole. The social contract between the noir hero and the femme fatale—social because it attempts to erect some community within the private space of *jouissance*—turns out, in these cases, to be an ineffectual and ultimately deadly stand-in for the social bond that classical detective fiction had earlier described.

Slavoj Žižek, following up on remarks made by Lacan in his "Seminar on 'The Purloined Letter,'" has noted that one of the differences between classical detection and the hard-boiled/noir variety is that in the former the detective accepts money for his services, while in the latter he does not.[30] It is Al Roberts (in *Detour*), however, who supplies the most revealing reason for the noir protagonist's *inability* to deal with symbolic currency. Reluctant to accept a ten-dollar tip for his piano playing, he spits out his definition of money: "a piece of paper crawling with germs." What happens, we have tried to argue, is this: the neutral, dead system of symbolic community and exchange that had supported the classical world has given way in noir to a world that crawls with private enjoyment and thus rots the old networks of communication. These different relations to money do not mean that the detective is separated from the space of the crime, while the noir hero is imbedded in it. As I have argued, the space of detection is a deep one because it is engaged by the desire of the detective, while the space of noir, empty of desire, is flat and unengageable. There is in noir no deep space for the hero to be imbedded in; he remains wholly external to the cities through which he passes. The spaces of detective fiction and film noir reveal respectively the paradoxical logics of modernism—a bounded space is abyssally infinite—and its postmodern inversion—an open or nomadic space, defined by sheer contiguity, is claustrophobically finite, encloses us within private and senseless being. This distinction requires another: between postmodernism and a second, parallel type of modernism, which is also dependent on the absence of a limit. Where in the first modern space the unlimited number of objects that come to be included there assume a universal equivalence, a commensurability; in the second objects are incommensurable. In postmodernism the modern aporia between commensurability and incommensurability is dissolved through an unbarring of the Other, that is, through an annihilation of the public sphere that created this aporia.

This is what concerns me: a growing sense that in theorizing sex we are engaged in a kind of "euthanasia of pure reason."[1] I borrow this last phrase from Kant, who used it to label one of two possible responses to the antinomies of reason, that is, to the internal conflicts of reason with itself. Reason, he said, falls inevitably into contradiction whenever it seeks to apply itself to cosmological ideas, to things that could never become objects of our experience. Faced with the apparent unresolvability of these conflicts, reason either clings more closely to its dogmatic assumptions or abandons itself to—and this is the option for which Kant reserved his impassioned put-down—a despairing skepticism. I will suggest that the attempt to contemplate sex also throws reason into conflict with itself and will here declare my opposition to the alternatives we face as a result, particularly to the latter, only because—in critical circles, at least—this is the one that currently claims our attention.

Judith Butler's strongly argued *Gender Trouble: Feminism and the Subversion of Identity* is an excellent contemporary example of this second alternative.[2] The uncontestable value of this book lies in the way it deftly shakes off all the remaining bits of sleepy dogmatism that continue to attach themselves to our thinking about sexual identity. The notion of sex as an abiding, a priori substance is fully and—if careful argument were enough to prevail—finally critiqued. Without in any way wishing to detract from the real accomplishments of this book or the sophistication of its argument, I would like to challenge some of its fundamental assumptions on the grounds that they may not support the political goals the book wants to defend. The problem, as I see it, with this exemplary book is that its happy voidance of the dogmatic option simply clears a space for the assertion of its binary opposite, if not for the "despairing skepticism" about which Kant warned us, then for skepticism's sunny slipside: a confident voluntarism. Having successfully critiqued the metaphysical notion that sex is a substance inscribed at the origin of our acts, our discourse, Butler defines sex as a "performatively enacted signification . . . one that, released from its naturalized interiority and surface, can occasion the parodic proliferation and subversive play of gendered meaning" (33). In other words, Butler proceeds as though she believes that the deconstruction of the fiction of innate or essential sex is also, or must lead to, a rejection of the notion that there is anything constant or invariable about sexual difference, that sex is anything but a construct of historically variable discursive practices into which we may intervene in order to sow "subversive confusion." All kinds of practices construct masculinity and femininity as discrete entities, and there is no denying the effectiveness, the reality of this construction, she argues; but if sex is something that is "made up," it can also be unmade. What's done, after all, can always be undone—in the order of signification, at least. What's familiar, naturalized, credible can be made strange: defamiliarized, denaturalized, "incredibilized." Negated.

First complex of questions: Are the alternatives offered here—sex is substance/ sex is signification—the only ones available? And if not, what else might sex be?

What Butler is primarily intent on undoing is "the stability of binary sex" (6), since she takes it to be the effect of practices seeking to install a compulsory heterosexuality. It is the very *twoness* of sex, the way it divides all subjects absolutely into two separate, mutually exclusive categories, that serves the aims of heterosexism. Now, this argument makes no sense unless we state its hidden assumption that two have a tendency to one, to couple. But from where does this assumption spring? From the conception of the binary terms, masculinity and femininity, as complementary. That is, it is only when we define the two terms as having a reciprocal relation, the meaning of the one depending on the meaning of the other and vice versa, that we incline them—more strongly, compel them—toward union, albeit one that is sustained through violent antagonisms. For, the complementary relation is, in Lacan's terms, an imaginary one; it entails both absolute union and absolute aggression.

Second complex of questions: Must sexual difference be conceived only as an imaginary relation? Or, is there a different way to think the division of subjects into two sexes, one that does not support a normative heterosexuality?

The stability of the male/female binary is not undone, however, simply by chipping away at the barrier that separates them, calling into question the neatness of their division. If the categories of woman, femininity, feminism cannot ultimately hold, Butler—taking a frequently advanced contemporary position—tells us, this is also due to the fact that these categories are crossed by all sorts of others—race, class, ethnicity, etc.—that undermine the integrity of the former list of categories. The very heterogeneity of the category of woman is evidenced in the opposition to feminism by women themselves. There will never and can never be a feminism unified in its politics.

Third complex of questions: Is sexual difference equatable with other categories of difference? Is one's sexual identity constructed in the same way, does it operate on the same level, as one's racial or class identity; or is sexual difference a different kind of difference from these others?

Fourth complex of questions: Is the heterogeneity of the category of women, the very failure of feminism to enlist all women, similar to the failure to enlist all men in a single cause? Is the fractiousness of feminism attributable solely to racial, professional, class differences? Why can't feminism forge a unity—an all—of women?

What is sex, anyway? My first question is also the one that initiates the inquiry of *Gender Trouble.* Echoing Freud's contention that sexual difference is not unambiguously marked either anatomically, chromosomally, or hormonally, that is, questioning the prediscursive existence of sex, Butler automatically assumes, as I noted earlier, that sex must be discursively or culturally constructed. But Freud himself *eschewed* the limitation of these alternatives; he founded psychoanalysis on the refusal to give way either to "anatomy or convention,"[3] arguing that neither of these could account for the existence of sex. While sex is, for psychoanalysis, never simply a natural fact, it is also never reducible to any discursive construction, to sense, finally. For what such a reduction would remain oblivious to is *the radical antagonism between sex and sense*. As Lacan put it, "Everything implied by the analytic engagement with human behaviour indicates not that meaning reflects the sexual, but that it makes up for it."[4] Sex is the stumbling block of sense. This is not to say that sex is prediscursive; we have no intention of denying that human sexuality is a product of signification, but we intend, rather, to refine this position by arguing that sex is produced by the internal limit, the failure of signification. It is only there where discursive practices falter—and not at all where they succeed in producing meaning—that sex comes to be.

Butler, of course, knows something about the limits of signification. She knows, for example, that there is no "*telos* that governs the process" (33) of discourse, that discursive practices are never complete. This is why she makes the claim that "*woman* itself is a term in process, a becoming, a constructing that cannot rightfully be said to originate or end" (33). So far so good—we find nothing here with which we would want to quarrel. The error, the subreption, occurs only in the next step when the argument no longer concerns only the term *woman* but becomes instead an argument about woman as such. For the thesis of the book is not that the meaning of the term *woman* has shifted and will continue to shift throughout history but that it is "never possible finally to become a woman" (33), that one's sexual identity is itself never complete, is always in flux. In other words, Butler concludes from the changing *concepts* of women something about the *being,* the *existence* of women. I will argue that her conclusion is illegitimately derived: we cannot argue that sex is incomplete and in flux because the terms of sexual difference are unstable. This is first of all a *philosophical objection;* to argue, as Butler is careful to do, that reason is limited is precisely to argue that reason is unable to move conclusively from the level of the concept to the level of being; it is impossible to establish the necessity of existence on the basis of the possibilities created by concepts.

To say that discourse is ongoing, always in process, is to acknowledge the basic, and by now much taken-for-granted, fact that within discourse there are no positive terms, only relations of difference. One term acquires meaning only through its difference from all the others—ad infinitum, since the final terms is never at hand. Put another way, the statement that discourse is ongoing simply acknowledges a *rule of language* that prescribes the way we must proceed in determining the value of a signifier. We would not be wrong to call this prescription a *rule of reason*—reason, since Saussure, being understood to operate not through the modalities of time and space (as Kant believed) but through the signifier. But his very rule entangles us in a genuine contradiction, an antinomy, such as troubled Kant in *The Critique of Pure Reason*. To be brief (we will return to these points later), this rule of language enjoins us not only to believe in the inexhaustibility of the process of meaning, in the fact that there will always be another signifier to determine retroactively the meaning of all that have come before, it also requires us to presuppose "all the other signifiers," the total milieu that is necessary for the meaning of one. The completeness of the system of signifiers is both demanded and precluded by the same rule of language. Without the totality of the system of signifiers there can be no determination of meaning, and yet this very totality would prevent the *successive* consideration of signifiers that the rule requires.

Kant argues that there is a legitimate solution to this contradiction, but first he attacks the illegitimate solutions that function by denying one of the poles of the dialectic. Saussure's displacement of his own notion of "pure difference" by the more "positive" notion of "determinant oppositions" is a type of illegitimate solution that may be referred to as the "structuralist solution."[5] Emphasizing the "synchronic perspective" of the linguist and his community, Saussure eventually decided to give priority to the contemporaneous system of signifiers operating at some (hypothetical) frozen moment: the present. Forgetting for his own purposes his important stipulation that meaning must be determined retroactively, that is, forgetting the diachronic nature of meaning, he ultimately founded the science of linguistics on the systematic totality of language. Thus, the structuralist argument ceased to be that the final signifier S_2 determines that which has come before, S_1 and became instead that S_2 determines S_1 *and* S_1 determines S_2; that is, reciprocal oppositions stabilize meanings between coexistent terms, and differential relations no longer threaten the transvaluation of all preceding signifiers.

A certain "poststructualist" response to this structuralist thesis has taken an antithetical position by simply ignoring the requirement for the completion of meaning. Butler's position in *Gender Trouble* fits into the second category of response to the antinomic rule of language; it notes merely that signification is always in process and then concludes from this that there is no stability of sex. Kant would argue that her error consists in illegitimately "attribut[ing] objective reality to an idea which is valid only as a rule" (288), that is, in confusing a rule of language with a description of the Thing-in-itself, in this case with sex. But this is misleading, for it seems to imply that sex is something that is beyond language, something that language forever fails to grasp. We can follow Kant on this point only if we add the proviso that we understand the Thing-in-itself to mean nothing but the impossibility of thinking—articulating—it. When we speak of language's failure with respect to sex, we speak not of its falling short of a prediscursive object but of its falling into contradiction with itself. Sex coincides with this *failure,* this inevitable contradiction. Sex is, then, the impossibility of completing meaning, not (as Butler's historicist/deconstructionist argument would have it) a meaning that is incomplete, unstable. Or, the point is that sex is the structural incompleteness of language, not that sex is itself incomplete. The Butler argument converts the progressive rule for *determining* meaning (the rule that requires us to define meaning retroactively) into a *determined* meaning. The Kantian/psychoanalytic argument, like this other, wants to desubstantialize sex, but it does so in a different way. First, it acknowledges rather than ignores the contradiction of the rule of reason. Then it links sex to the conflict of reason with itself, not simply to one of the poles of the conflict.

This constitutes a more radical desubstantialization of sex, a greater subversion of its conception as substance, than the one attempted by the Butler position. For sex is here not an *incomplete* entity but a totally empty one—it is one to which no predicate can be attached. By linking sex to the signifier, to the process of signification, Butler makes our sexuality something that communicates itself to others. While the fact that communication is a process, and thus ongoing, precludes a complete unfolding of knowledge at any given moment, further knowledge is still placed within the realm of possibility. When, on the contrary, sex is *disjoined* from the signifier, it becomes that which does not communicate itself, that which marks the subject as unknowable. To say that the subject is sexed is to say that it is no longer possible to have any knowledge of *him* or *her. Sex serves no other function than to limit reason, to remove the subject from the realm of possible experience or pure understanding.* This is the meaning, when all is said and done, of Lacan's notorious assertion that "there is no sexual relation": sex, in opposing itself to sense, is also, by definition, opposed to relation, to communication.[6]

This psychoanalytical definition of sex brings us to our third complex of questions, for, defined not so much by discourse as by its default, sexual difference is unlike racial, class, or ethnic differences. Whereas these differences are inscribed in the symbolic, sexual difference is not: only the failure of its inscription is marked in the symbolic. Sexual difference, in other words, is a real and not a symbolic difference. This distinction does not disparage the importance of race, class, or ethnicity, it simply contests the current doxa that sexual difference offers the same *kind* of description of the subject as these others do. Nor should this distinction be used to isolate considerations of sex from considerations of other differences. It is always a sexed subject who assumes each racial, class, or ethnic identity.

Why insist, then, on the distinction? The answer is that the very sovereignty of the subject depends on it, and it is only the conception of the subject's sovereignty that stands any chance of protecting difference in general. It is only when we begin to define the subject as *self-governing,* as subject to its own laws, that we cease to consider her as *calculable,* as subject to laws already known and thus manipulable. It is only when the sovereign incalculability of the subject is acknowledged that perceptions of difference will no longer nourish demands for the surrender of difference to processes of "homogenization," "purification," or any of the other crimes against otherness with which the rise of racism has begun to acquaint us. This does not mean that we would support a conception of the subject as preexistent or in any way transcendent to the laws of language or the social order, a subject who calculates, using the laws of language as a tool to accomplish whatever goal she wishes. The subject who simply does or believes as she wishes, who makes herself subject only to the law she *wants* to obey, is simply a variation on the theme of the calculable subject. For it is easy to see that one is quickly mastered by one's sensuous inclinations, even as one seeks to impose them.

The only way to resolve this particular antinomy—the subject is *under* (i.e., the determined effect of) the law/the subject is *above* the law— is to demonstrate that, as Etienne Balibar has recently put it,

> she is neither only above, nor only under the law, but *at exactly the same level as it.* . . . Or yet another way: there must be an exact correspondence between the absolute activity of the citizen (legislation) and [her] absolute passivity (obedience to the law, with which one does not "bargain," which ones does not "trick") . . . in Kant, for example, this metaphysics of the subject will

proceed from the double determination of the concept of right as freedom and as compulsion.[7]

To claim that the subject is at *the same level as the law* is not equivalent to claiming that she *is* the law, since any conflation of subject with law only reduces her, subjects her absolutely, *to* the law. At the same level as and yet not the law, the subject can only be conceived as the failure of the law, of language. *In* language and yet *more than* language, the subject is a cause for which no signifer can account. Not because she transcends the signifier but because she inhabits it *as limit*. This subject, radically unknowable, radically incalculable, is the only guarantee we have against racism. This is a guarantee that slips from us whenever we disregard the nontransparency of subject to signifier, whenever we make the subject coincide with the signifier rather than its misfire.

To my first, philosophical objection to the Butler definition of sex one must add not only the previous ethical objection but a psychoanalytical one as well. I noted already that there was a crucial difference between hers and the psychoanalytic position on sex. I want now to go further by exposing the "total incompatibility" of the two positions. I choose this phrase in order to echo the charge raised against Jung by Freud, whose characterization of the former's stance in regard to the libido is applicable to our discussion. This stance, Freud says, "pick[s] out a few cultural overtones from the symphony of life and . . . once more fail[s] to hear the mighty and powerful melody of the [drives]."[8] Freud here accuses Jung of evacuating the libido of all sexual content by associating it exclusively with cultural processes. It is this association that leads Jung to stress the essential plasticity or malleability of the libido: sex dances to a cultural tune. Freud argues, on the contrary, that sex is to be grasped not on the terrain of culture but on the terrain of the drives, which—despite the fact that they have no existence outside culture—are not cultural. They are, instead, the other of culture and, as such, are not susceptible to its manipulations.

Sex is defined by a law (of the drives) with which (to return to Balibar's phrase) "one does not 'bargain,' which one does not 'trick.'" Against the Jungian and contemporary critical belief in the plasticity of sex, we are tempted to argue that, from the standpoint of culture, *sex does not budge.* This is to say, among other things, that *sex, sexual difference, cannot be deconstructed,* since deconstruction is an operation that can be applied only to culture, to the signifier, and has no purchase on this other realm.[9] To speak of the deconstruction of sex makes about as much sense as speaking about foreclosing a door; action and object do not belong to the same discursive space. Thus we will argue that while the subject—who is not pinned to the signifier, who is an effect, but not a realization of social discourses—is, in this sense, free of absolute social constraint, he or she is nevertheless *not* free to be a subject any which way: within any discourse the subject can only assume either a male or a female position.

The Jungian—and contemporary "neo-Jungian"—position, remaining deaf to the "melody of the drives," does not recognize this compulsory dimension of sex, its inescapability. Focusing merely on the cultural "free" play of the signifier, this position disjoins freedom from compulsion: it is for this very reason *voluntarist,* despite all its own precautions, despite all the steps taken to inoculate itself against this charge. *Gender Trouble,* for example, is not careless on this point. The book's conclusion anticipates and attempts a defense against the accusation of voluntarism that it knows awaits it. Redefining the notion of agency, the final chapter aims to locate the subject "on the same level as" language, neither above (where the naive notion of agency would place it) nor below it (where it would be positioned by a determinist notion of construction). What's missing, however, and what thus leaves Butler defenseless before the charge she tries to sidestep, is any proper notion of the unsurpassable limit, the impossibility that hamstrings every discursive practice. Even when she speaks of compulsion and failure, she says this:

> If the rules governing signification not only restrict, but enable the assertion of alternative domains of cultural intelligibility, i.e., new possibilities for gender that contest the rigid codes of hierarchical binarisms, then it is only *within* the practices of repetitive signifying that a subversion of identity becomes possible. The injunction to *be* a given gender produces necessary failures. . . . The coexistence or convergence of [different] discursive injunctions produces the possibility of a complex reconfiguration and redeployment. (145)

What we are provided with here is a description of the *effect* of the inherent failure of discourse—a riot of sense in which one meaning constantly collides with another; a multiplication of the possibilities of each discourse's meaning—but no real acknowledgment of its cause: the impossibility of saying everything in language. We repeat, Freud taught us, because we cannot remember. And what we cannot remember is that which we never experienced, never had the possibility of experiencing, since it was never present as such. It is the deadlock of language's conflict with itself that produces this experience of the inexperienceable (which can neither be remembered nor spoken); it is this deadlock that thus necessitates repetition. But the constraint proper to repetition is occluded in the sentences quoted here, and so, too, is sex. Sex is that which cannot be spoken by speech; it is not any of the multitude of meanings that try to make up for this impossibility. In eliminating this radical impasse of discourse, *Gender Trouble,* for all its talk about sex, eliminates sex itself.

Sex does not budge, and it is not heterosexist to say so. In fact, the opposite may be true. For it is by making it conform to the signifier that you oblige sex to conform to social dictates, to take on social content. In the end, Butler, wanting to place the subject on the same level as language, ends up placing her *beneath* it, as its realization. Freedom, "agency," is inconceivable within a schema such as this.

The Phallic Function

Let me now confront the objections I know await me. I have been presenting the psychoanalytic position using arguments borrowed from critical philosophy. And yet the subject posed by this philosophy—sometimes referred to as the "universal" subject, as opposed to the concrete individual—seems, by definition, to be *neuter,* to be *un*sexed, while the subject of psychoanalysis is, equally by definition, always sexed. How, then, does the sexually differentiated subject enter the framework of critical philosophy? By what route have we arrived at what will no doubt appear to be the oxymoronic conclusion that the "universal" subject is *necessarily* sexed?

But why, we may ask in our turn, is it so readily assumed that the philosophical subject must be neuter? From our perspective it is this assumption that seems unwarranted. What grounds it, those who hold it suppose, is the subject's very definition as constitutionally devoid of all positive characteristics. From this we may infer that those who desexualize the subject regard sex as a positive characteristic. Everything we have said so far boils down to a denial of this characterization. When we stated, for example, that sexual difference is not equatable with other kinds of difference, we were saying that it does not positively describe the subject. We could put it this way: *male and female, like being, are not predicates, which means that rather than increasing our knowledge of the subject, they qualify the mode of the failure of our knowledge.*

We have been defining the subject as the internal limit or negation, the failure of language—this in order to argue that the subject has no substantial existence, that it is not an object of possible experience. If this subject is thought to be unsexed, it is not only because sex is naively assumed to be a positive characteristic but also because failure is assumed to be singular. If this were true, if language—or reason—had only one mode of misfire, then the subject would in fact be neuter. But this is not the case; language and reason may fail in one of two different ways. The distinction between these modalities of misfire—between the two ways in which reason falls into contradiction with itself—was first made by Kant in *The Critique of Pure Reason* and was employed again in *The Critique of Judgment*. In both works he demonstrated that the failure of reason was not simple, but foundered upon an antinomic impasse through two separate routes; the first was mathematical, the second dynamical.

Many have attempted to locate sexual difference in Kant's texts, but what they in fact were looking for was sexual bias or sexual indifference. Some have discerned in the descriptions of the beautiful and the sublime, for example, a differentiation of a sexual sort. These critics have—if I may say so—been looking for sex in all the wrong places. I am proposing that sexual difference can, indeed, be found in Kant, not in an accidental way, in his use of adjectives or examples, but, fundamentally, in his distinction between the mathematical and the dynamical antinomies. That is to say, *Kant was the first to theorize, by means of this distinction, the difference that founds psychoanalysis's division of all subjects into two mutually exclusive classes: male and female.*

I intend, then, for the rest, to interpret psychoanalysis's sexuation of the subject in terms of Kant's analysis of the antinomies of reason. More specifically my focus will be on the formulas of sexuation proposed by Lacan in his Seminar XX: *Encore*. In this seminar Lacan reiterates the position of psychoanalysis with regard to sexual difference: our sexed being, he maintains, is not a biological phenomenon, it does not pass through the body, but "results from the logical demands of speech."[10] These logical demands lead us to an encounter with a fundamental bedrock or impasse when we inevitably stumble on the fact that "saying it all is literally impossible: words fail."[11] Moreover, we are now in a position to add, they fail in two different ways, or, as Lacan puts it in *Encore*, "There are two ways for the affair, the sexual relation, to misfire. . . . There is the male way . . . [and] the female way."[12]

The formulas of sexuation, as they are drawn in "A Love Letter," the seventh session of the seminar, look like this:[13]

$$\exists x \quad \overline{\Phi x} \qquad \overline{\exists x} \quad \overline{\Phi x}$$

$$\forall x \quad \Phi x \qquad \overline{\forall x} \quad \Phi x$$

Each of the four formulas is a simple logical proposition and, like all propositions, has both a *quantity* and a *quality*. The quantity of a proposition is determined by the quantity of its subject term; the symbols $\forall$ and $\exists$ are quantifiers, that is, they indicate the quantity of the subject term. $\forall$, the universal quantifier, is shorthand for words such as *every, all, none;* but it is important to note that proper nouns are also considered universals. $\exists$, the existential quantifier, stands for words such as *some, one, at least one, certain, most.* The quality of a proposition is determined by the quality of its copula, either affirmative or negative. The affirmative is unmarked, while the negative is marked by a bar placed over the predicate term.

Since the symbol Φ is already familiar to us from Lacan's other texts, a translation of the propositions is now possible:

There is at least one x that is not submitted to the phallic function	There is not one x that is not submitted to the phallic function
All x's are (every x is) submitted to the phallic function	Not all (not every) x is submitted to the phallic function

The left side of the schema is designated the male side, while the right side is female. The first thing to notice is that the two propositions that compose each side appear to have an *antinomic* relation to each other, that is, they appear to contradict each other. How have these apparent antinomies been produced, and how do they come to be designated by the terms of sexual difference? Before answering these questions, we need to know a little more about the formulas.

Lacan abandons two of the terms of classical logic that we used in the previous description; instead of *subject* and *predicate,* he uses the terms *argument* and *function.* This substitution marks a conceptual difference: the two classes, male and female, are no longer formed by gathering together subjects with similar attributes as was the case with the older terms. The principle of sorting is no longer descriptive, that is, it is not a matter of shared characteristics or a common substance. Whether one falls into the class of males or females depends, rather, on where one places oneself as argument in relation to the function, that is, which enunciative position one assumes.

What legitimates Lacan's abandonment of some of the terms, and even some of the premises, of classical logic is the function—the phallic function—that appears in each of the four propositions. This function, and particularly the fact that it does appear on both sides of the table, has been at the center of controversy since Freud first began elaborating his theory of feminine sexuality. Feminists have always revolted against the notion that the phallus should be made to account for the existence of both sexes, that the difference between them should be determined with reference to this single term. They have deplored what they have understood to be a reduction of difference to a simple affirmation or negation: having or not having the phallus. But this complaint strikes out against the wrong target, for the peculiarity, or singularity, of the phallic signifier is due precisely to the fact that it ruins the possibility of any simple affirmation or negation. It is the phallic signifier that is responsible for the production on each side of the table not of a simple statement but of two conflicting statements. Each side is defined both by an affirmation and a negation of the phallic function, an inclusion and exclusion of absolute (nonphallic) *jouissance.* Not only is the notorious "not-all" of the female side—not all are submitted to the phallic function—defined by a fundamental undecidability regarding the placement of woman within the class of things submitted to phallic rule, but the male side embraces a similar undecidability: the inclusion of *all* men within the domain of phallic rule is conditioned by the fact that *at least one* escapes it. Do we count this "man escaped" among the all, or don't we? What sort of a "man" is it whose *jouissance* is not limited to the male variety; and what sort of an "all" is it that is missing one of its elements?

So you see, there's no use trying to teach psychoanalysis about undecidability, about the way sexual signifiers refuse to sort themselves out into two separate classes. It's no use preaching deconstruction to psychoanalysis because it already knows all about it. Bisexuality was long a psychoanalytical concept before it was ever a deconstructionist one. *But the difference between deconstruction and psychoanalysis is that the latter does not confuse the fact of bisexuality—that is, the fact that male and female signifiers cannot be distinguished absolutely—with a denial of sexual difference.* Deconstruction falls into this confusion only by disregarding the difference between the ways in which this failure takes place. Regarding failure as uniform, deconstruction ends up collapsing sexual difference into sexual indistinctness. This is in addition to the fact that, on this point at least, deconstruction appears to be duped by the pretention of language to speak of being, since it equates a confusion of sexual signifiers with a confusion of sex itself.

This, in brief, is the lesson of the formulas of sexuation; it is a lesson learned from Kant, as I will now try to show in greater detail. First, however, we need to say a bit more about the phallic function that is the source of all this undecidability. Its appearance—on *both* sides of the table—indicates that we are concerned with speaking beings, beings, according to Lacan's translation of the Freudian concept of castration, who surrender their access to *jouissance* upon entering language. This not only restates what we have been arguing all along—it is the impasses of *language* that create the experience of the inexperienceable, the unsayable— it also exposes the foolishness of that reading of Lacan's theory of sexual difference which asserts that it strands woman on a dark continent, outside language. Each side of the table describes a different impasse by means of which this question of the outside of language is raised, a different manner of revealing the essential powerlessness of speech. But while the phallic function produces on each side a failure, it does not produce a symmetry between the sides.

The Female Side: Mathematical Failure

We are not going to begin our reading, as is customary, on the left, but rather on the right, or female, side of the formulas. As opposed to the fairly common prejudice that psychoanalysis constructs the woman as secondary, as a mere alteration of the man, the primary term, these formulas suggest that there is a kind of priority to the right side. This reading of the formulas is consistent with the privilege given the mathematical antinomies by Kant, who not only deals with them first but also grants the mathematical synthesis a more immediate type of certitude than its dynamical counterpart. In Kant's analysis, it is the dynamical antinomies (the "male side" of the formulas, in our reading) that appear in many ways secondary, a kind of *resolution* to a more fundamental *irresolvability,* a total and complete impasse manifested by the mathematical conflict. One of the things we will want to attend to while investigating the differences between these two modes of conflict is the way the very notions of conflict and solution shift from the first mode to the second. (Finally, however, this notion of the priority of one of the sexes or antinomies over the other must be regarded as a mirage. Rather than two species of the same genus, the sexes and the antinomies should be read as positions on a Moebius strip.) There is an unmistakable asymmetry between the mathematical and the dynamical antinomies: on moving from one to the other, we seem to enter a completely different space. Rather than remaining baffled by this difference, as so many of Kant's commentators have been, rather than ascribing it to a confusion of thought, we will try, with the help of Lacan, to draw out the logic that sustains it.

What is a mathematical antinomy; how would we describe the conflict that defines it? Kant analyzes two "cosmological ideas" that precipitate this variety of conflict; we will discuss only the first, since it is this one that seems to us to correspond most closely to the antinomy found on the "female side" of the formulas of sexuation. The first antinomy is occasioned by the attempt to think the "world," by which Kant means "the mathematical total of all phenomena and the totality of their synthesis" (237), that is to say, the universe of phenomena such that it is no longer necessary to presuppose any other phenomenon that would serve as the condition for this universe. Reason aims, then, at the unconditioned whole, the absolute all of phenomena. This attempt produces two conflicting propositions regarding the nature of this all—a thesis: the world has a beginning in time and is also limited in regard to space; and its antithesis: the world has no beginning and no limits in space but is, in relation both to time and space, infinite.

After examining both arguments, Kant concludes that while each successfully demonstrates the falsity of the other, neither is able to establish convincingly its own truth. This conclusion creates a skeptical impasse from which he will have to extricate himself, since one of the basic tenets of his philosophy, which opposes itself to skepticism, is that every problem of reason admits of a solution. The solution he arrives at is the following: rather than despairing over the fact that we cannot choose between the two alternatives, we must come to the realization that we need not choose, since both alternatives are false. That is to say, the thesis and antithesis statements, which initially appeared to constitute a *contradictory* opposition, turn out upon inspection to be *contraries*.

In logic, a contradictory opposition is one that exists between two propositions of which one is the simple denial of the other; since the two together exhaust the entire range of possibilities, the truth of one establishes the falsity of the other, and vice versa. Contradiction is a zero-sum affair. The negation, which bears on the copula, leaves nothing beyond itself; it completely annihilates the other proposition. A contrary opposition, on the other hand, is one that exists between two propositions of which one does not simply deny the other but makes an assertion in the direction of the other extreme. The negation, which bears this time only on the predicate, does not exhaust all the possibilities but leaves behind something on which it does not pronounce. For this reason *both* statements may simultaneously be false.

In order to make this logic less abstract, Kant resorts to an uncharacteristically pungent example that successfully illustrates what is at stake in the mathematical antinomies. He opposes the statement "Bodies smell good" to a contrary, "Bodies smell bad," in order to show that the second does not simply negate the first (for which "Bodies are not good-smelling" would have been sufficient) but goes on to posit another smell, this time a bad one. While it is not possible for both of these propositions to be true—since fragrance and foulness cancel each other out—it is possible for both to be false—since neither takes into account another possibility, that bodies may be odor-free.

To illustrate this logical point differently, we might note that it is the structure of contrary opposition that produces the "When did you stop beating your wife?" joke. The form of the question, while seeming to allow the addressee to supply any answer he chooses, in fact allows him only to choose among contraries. It does not allow him to negate the accusation implicit in the question.

Kant avoids the skeptical impasse by refusing to answer the question "Is the world finite or infinite?" and by instead negating the assumption implicit in the question: the world *is*. As long as one assumes that the world exists, the thesis and antithesis of the cosmological antinomy have to be regarded as contradictory, as mutually exclusive and exhaustive alternatives. One is thus forced to choose. But once this assumption is shown to be ill-founded, neither alternative need be taken as true; a choice is no longer necessary. The solution to this antinomy, then, lies in demonstrating the very incoherency of this assumption, the *absolute impossibility* (294) (Kant's words) of the world's existence. This is done

by showing that the world is a self-contradictory concept, that the absolute totality of an endless progression is inconceivable, by definition.

How so? If the world is an object of experience, as those so eager
to determine its magnitude suppose, then the conditions of the possibility
of experience must be met in conceiving it. Thus, the essential bankruptcy
of the idea of the world will be made visible by the demonstration of its
inability to meet these formal conditions. These conditions specify that a
possible object of experience must be locatable through a progression or
regression of phenomena in time and space. The concept of an absolute
totality of phenomena, however, precludes the possibility of such a *succession* because it is graspable only as the *simultaneity* of phenomena. The
rule of reason that requires us to seek after conditions is therefore abridged
by the conception of the rule's total satisfaction, that is, by the conception
of the world. Adherence to the rule and the complete satisfaction of the
rule are, it turns out, antinomic. The world is an object that destroys the
means of finding it; it is for this reason illegitimate to call it an object at
all. A universe of phenomena is a true contradiction in terms; *the world
cannot and does not exist.*

Having demonstrated the impossibility of the existence of the
world, Kant can then dismiss both the thesis and the antithesis statements.
This is indeed what he does when he states his solution twice, first in a
negative and then in an affirmative form. "The world has no beginning
in time and no absolute limit in space," is the negative solution; it denies
the thesis without going on, as the antithesis does, to make a counteras-
sertion. There can be no limit to phenomena in the phenomenal realm,
for this would require the existence of a phenomenon of an exceptional
sort, one that was not itself conditioned and would thus allow us to halt
our regress, or one that took no phenomenal form, i.e., that was empty:
a void space or a void time. But clearly these self-contradictions admit of
no real possibilities. No phenomena are exempt from the rules of reason
that alone make them objects of our experience. Or, *there is no phenomenon*

that is not an object of possible experience (or not subject to the rule of regress): $\overline{\exists}x \quad \overline{\Phi}x$.

Kant then goes on to dismiss the antithesis by stating that "the regress in the series of phenomena—as a determination of the cosmical quantity, proceeds *indefinitum*" (294). That is, our acknowledgment of the absence of a limit to the set of phenomena does not oblige us to maintain the antithetical position—that they are *infinite*—rather, it obliges us to recognize the basic *finitude* of all phenomena, the fact that they are inescapably subject to conditions of time and space and must therefore be encountered one by one, indefinitely, without the possibility of reaching an end, a point where all phenomena would be known. The status of the world is not infinite but indeterminate. *Not-all phenomena are a possible object of experience:* $\overline{\forall}x \quad \Phi x$.

The solution offered by Kant's critical philosophy must be stated twice so as to guard against any possible misunderstanding. For the simple statement that there is no limit to phenomena will imply to those given to transcendental illusions that the world is limitless, whereas the simple statement that that not all phenomena can be known will imply that at least one phenomenon escapes our experience.

Now, it should be obvious that the formulas we have produced from Kant's two statements regarding the solution of the first mathematical antinomy formally reduplicate those that Lacan gives for the woman, who, like the world, does not exist. But how can this parallel between woman and world be sustained; how is it that Lacan can speak of the nonexistence of the woman? Our response must begin with Lacan's own explanation: *"In order to say 'it exists,' it is also necessary to be able to construct it, that is to say, to know how to find where this existence is."*[14] You will be able to hear in this explanation its Kantian tones, but you should hear in it as well echoes of Freud, who argued that in order to find an object, you must also be able to refind it. If the woman does not exist, this is because she cannot be refound. At this point my explanatory restatement of Lacan's not very well understood dictum will seem no less

opaque than its original. My intention, however, is to clarify this explanation as I proceed through the explication of the dynamical antinomies
and, by this, further to establish the link between Kant and Freudian
psychoanalysis.

For the moment let us continue to attend to the purely Kantian
tones of Lacan's statement. Lacan is undoubtedly arguing that a concept
of woman cannot be constructed because the task of fully unfolding her
conditions is one that cannot, in actuality, be carried out. Since we are
finite beings, bound by space and time, our knowledge is subject to
historical conditions. Our conception of woman cannot "run ahead" of
these limits and thus cannot construct a concept of the whole of woman.
But how does this Kantian position differ from the one articulated by
Butler and others? Is our position really so much at odds with the one
that now so often poses itself against every universalism: there is no
general category of woman or of man, no general category of the subject;
there are only historically specific categories of subjects as defined by
particular and diverse discourses? What is the difference between our
interpretation of "the woman does not exist" and the following one: we
are misguided when we make claims for the existence of the woman, for

> the category of "women" is normative and exclusionary and
> invoked with the unmarked dimensions of class and racial priv-
> ilege intact. In other words, the insistence upon the coherence
> and unity of the category of women has effectively refused the
> multiplicity of culture, social, and political intersections in which
> the concrete array of "women" are constructed. (Butler, 14)

Here it is being suggested that the universal category of woman contra-
dicts and is contradicted by current work that investigates the class and
racial differences among women as they are constructed by various practices. The logic of the argument is Aristotelian; that is, it conceives the
universal as a positive, finite term ("normative and exclusionary") that

finds its limit in another positive, finite term (particular women or "the concrete array of 'women'"). The negation of the all produces, then, the particular. The condemnation of the "binarism of sex" that is launched from this position firmly grounds itself in a binary logic that conceives the universal and the particular as exhaustive possibilities.

Kant had something else in mind when he argued that the mathematical antinomies demonstrated the limits of reason. His point—which bears repeating—is that our reason is limited because *the procedures of our knowledge have no term, no limit; what limits reason is a lack of limit.* This insight is compromised—not confirmed—whenever we conceive the not-all on the side of extension;[15] that is, whenever we conceive the negation of the world, or of universal reason and its pretension to be able to speak of all phenomena, as simply implying that all we may properly know are finite, particular phenomena. For in this case, we simply supply reason with an *external* limit by supposing a segment of time, the future, that extends beyond and thereby escapes reason. This eliminates from reason its *internal* limit, which alone defines it.

Recall that Kant maintained that the first antinomy provided indirect proof of "the transcendental ideality of phenomena." Here is the proof as Kant summarizes it:

> If the world is a whole existing in itself, it must be either finite or infinite. But it is neither finite nor infinite—as has been shown, on the one side by the thesis, on the other side, by the antithesis. Therefore the world—the content of all phenomena—is not a whole existing in itself. It follows that phenomena are nothing, apart from our representations. (286)

Kant's logic would appear to be flawed if the negation contained in the penultimate statement were taken as a *limitation* of all phenomena, or of the world, to particular phenomena. It is possible to pass to his conclusion only if one takes the penultimate statement as an *indefinite judgment.*[16] That is, what is involved here is not the negation of a copula such that "all phenomena" is completely canceled or eliminated, leaving its complement—some or particular phenomena—to command the field, but rather the affirmation of a negative predicate. Which is to say, Kant is urging that the only way to avoid the antinomies in which the idea of world entraps us is to affirm that the world is not a possible object of experience without pronouncing beyond this on the existence of the world. This conceives reason as limited by nothing but its own nature (its dependence on the merely regulative idea of totality), as *internally* limited.

This is the very crux of the difference between the Kantian position and the historicist one. Or, we should say, between the Kantian-*Lacanian* position and the historicist one, since Lacan adopts a similar stance with regard to the woman. When he says "The Woman is not-all," he demands that we read this statement as an *indefinite judgment.* Thus, while he does indeed claim, as his readers have often been horrified to observe, that the idea of the woman is a contradiction of reason, and that she therefore does not exist, he also claims, and this has not been as readily observed, that her existence *cannot* be contradicted by reason—nor, obviously, can it be confirmed. In other words, he leaves open the possibility of there being something—a feminine *jouissance*— that is unlocatable in experience, that cannot, then, be said to exist in the symbolic order. The ex-sistence of the woman is not only *not* denied, it is also not condemnable as a "normative and exclusionary" notion; on the contrary, the Lacanian position argues that it is only by refusing to deny—or confirm—her ex-sistence that "normative and exclusionary" thinking can be avoided. That is, it is only by acknowledging that a concept of woman *cannot* exist, that it is structurally impossible within the symbolic order, that each historical construction of her can be challenged. For, after all, nothing prohibits these historical constructions from asserting their universal truth; witness the historical assertion that a general, transhistorical category of woman *does not* exist. The truth of this assertion is simply not available to a historical subject.

Let us be clear that one of the consequences of the Lacanian argument is that it, too, like historicism, calls into question the collectibility of women into a whole. It thus also regards all efforts at a coalition politics as problematic. But unlike the historicists, Lacan sees the collectibility of women as imperiled not by the external collisions of different definitions but by the internal limit of each and every definition, which fails somehow to "encompass" her. Lacan's position opens out onto a beyond that it is impossible to confirm or deny.

Judging from the feminist brouhaha that has surrounded the reference to this beyond, we can safely assume that it needs further explanation and defense. It has frequently been taken to consist of one more relegation of the woman to the outside of language and the social order, one more attempt to banish her to some "dark continent" (as if any form of life had ever been found to survive within the dead structures of language!). We must therefore be more explicit about just what is meant by the "failure of the symbolic" with respect to the woman, what is signaled by the indefinite judgment. The symbolic fails to constitute not the *reality* but, more specifically, the *existence* of the woman. To be more precise: what fails, what becomes impossible, is the rendering of a judgment of existence. As long as it can be demonstrated that world or woman cannot form a whole, a universe—that is, that there is no limit to phenomena of language, no phenomenon that is not an object of experience, no signifier whose value does not depend on another—then the possibility of judging whether or not these phenomena or these signifiers give us information about a reality independent of us vanishes. In order to be able to declare that a thing exists, it is necessary also to be able to conclude otherwise—that it does not. But how is this second, negative judgment possible if there is no phenomenon that is not an object of our experience, that is, if there are no metaphenomena that escape our experience and are thus able to challenge the validity of those that do not?

The lack of a limit to phenomena (and to signifiers) precludes precisely this: a metalanguage, without which we are restricted to endless affirmation, that is, to affirming without end—and without being able to negate any—the contingent series of phenomena that present themselves to us. There is, as Freud said of the unconscious, no "no" where no limit is possible. And as with the unconscious, so here, too, contradiction is necessarily ignored, since everything has to be considered equally true. There are no available means of eliminating inconsistency where nothing may be judged false.

So, whereas historicist feminists currently propose that we regard the aggregation of "female subject positions" as the solution to the "riddle of femininity," that is, that we acknowledge the *differences* in these various constructions of woman and the nonnecessity of their relation to each other in order finally to lay to rest the question of what a woman is, Lacan proposes that this "solution" is a datum in need of explanation. *Why* is it—Lacan requires us not to rest content with the observation but to inquire further—*why* is it that woman does not form an all? Why is it that we must see in the discursive constructions of women a series of differences, and never encounter among them woman as such? Lacan answers that the woman is not-all because she lacks a limit, by which he means she is not susceptible to the threat of castration; the "no" embodied by this threat does not function for her. But this may be misleading, for while it is true that the threat has no purchase on the woman, it is crucial to note that the woman is the consequence and not the cause of the nonfunctioning of negation. She is the failure of the limit, not the cause of the failure.

In sum, woman is there where no limit intervenes to inhibit the progressive unfolding of signifiers, where, therefore, a judgment of existence becomes impossible. This means that everything can be and is said about her, but that none of it is subject to "reality testing"—none of what is said amounts to a confirmation or denial of her existence, which thereby eludes every symbolic articulation. The relation of the woman to the symbolic and to the phallic function is considerably complicated by this argument. For it is precisely because she is totally, that is, limitlessly inscribed within the symbolic that she is in some sense wholly outside it, which is to say the question of her existence is absolutely undecidable within it.

From this we are obliged to recognize that the woman is indeed a product of the symbolic. But we must also recognize that in producing her, the symbolic does not function in the way that we are accustomed to thinking it does. Ordinarily we think of the symbolic as synonymous, in Lacanian terms, with the Other. The Other is, however, by definition that which guarantees our consistency, and, as we have seen, there is no such guarantee where the woman is concerned. She, or the symbolic that constructs her, is fraught with inconsistencies. We are thus led to the conclusion that the woman is a product of a "symbolic without an Other." For this newly conceived entity, Lacan, in his last writings, coined the term *lalangue*. Woman is the product of *lalangue*.

The Male Side: Dynamical Failure

If we were to play by the rules of historicism, we would have to argue that, like the woman, the man does not exist, that no general category of man is instantiated in the multiplicity of male subject positions that every era constructs. Thus, a nominalist argument, like a kind of theoretical solvent, currently manages to dissolve the categories of man and woman alike. According to Lacan, however, we *cannot* symmetrically argue that the man does not exist. We have, if the left-hand side of the sexuation table is to be believed, no problem in locating him, in proclaiming his existence.

This statement may come as a surprise—and not only to historicists. For our discussion has led us to assume that the rule of reason, which impels us to seek after a totality of conditions, must forever render any judgment of existence impossible. We are therefore unprepared for

Summary of the Argument of "Sex and the Euthanasia of Reason"

Dynamical/Male	Mathematical/Female
Thesis: Causality according to the laws of nature is not the only causality operating to originate the world. A causality of freedom is also necessary to account fully for these phenomena.	Thesis: The world has a beginning ~~in~~ time and is also ~~limited~~ in regard to ~~space.~~
Antithesis: There is no such thing as freedom, but everything in the world happens solely according to the laws of nature.	Antithesis: The world has no ~~beginning~~ and no limits in ~~space,~~ but is, in relation ~~both~~ to time and space, infinite.
$\exists x \qquad \overline{\Phi}x$ $\forall x \qquad \Phi x$	$\overline{\exists}x \qquad \overline{\Phi}x$ $\overline{\forall}x \qquad \Phi x$

the conjuring away of this impossibility, which seems to be implied by the confirmation of the existence of man. A similar surprise is regularly expressed by Kant's commentators, who wonder at the sudden ease with which a resolution of the dynamical antinomies is found. Where thesis and antithesis of the mathematical antinomies were both deemed to be false because both illegitimately asserted the existence of the world (or the composite substance), the thesis and antithesis of the dynamical antinomies are both deemed by Kant to be true. In the first case, the conflict between the two propositions was thought to be irresolvable (since they made contradictory claims about the same object); in the second case, the conflict is "miraculously" resolved by the assertion that the two statements do not contradict each other. If it were merely a matter of the thesis, one would have no difficulty in accepting this argument: the thesis, "Causality according to the laws of nature is not the only causality operating to originate the phenomena of the world. A causality of freedom is also necessary to account fully for these phenomena," concedes the importance of natural causality and merely insists on a supplement of freedom. It is, however, not so easy to bring the antithesis in line with Kant's denial of contradiction. The statement "There is no such thing as freedom, but everything in the world happens solely according to the laws of nature" manifestly resists or negates the thesis. If we are to accept Kant's argument that both statements are simultaneously true, we are going to have to do so *despite* the clear contradiction. In short, we will have to avail ourselves of a non-Aristotelian logic—just as we did with the mathematical antinomies.

We will not be concerned in what follows with the specifics of Kant's arguments about the cosmological ideas of freedom and God so much as with the way the second set of antinomies overcomes the impasse presented by the first set. We must also note that the left-hand, or male, side of the formulas of sexuation repeats the logic of Kant's resolution: "There is at least one x that is not submitted to the phallic function" and "All x's are submitted to the phallic function" are both taken to be true, despite the fact that the antithesis's claim to inclusiveness is obviously falsified by the thesis, that is, the all of the antithesis is negated by the thesis.

And yet Kant says that the antithesis is *true;* he confirms the existence of the all, the universal, just as Lacan confirms the existence of the universe of men. Since the existence of the universe was regarded in the case of the woman as impossible because no limit could be found to the chain of signifiers, it would be smart to assume that the formation of the all on the male side depends on the positing of a limit. But this resolution is more easily surmised than supported, since we were presented on the female side with good reasons for believing that the positing of a limit was impossible, that there could be no metaphenomena, no metalanguage. We cannot, on the male side, depart from the well-established rule of reason—nor do we.

In fact, the limit on the "sinister," or dynamical, side does not produce the possibility of metalanguage but simply covers over its lack. This is accomplished by adding to the series of phenomena (or signifiers) a negative judgment regarding what cannot be included in the series. The phrase "There is no such thing as freedom," which appears in the antithesis of the third antinomy (to take this one as an example), serves precisely this function, the function of limit. By means of this negative judgment, the inconceivability of freedom is conceptualized and the series of phenomena ceases to be open ended; it becomes a closed set, since it now includes—albeit in negative form—that which is excluded from it: that is, it now includes *everything*. You will note that this *everything* appears as a consequence in the second phrase of the third antinomy's antithesis: "But everything in the world happens solely according to the laws of nature." Suddenly the world, which was prohibited from forming in the mathematical antinomies, comes into being on the dynamical side.

In speaking of this imposition of a limit as an addition, as a *supplementation* of natural causality, we have in fact presented the thesis version of what takes place. But another equally accurate, equally true description is offered by the antithesis. According to this version, what is involved in the shift from the female to the male side is a *subtraction*. Recall Kant's complaint that the thesis and antithesis of the mathematical antitheses both overstepped their official functions, since they both "enounce[d] more than [was] requisite for a full and complete contradiction" (285); that is, both said *too much*. A surplus, because illegitimate, affirmation of existence burdened each statement. On the dynamical side, this surplus is *subtracted* from the phenomenal field and—we can look at it this way—it is this subtraction that installs the limit. The removal or separation of freedom from the realm of mechanical causality is what dissolves the radical inconsistency, the absolute impasse, on the dynamical side. Where the mathematical field was defined by the homogeneity of its elements (which were all phenomena, objects of experience) and the inconsistency of its statements (since none could be counted false), the dynamical field is defined by the heterogeneity of its elements (the result of the *separation* of the two types of causality, sensuous and intelligible, into different realms) and—what? What is it that corresponds on this side to the inconsistency on the other? Incompleteness.[17] That is, the all forms on the dynamical side, but it is missing an element: freedom. The initial cause cannot be tolerated by, or disappears from, the mechanical field that it founds.[18] Which means that on this side it will always be a matter of saying *too little*.[19]

In Lacan's formulas, the parallels between the two sides are more visible, since the same symbols are used throughout. Thus we can see that the question of existence is carried over directly to the dynamical side. That is to say, the surplus declarations of existence that caused the conflict on the female side are silenced on the male side because it is precisely existence—or being—that is *subtracted* from the universe that forms there. This is how one should read Lacan's placing of the existential quantifier as the limit of the all, which is ruled by the universal quantifier. If, therefore, a world (operating solely according to the laws of nature) or universe (of men) can be said to exist on the dynamical or male side, we must not forget that it is merely a conceptual existence that is being claimed for it. Being as such escapes the formation of the concept of world. The universe that forms is thus defined by a certain impotence, since everything can be included therein *except* being, which is heterogeneous to the conceptual world.

That thesis and antithesis—$\exists x \ \overline{\Phi}x$ and $\forall x \ \Phi x$—must both be stated and judged to be simultaneously true is explained, then, by the paradoxical status of the limit, which cannot be understood as entirely missing or as entirely included in the set of men. For, as Kant taught us, if one were to say that a man existed, one would add absolutely nothing to this man, to the concept of man. Thus we could argue that this concept lacks nothing. And yet it does not include being and is in this sense inadequate, since the concept cannot include the fact that the thing named by it does in fact exist.

This brings us back the question of "reality testing" that we raised earlier. We had promised that this procedure, which was ruled out as impossible on the female side, would finally come into play on the male side. We continue to maintain this, though this is clearly the occasion to clarify what reality testing *is* in Freudian terms. There is no more appropriate place to begin than Freud's essay "Negation," since that text is framed in almost the same terms as we, after Kant and Lacan, have been framing our discussion. When Freud makes the comment "With the help of the symbol of negation, thinking frees itself from the restrictions of repression and enriches itself with material that is indispensable for its proper functioning,"[20] we should be reminded immediately of the dynamical antinomies. For the symbol of negation is precisely the limit that allowed Kant, in the dynamical antinomies, to assert a knowledge of "everything in the world," where, in the mathematical antinomies, he was forced to admit that reasoning on the world fails. In the dynamical antinomies, Kant, too, gives himself material, an object of thought, even though, in the earlier conflict, reason was denied the possibility of any such object and was condemned merely to "dispute about nothing" (283).

What does Freud say about the process of reality testing? He says, first of all, something he has been saying since the *Project* (1895) and that he said most memorably in *The Three Essays on a Theory of Sexuality* (1905): the finding of an object is the refinding of it. Here, the aim of reality testing "is not to find an object in real perception which corresponds to the one presented, but to *re-find* such an object, to convince oneself that it is still there."[21] He says also that one of the problems that presents itself to this process is that

> the reproduction of a perception as a presentation is not always a faithful one; it may be modified by omissions, or changed by the merging of various elements. In that case, reality-testing has to ascertain how far such distortions go. But it is evident that a

precondition for the setting up of reality-testing is that objects shall have been lost which once brought real satisfaction.[22]

Contrary to the common misperception, reality testing is not described here as a process by which we match our perceptions against an external, independent reality. In fact, it is the permanent *loss* of that reality—or real: a reality that was never present as such—that is the precondition for determining the objective status of our perceptions. Not only is the real unavailable for comparison with our perceptions but, Freud concedes, we can assume that the latter are always somewhat distorted, inexact. What, then, accounts for the distinction between subjective and objective perceptions; what intervenes to transform the welter of conflicting, distorted phenomena into the conviction that our experience is objective? The answer, which should now be half-guessed, goes something like this: to the multitude of our perceptions something is added that is not a new perception, new sensible content; instead this addition is intelligible and contentless: a negative judgment that marks the limit of our perceptions and hence the loss of the object that "brought real satisfaction." The negative judgment excludes this object from thought—or, more precisely, the exclusion of this object makes thought possible. Which means that the term *exclusion* is not entirely accurate insofar as it may tend to imply a nonrelation between the real object and the object of thought, while Freud suggests a definite relation between these two terms. For fleeting perceptions seem to acquire the weight of objectivity only when they are weighted or anchored by the excluded real object. That is, it is only when our perceptions come to refer themselves to this lost object of satisfaction that they can be deemed objective. Referring themselves to the object, they come to be understood as manifestations of it. So, the object is excluded from perceptions, but not simply, since it now functions as that which is "in them more than them": the guarantee of their objectivity. If Freud prefers to name the process of reality testing by the redoubled verb *refind* rather than *find,* this is not only because the lost object can never be directly found and must instead be refound in its manifestations but also because it is found a number of times, again and again, in a multitude of perceptions that, however different they are from each other (the distortions, the modifications), must nevertheless be counted as evidence of the same inaccessible reality that they are all—the whole phenomenal universe—powerless to contain. Thus, while guaranteeing that perceptions designate some objective, independent reality, the negative judgment maintains—must maintain—this reality as ungraspable, for if it were to assume a phenomenal form, it would become merely another perception; in which case the universe of thought would collapse.

To return to our discussion of sexual difference, there should now be no confusion about the fact that if the man, unlike the woman, can be claimed to exist, his ex-sistence or being remains inaccessible nevertheless, since it escapes the conceptual or symbolic field in which his existence takes shape. If the differences among men may be disregarded, and one man can be substituted for another because they are manifestations of the same thing, what this thing is is still unknown and must remain so. Correlatively, no man can boast that he embodies this thing—masculinity—any more than any concept can be said to embody being.

All pretentions of masculinity are, then, sheer imposture; just as every display of femininity is sheer masquerade. Through his desubstantialization of sex, Lacan has allowed us to perceive the fraudulence at the heart of every claim to positive sexual identity. And he has done this equally for men and for women. Which is not to say that he has treated them symmetrically or conceived them as complements of each other. A universe of men and women is inconceivable; one category does not complete the other, make up for what is lacking in the other. Were one to believe in the possibility of such a universe, one would believe in the sexual relation, with all its heterosexist implications.

But Lacan does not. On the contrary, he shows us exactly why the heterosexist assumption—which may be formulated thus: men love women and women love men—is not a legitimate proposition. For it presupposes that a universal quantifier, an *all,* modifies both *men* and *women,* and this is precisely what the formulas contest. While the universe of women is, as we have argued at length, simply *impossible,* a universe of men is possible only on the condition that we except something from this universe. The universe of men is, then, an illusion fomented by a *prohibition:* do not include everything in your all! Rather than defining a universe of men that is complemented by a universe of women, Lacan defines man as the prohibition against constructing a universe and woman as the impossibility of doing so. The sexual relation fails for two reasons: it is impossible and it is prohibited. Put these two failures together; you will never come up with a whole.

Sexual Difference and the Superego

This argument has given itself just two tasks: to challenge the assumptions about sex harbored, often in common, by historicist and deconstructionist positions; and to clarify the alternative offered in Lacan by making explicit his debt to critical philosophy. It would require much more time and space than I have here to develop the implications of this alternative theory of sexual difference. But I do not want to close this chapter of my investigation without at least noting one important point and suggesting a path for pursuing it. The point is this: the Kantian account of the dynamical antinomies and the Lacanian account of the male antinomies both align themselves with the psychoanalytical description of the superego.

In *The Critique of Judgment,* Kant, speaking of the dynamically sublime,[23] invokes images of threatening rocks, thunderclouds, volcanoes, hurricanes, terrifying images of a mighty and potentially destructive nature that nevertheless have, he says, "no dominion over us."[24] The "as if" quality that attaches itself to the dynamically sublime has often struck commentators as curious. What does Kant mean by speaking of a fearful object of which we actually have no fear? He means that from our position in the phenomenal world, we can formulate only the *possibility* of this terrible force and not its *existence,* just as we can formulate only the possibility and not the existence of God, freedom, the soul. This possibility of a realm beyond, unlimited by our phenomenal conditions, is precisely dependent on the foreclosure of the judgment of existence.

This same explanation accounts for the paradoxes of the superego. Here, again, the ferocity of the superego is not exactly to be feared, for this ferocity depends not on the harshness of its prohibitions (in the sense that the superego might be positively imagined as a kind of strict father or that his interdictions might be positively spelled out) but on the conversion of the father into an impossible real, that is, a being on whose existence we cannot pronounce. The prohibition proper to the superego renders something unsayable and undoable, to be sure, but it does not say *what* we should not say or do; it merely imposes a limit that makes everything we do and say seem as nought compared to what we cannot. As Lacan explains, "The superego . . . [the commandment "Enjoy!"] is the correlative of castration, which is the sign that adorns our admission that the *jouissance* of the Other, the body of the Other, is only promised in infinity."[25]

Yet once we establish that this logic of the limit or exception defines the dynamical antinomies, the male subject, and the superego, we have a problem, or so it seems on first blush. For we now appear to lend support to the notorious argument that presents woman as constitutionally indisposed to developing a superego and thus susceptible to an ethical laxity. In response to this, all we can suggest at this point is that the field of ethics has too long been theorized in terms of this particular superegoic logic of exception or limit. It is now time to devote some thought to developing an ethics of inclusion or of the unlimited, that is, an ethics proper to the woman. Another logic of the superego must commence.

Notes

Chapter 1

1. Peter Dews, "The *Nouvelle Philosophie* and Foucault," *Economy and Society* 8, no. 2 (May 1979), p. 134. This essay is an excellent account of Foucault's theoretical relation to the events of May 1968 and the reactions to them.

2. Meaghan Morris and Paul Patton, eds., "Powers and Strategies," in *Michel Foucault: Power, Truth, Strategy* (Sydney: Feral Publications, 1967), p. 52.

3. See, for example, "Human Rights and the Welfare State," in *Democracy and Political Theory* (Minneapolis: University of Minnesota Press, 1988) and "Politics and Human Rights," in *The Political Forms of Modern Society: Bureaucracy, Democracy, Totalitarianism* (Cambridge, MA: The MIT Press, 1986), both by Claude Lefort.

4. Morris and Patton, "Truth and Power," in *Michel Foucault*, p. 33.

5. Lefort, "The Permanence of the Theological Political," in *Democracy and Political Theory*, p. 218.

6. Foucault never abandons, however, the notion that different, even directly contradictory, discourses must be shown to occupy the same space, that there must be some account of their common condition. But there are some Foucauldians who are less vigilant on this point; the discourses they analyze are conceived as more completely autonomous. The emphasis in these instances shifts to the conflicts that arise between discourses, and the space that supports them becomes absent rather than empty.

7. Morris and Patton, *Michel Foucault*, p. 33.

8. For this encounter between the students and Lacan, see "Impromptu at Vincennes," in *Television/A Challenge to the Psychoanalytic Establishment*, ed. Joan Copjec, trans. Denis Hollier, Rosalind Krauss, and Annette Michelson (New York: W. W. Norton, 1990).

9. See Juliet Flower MacCannell's *The Regime of the Brother: After the Patriarchy* (New York and London: Routledge, 1991) for an excellent book-length theorization of this society.

10. This reading of the death drive is brilliantly stated in Gilles Deleuze's chapter "The Death Instinct" in his *Coldness and Cruelty* (New York: Zone Books, 1991).

11. Jacques Lacan, "The direction of the treatment and the principles of its powers," in *Ecrits: A Selection,* trans. Alan Sheridan (New York: W. W. Norton, 1977), p. 240.

12. Ibid., p. 257.

Chapter 2

1. In *The Four Fundamental Concepts of Psycho-Analysis,* ed. Jacques-Alain Miller, trans. Alan Sheridan (London: The Hogarth Press and the Institute of Psycho-Analysis, 1977, p. 274), Lacan speaks of the "phantasies" of the "mass media," as he very quickly suggests a critique of the familiar notion of "the society of the spectacle." This notion is replaced in Lacan by what might be called "the society of [formed from] the nonspecularizable."

2. *Liddell and Scott's Greek-English Lexicon,* 1906; all translations of ancient Greek terms are from this source.

3. Jacques Lacan, *Television/A Challenge to the Psychoanalytic Establishment,* ed. Joan Copjec, trans. Denis Hollier, Rosalind Krauss, and Annette Michelson, (New York: W. W. Norton, 1990) p. 3.

4. Mary Ann Doane points out that it is our very fascination with the model of the screen as mirror that has made it resistant to those theoretical objections that she herself makes ("Misrecognition and Identity," *Ciné-Tracts,* no. 11 [Fall 1980], p. 28.

5. Mary Ann Doane, Patricia Mellencamp, and Linda Williams, eds., *Re-vision* (Los Angeles: The American Film Institute, 1984), p. 14. The introduction to this very useful collection of essays also attempts to detail some of the historical shifts in feminist theories of representation; I am only attempting to argue the need for one more shift, this time away from the panoptic model of cinema.

6. See, especially, Teresa de Lauretis, *Technologies of Gender* (Bloomington: Indiana University Press, 1987).

7. F. S. Cohen, in "What is a question?" makes this important distinction clearly: "Indetermination or doubt is not, as is often maintained, a wavering between different certainties, but the grasping of an incomplete form" (*The Monist,* no. 38 [1929], p. 354, n. 4).

8. Michel Foucault, *Power/Knowledge,* ed. Colin Gordon (New York: Pantheon, 1986), p. 186. The interview with Lucette Finas in which this statement occurs was also published in *Michel Foucault: Power, Truth, Strategy,* ed. Meaghan Morris and Paul Patton (Sydney: Feral Publications, 1979). The statement is quoted and emphasized in Mark Cousins and Athar Hussain's excellent book *Michel Foucault* (New York: St. Martin's Press, 1984), p. 244.

9. Although some might claim that it was the introduction of the linguistic model into film studies that initiated the break, it can be more accurately argued that the break was precipitated by a shift in the linguistic model itself—from an exclusive emphasis on the relation between signifiers to an emphasis on the relation between signifiers and the subject, their signifying effect. That is, it was not until the *rhetorical* aspect of language was made visible—*by means of the concept of the apparatus*—that the field of film studies was definitively reformed. I am arguing, however, that once this shift was made, some of the sophistications introduced by semiology were, unfortunately, forgotten.

To define a *break* (rather than a continuity) between what is often referred to as "two stages," or the first and second semiology, is analogous to defining a break between Freud's first and second concept of transference. It was only with the second, the privileging of the analyst/analysand relationship, that psychoanalysis (properly speaking) was begun. Biography rather than theory is the source of the demand for the continuity of these concepts.

10. The best discussion of the relations between Bachelard and Althusser can be found in Etienne Balibar, "From Bachelard to Althusser: the concept of 'epistemological break,'" *Economy and Society* 5, no. 4 (November 1976), pp. 385–411.

11. This image of the scientist discontinuous with him- or herself can be given a precise figuration, the alchemical image of the Melusines: creatures composed partially of inferior, fossilelike forms that reach back into the distant past (the imaginary) and partially of superior, energetic (scientific) activity. In *The Poetics of Space* (Boston: Beacon Press, 1969), p. 109, Bachelard, whose notion of the unconscious is more Jungian than Freudian, refers to this image from Jung's *Psychology and Alchemy*.

12. The one reservation Metz has to the otherwise operative analogy between mirror and screen is that, at the cinema, "the spectator is absent from the screen: contrary to the child in the mirror" (Christian Metz, *The Imaginary Signifier* [Bloomington: Indiana University Press, 1982] p. 48). Jacqueline Rose clarified the error implied in this reservation by pointing out that "the phenomenon of transitivism demonstrates that the subject's mirror identification can be with another child," that one always locates *one's own image in another* and thus the imaginary identification does not depend on a literal mirror ("The Imaginary," in *Sexuality in the Field of Vision* [London: Verso, 1986], p. 196). What is most often forgotten, however, is the corollary of this fact: one always locates *the other in one's own image*. The effect of *this* fact on the constitution of the subject is Lacan's fundamental concern.

13. Lacan, *The Four Fundamental Concepts,* p. 81.

14. It was Jean-Louis Baudry who first formulated this definition of the impression of reality. See his second apparatus essay, "The Apparatus," in *Camera Obscura* 1 (Fall 1976), especially pp. 118–119.

15. Metz's two-stage scenario is critiqued by Geoffrey Nowell-Smith in "A Note on History/Discourse," (*Edinburgh '76,* pp. 26–32); and by Mary Ann Doane in "Misrecognition and Identity."

16. I have elsewhere referred to the gaze as "metempsychotic": although it is a concept abhorrent to feminist reason, the target of constant theoretical sallies, the gaze continues to reemerge, to be reincorporated, as an assumption of one film analysis after another. The argument I am making is that it is because we have not properly determined what the gaze is, whence it has emerged, that we have been unable to eliminate it. It is generally argued that the gaze is dependent on psychoanalytic structures of voyeurism and fetishism, presumed to be male. I am claiming instead that the gaze arises out of *linguistic* assumptions and that these assumptions, in turn, shape (and appear to be naturalized by) the psychoanalytic concepts.

17. Mikkel Borch-Jacobsen's interesting book, *The Freudian Subject* (Stanford: Stanford University Press, 1988) grapples with this *necessary* distinction—with results very different from Lacan's.

18. Paul Hirst, "Althusser's Theory of Ideology," *Economy and Society* 5, no. 4 (November 1976), pp. 385–411.

19. Mikkel Borch-Jacobsen, in "The Law of Psychoanalysis," (*Diacritics* [Summer 1985] pp. 26–36), discusses Freud's argument with Kant in *Totem and Taboo.* This article relies, it appears, on Lacan's work in *The Ethics of Psychoanalysis,* ed. Jacques-Alain Miller, trans. Dennis Porter (New York: W. W. Norton, 1992) and the unpublished seminar on anxiety: see especially the session of December 12, 1962, where Lacan defines obsession as that which *covers over the desire in the Other with the Other's demand.* This remark relates obsessional neurosis to a certain (Kantian) concept of moral consciousness.

20. Sigmund Freud, *The Standard Edition of the Complete Psychological Works of Sigmund Freud,* trans. James and Alix Strachey (London: The Hogarth Press and the Institute of Psycho-Analysis, 1953–1974), vol. 13, pp. 69–70.

21. In order to dissociate his concept of science from that of idealism, conventionalism, and formalism, Bachelard formulated the concept of "applied rationalism": a scientific concept must integrate within itself the conditions of its realization. (It is on the basis of this injunction that Heisenberg could dismiss as illegitimate any talk of an electron's location that could not also propose an experimental method of locating it.) And in order to dissociate his concept of science from that of the positivists, empiricists, and realists, Bachelard formulated the concept of "technical materialism": the instruments and the protocols of scientific experiments must be theoretically formulated. The system of checks and balances according to which these two imperatives operate is what Bachelard normally means by *orthopsychism.* He extends the notion in *Le rationalisme appliqué,* however, to include the formation of the scientific subject.

22. Gaston Bachelard, *Le rationalisme appliqué* (Paris: Presses Universitaires de France, 1949), pp. 65–81.

23. Gaston Bachelard, *The New Scientific Spirit* (Boston: Beacon Press, 1984), p. 32.

24. Lacan, *Television,* p. 7.

25. Lacan, *The Four Fundamental Concepts,* p. 106.

26. See especially Jean-Louis Baudry, "Ideological Effects of the Basic Cinematographic Apparatus" (first published in French in *Cinéthique,* nos. 7–8 [1970] and, in English, in *Film Quarterly,* no. 28 [Winter 1974–1975]) and Jean-Louis Comolli,

"Technique and Ideology: Camera, Perspective, Depth of Field" (first published in French in *Cahiers du cinéma,* nos. 229, 230, 231, and 233 [1970–1971] and circulated in English translation as a British Film Institute off-print). This historical continuity has been taken for granted by film theory generally. For a history of the *non*continuity between Renaissance techniques of observation and our own, see Jonathan Crary, *Techniques of the Observer.* (Cambridge, MA: The MIT Press, 1990). In this book, Crary differentiates the camera obscura from the physiological models of vision that succeeded it. Lacan, in his seminars on the gaze, refers to both these models as they are represented by the science of optics and the philosophy of phenomenology. He exhibits them as two "ways of being wrong about this function of the subject in the domain of the spectacle."

27. Lacan, *The Four Fundamental Concepts,* p. 96.

28. The questions Moustapha Safouan poses to Lacan during Seminar XI (*The Four Fundamental Concepts,* p. 103) force him to be quite clear on this point: "Beyond appearance there is nothing in itself, there is the gaze."

29. This is the title given to the last session of the seminar published as *The Four Fundamental Concepts.* Although the "you" of the title refers to the analyst, it can refer just as easily to the ideal image in the mirror.

30. Jacqueline Rose's "Paranoia and the Film System" (*Screen* 17, no. 4 [Winter 1976–1977]) is a forceful critique (directed specifically at Raymond Bellour's analyses of Hitchcock, but also at a range of film-theoretical assumptions) of that notion of the cinema that sees it as a successful resolution of conflict and refusal of difference. Rose reminds us that cinema, as "technique of the imaginary" (Metz), necessarily unleashes a conflict, an aggressivity, that is irresolvable. While I am, for the most part, in agreement with this important essay, I am arguing here that aggressivity is *not* dependent on the shot-countershot structure. It is not the reversibility of the look but the unreturned look, the look that will not turn the subject into a fully observable being, that threatens the subject. Lacan says himself (*The Ego in Freud's Theory and in the Technique of Psychoanalysis* [New York and London: W. W. Norton, 1978], p. 232), "The phenomenon of aggressivity isn't to be explained simply on the level of imaginary identification."

31. Lacan, *The Four Fundamental Concepts,* p. 99.

32. In "Another Lacan," (*Lacan Study Notes* 1, no. 3) Jacques Alain Miller is concerned to underline the clinical dimension of Lacan's work, particularly his concept of "the pass." The difference between the "deconstructionist" and the Lacanian notion of fantasy is, thus, also made clear.

Chapter 3

1. Sigmund Freud, *The Standard Edition of the Complete Psychological Works of Sigmund Freud* (*SE*), trans. James and Alix Strachey, (London: The Hogarth Press and the Institute of Psycho-Analysis, 1953–1974), vol. 21, p. 82.

2. Ibid., p. 89.

3. Ibid., p. 92.

4. See especially Mary Ann Doane's *The Desire to Desire* (Bloomington: Indiana University Press, 1987) in which Doane shows how the "woman's film" of the 1940s made the female spectator's pleasure simultaneous with a masochistic viewing position. Her historically specific argument is subtle and convincing. I object not to this kind of argument but rather to a general alignment of female pleasure and masochism such as one finds, for example, in the works of Raymond Bellour.

5. Freud, *SE*, p. 91.

6. Samuel Beckett, *Watt* (New York: Grove, 1972), p. 175.

7. Freud, *SE*, vol. 8, p. 209.

8. Henri Bergson, "Laughter," in *Comedy* (New York: Doubleday, 1956).

9. Bergson's theories also had a great impact on literary and artistic modernism. For Bergson, the artist was one who was free of the necessity to view the world in terms of its practical utility and was thus capable, through the unique qualities of his or her perception, to "create," that is, to modify phenomenal reality through the active engagement of mind. Art, then, is seen to occupy a realm separate from that of the everyday. The "postmodern" attention of art and literature to the practices of everyday life and the erasure of the absolute boundaries between the "scientific" and the "artistic" text signal, in this respect at least, a waning of the influence of Bergson.

10. Bergson, *An Introduction to Metaphysics,* trans. T. E. Hulme (New York: Bobbs-Merrill, 1955), p. 37.

11. Freud, *SE,* vol. 18, p. 36.

12. Within psychoanalysis itself the concept of the death drive has been repeatedly questioned and rejected. In response to one such repudiation, made this time by

Rudolph Lowenstein, Lacan wrote, "It is certain that man distinguishes himself in the biological domain, in that he is the only being who commits suicide, who has a superego" (quoted in Elisabeth Roudinesco, *La bataille de cent ans,* vol. 2 [Paris: Seuil, 1986], p. 136). Man [*sic*] distinguishes himself also as the only being who speaks, and it is because of *this* that he acquires the other distinction.

13. Jacques Lacan, in *The Ethics of Psychoanalysis,* trans. Dennis Porter (New York: W. W. Norton, 1992), clearly constructs this distinction; in doing so he states straightforwardly that the death drive is "a function of the signifying chain" and thus "is to be situated in the historical domain" (p. 205).

14. Samuel Alexander, another "evolutionary" philosopher, is cited by Louis S. Sass in "Introspection, Schizophrenia, and the Fragmentation of the Self" (*Representations* 19 [Summer 1987]) in support of a definition of schizophrenia that runs directly counter to current Lacanian-influenced literary definitions. An analysis of the refutation of Bergsonian/Janetist, that is, "evolutionary," psychiatry by the structural psychoanalysis of Clérambault/Lacan would reveal the problems inherent in Sass's definition.

15. Aristotle also speculates etymologically that the term *automaton* may be derived from *maten,* "in vain."

16. Jacques Lacan, *The Four Fundamental Concepts of Psycho-Analysis,* ed. Jacques-Alain Miller, trans. Alan Sheridan (London: The Hogarth Press and the Institute of Psycho-Analysis, 1977), p. 23.

17. Aristotle, *Physics,* I. 7, 189b.

18. Aristotle, *De Motu Animalium,* 7.

19. Jacques Lacan, "L'Angoisse," unpublished seminar, May 8, 1963.

20. Jacques Lacan, *Television/A Challenge to the Psychoanalytic Establishment,* ed. Joan Copjec, trans. Denis Hollier, Rosalind Krauss, and Annette Michelson (New York: W. W. Norton, 1990), p. 6.

21. Samuel Beckett, *Murphy* (New York: Grove Press, 1959), p. 18.

22. Lacan's fullest discussion of the creation ex nihilo of the subject can be found in *The Ethics of Psychoanalysis.*

23. Samuel Weber, "Closure and Exclusion," *Diacritics* 10, no. 2 (Summer 1980).

24. Ibid., p. 44.

25. Jacques Derrida, "Signature, Event, Context," *Glyph* 1 (1977), p. 194. This essay, an extended critique and celebration of J. L. Austin's theory of speech acts, is followed by a second text, "Limited, Inc.," (*Glyph* 2 [1977]), which makes many of the same points as the first, this time in response to John Searle's clumsy defense of Austin.

26. Samuel Weber, "Introduction," in *Demarcating the Disciplines* (Minneapolis: University of Minnesota Press, 1986), p. ix.

27. Jacques Lacan, *Encore* (Paris: Seuil, 1975), p. 13.

28. See, for example, Erik Porge, *Se compter trois: Le temps logique de Lacan* (Paris: Eres, 1989), pp. 119–127.

29. Lacan, *The Four Fundamental Concepts,* p. 22. A sentence quoted earlier in this chapter can now be completed: "Cause is to be distinguished from that which is determinate in a chain, in other words the *law.*" Cause is both what escapes and founds the law.

30. J. L. Austin, "A Plea for Excuses," *Proceedings of the Aristotelian Society, no.* 57 (1956–58). Austin demonstrates in this paper an interest in context and failure similar to that revealed in his work on speech act theory.

31. H. L. A. Hart and A. M. Honoré, *Causation in the Law* (Oxford: Clarendon Press, 1959).

32. It seems likely that Lacan's interest in the burning child dream owes something to the tradition of philosophy that makes fire an almost emblematic phenomenon for the consideration of cause.

Chapter 4

I would like to thank Rachel Bowlby and Abigail Solomon-Godeau for assisting me with the photographic research for this chapter and for their helpful comments.

1. Joseph Kessel, "Un soir, rive gauche . . . ," *Le Figaro,* December 4, 1934; reprinted in Yolande Papetti, Bernard De Fréminville, Françoise Valier, and Serge Tisseron, *La passion des étoffes chez un neuro-psychiatre, G. G. de Clérambault* (Paris: Solin, 1981), p. 112.

2. "Le docteur Clérambault médicin chef de l'infirmeries spéciale du Dépôt s'est donné la mort," *Le Figaro,* November 20, 1934; reprinted in Papetti et al., *La passion des étoffes,* p. 111.

3. Jacques Lacan, "Propos sur la causalité psychique, in *Ecrits* (Paris: Seuil, 1966), p. 168.

4. Catherine Clément, *The Lives and Legends of Jacques Lacan,* trans. Arthur Gold-hammer (New York: Columbia University Press, 1983), p. 55. Clérambault is given a bit more attention in Elisabeth Roudinesco's *La bataille de cent ans: Histoire de la psychanalyse en France* (Paris: Seuil, 1986) and in David Macey's amazingly hasty *Lacan in Contexts* (London: Verso, 1988).

5. See note 1.

6. Quoted by Slavoj Žižek in ". . . Le plus sublime des hysteriques," in *Hystérie et obsession: Recueil des rapport de la Quatrième Rencontre internationale* (Paris: Navarin, 1985), p. 335.

7. I am using the word *pathological* in Kant's sense to refer to the empirical subject who *suffers* a range of feelings and sentiments in relation to everyday objects.

8. Malek Alloula, *The Colonial Harem,* trans. Myena and Wlad Godzich (Minneapolis: University of Minnesota Press, 1986). In her *Images of Women: The Portrayal of Women in Photography of the Middle East, 1860–1950* (London: Quartet Books, 1988), Sarah Graham-Brown presents Clérambault's photographs as a simple reverse striptease in which the body is gradually covered up rather than revealed; this interpretation misses the essential difference between Clérambault's photographs and those displayed in *The Colonial Harem.* Incidently, Graham-Brown repeats the error we find in *La passion des étoffes:* both lead us to believe that Clérambault took photographs only of women. This is not so; he also took many photographs of men.

9. Elisabeth Renard, *Le Docteur Gaëtan Gatian de Clérambault: Sa vie et son oeuvre (1872–1934)* (Paris: Librairie de François, 1942), p. 63.

10. G. G. de Clérambault, "Recherches technologiques sur la drapé," published originally in *Bulletin de la société d'ethnographie de Paris,* April 15, 1931, and reprinted in Papetti et al., *La passion des étoffes,* pp. 52–57.

11. This "master of classical dress" was, according to Renard (*Le Docteur,* p. 62), a man named Heuzey.

12. G. G. de Clérambault, "Classification des costumes drapés," address delivered on May 5, 1928; the resume of this lecture is reprinted in Papetti et al., *La passion des étoffes,* pp. 49–52.

13. Kessel, "Un soir," p. 112.

14. For a list of Grand Prix designs, see Donald D. Egbert, *The Beaux-Arts Tradition in French Architecture* (Princeton: Princeton University Press, 1980).

15. It was Viollet-le-Duc who initiated the attack; the winning entry, submitted by F. W. Chabrol, triumphed over two designs in the Islamic style, submitted by Emmanuel Brune and A. F. V. Dutert.

16. Clérambault, "Classification," p. 49.

17. Even Paul Guiraud, a supporter of Clérambault, concedes this description of him in the preface to G. G. de Clérambault, *Oeuvre psychiatrique* (Paris; PUF, 1942).

18. Cited in Demetrius Porphyrios, "The 'End' of Styles," *Oppositions,* no. 8 (Spring 1977), p. 120. My discussion of architectural "type" is derived primarily from this essay; from Anthony Vidler's "The Idea of Type," published in this same issue of *Oppositions;* and from Vidler's "The Third Typology," in *Rational Architecture* (Brussels: Archives d'architecture moderne, 1978).

19. Clérambault, "Classification," p. 49.

20. Le Corbusier in *L'architecture vivante,* (August 1927), cited by Vidler in "The Third Typology," p. 30.

21. Georges Canguilhem, "What Is Psychology?" *I&C* 7 (1980), p. 46.

22. Ibid., p. 47. Although Canguilhem privileges utilitarianism in his discussion, he sees it as forwarding a definition of man more as a tool*maker* than a tool. But he does not consider the issue of pleasure that is so central to utilitarianism and that forms the basis of our claim that utilitarianism was already, and not just a perlude to, instrumentalism.

23. This is a point often underlined. Canguilhem makes it, as do Jacques Lacan (in *The Ethics of Psychoanalysis,* ed. Jacques-Alain Miller, trans. Dennis Porter [New York: Norton, 1992]) and the fictional Teufelsdröckh (in Thomas Carlyle, *Sartor Resartus, The Life and Opinions of Herr Teufelsdröckh,* published serially in *Fraser's Magazine,* 1833–1834): "The end of Man is an Action, and not a Thought." See also Edmond Doutté, *Missions au Maroc* (Paris: Paul Geuthner, 1914), in which a journey to Morocco is presented precisely as an undertaking engaged more as an effort of *will* than as a search for knowledge (p. ix).

24. The literature on this subject is extensive; I cite here only a few recent and particularly relevant examples: Elizabeth Wilson, *Adorned in Dreams: Fashion and Modernity* (Berkeley: University of California Press, 1985); Peter Wollen, "Fashion/Orientalism/The Body," *New Formations,* no. 1 (1987); Kaja Silverman, "Fragments of a Fashionable Discourse," in *Studies in Entertainment,* ed. Tania Modleski (Bloomington: Indiana University Press, 1986); Annie Ochonisky, "La mode et le vêtement," *L'evolution psychiatrique* 52, no. 1 (1987).

This history of modern fashion begins around 1850 as, essentially, "feminine" fashion. Charles Frederic Worth opened his store in Paris in 1858, thus beginning the phenomenon of "haute couture." But by the 1920s there were increasing demands that women also renounce their interest in individual clothing styles and adopt a more uniform appearance. In England, for example, the Fashion of the Month League made recommendations about what women should wear, and there were several proposals for a Ministry of Fashion that would steer women toward the proper social attire. The most sinister aspect of this movement was its link with eugenics; at the moment this link was forged, the argument for the adoption of a simpler style of dress was that it would prevent those with unattractive bodies from disguising themselves and thus gaining the (sexual) opportunity of reproducing them. See, for this argument, J. C. Flugel, *The Psychology of Clothes,* 3rd ed. (London: The Hogarth Press, 1950). One sees here the principle of egalitarianism careening grotesquely off course, all the while supported by a principle of maximum happiness: the body, it is argued, must be duly valued, not necessarily for its own sake but for that of future generations (p. 223).

25. Ibid., p. 113.

26. Ibid., p. 183.

27. J.-N. L. Durand, *Précis des leçons d'architecture données a l'Ecole Royale Polytechnique* (Paris, 1819), p. 6. Of the historical studies I have read of this period in architecture, only one mentions this aspect of Durand's theory; Alberto Pérez-Gómez (*Architecture and the Crisis of Modern Science* [Cambridge, MA: The MIT Press, 1984]) calls Durand's statement "terrifying": "This materialistic premise became the basis of the ethics and aesthetics of technology, and it still underlies the most popular historical and ideological conceptions inherited from the nineteenth century. Only after Durand would it be important for architecture to provide 'pleasure' or that it be 'nice' rather than truly meaningful" (p. 299). Pérez-Gómez's phenomenological approach is, however, much different from my own, and we thus find different reasons to worry about this emphasis on pleasure.

28. Durand, *Précis,* p. 20.

29. Lacan, *The Ethics of Psychoanalysis,* p. 196 (translation modified). In Lacan's seminar, utilitarianism is treated not as a minor and somewhat quaint English philosophy concerned merely with the distribution of goods but as the clearest articulation of a revolution in ethics that unseated Aristotelian ethics in the nineteenth century. It is in this broader sense that I use the term *utilitarianism* throughout this chapter.

30. Jacques-Alain Miller, "Jeremy Bentham's Panoptic Device," *October,* no. 41 (Summer 1987), first published as "Despotisme de l'utile," *Ornicar?,* no. 3 (May 1975).

31. Clérambault, "Définition de l'automatisme mental," in *Oeuvre psychiatrique,* pp. 492–494. Clérambault had, however, been elaborating this concept in his teaching since 1919; three case studies, dated 1920 and accompanied by commentary, are also published in his collected works. This is not the place for a discussion of this important concept, but the crucial point is that while the whole of psychiatry was busy tracing psychic automatism to delirious *ideas,* Clérambault argued that these ideas (of persecution, hypochondria, etc.) were secondary *effects* of the illness, provoked as reactions to the morbid state. For a helpful discussion of mental automatism, see Jacques-Alain Miller, "Teachings of the Case Presentation," in *Returning to Freud: Clinical Psychoanalysis in the School of Lacan,* ed. and trans. Stuart Schneiderman (New Haven: Yale University Press, 1980).

32. Canguilhem, "What Is Psychology?" p. 44. The work of Charles Darwin is, of course, relevant here, for, with the publication in 1859 of *The Origin of Species,* the mind was also conceived as a crucial instrument in the struggle for survival.

33. See, for example, Charles Blondel, "L'activité automatique et l'activité synthétique," in *Nouveau traité de psychologie,* ed. Georges Dumas, vol. 4 (Paris: Alcan, 1934).

34. The French psychiatrist Henry Ey is one of the most prominent exponents of this notion and of the "evolutionary" psychiatry to which it belongs. His "Outline of an Organo-Dynamic Conception of the Structure, Nosography, and Pathogenesis of Mental Diseases," published in *Psychiatry and Philosophy,* ed. Maurice Natanson (New York: Sprinter, 1969) is a clear statement of the position Lacan attacks in "Propos sur la causalité psychique."

35. See Hugh Kenner, *The Counterfeiters* (New York: Doubleday, 1973) for an extremely lively exposition of this thesis.

36. One of the purposes of Turing's article was to show up the question "Can machines think?" as meaningless; since man was defined by what he did rather than what he thought, what sense would there be in comparing man and machine in terms of their abilities to think?

37. Andreas Huyssen has shown, in "The Vamp and the Machine: Technology and Sexuality in Fritz Lang's *Metropolis*," (*New German Critique,* nos. 24–25 [Fall/Winter 1981–1982]), that while androids were, in the eighteenth century, seen as a tribute to the genius of man, they were treated, in nineteenth-century literature, as threats to man's existence. As Huyssen says, "It is not hard to see that this literary phenomenon reflects the increasing technologization of human nature and the human body which reached a new stage in the early 19th century" (pp. 225–226).

38. Sigmund Freud, *Civilization and Its Discontents,* in *The Standard Edition of the Complete Psychological Works of Sigmund Freud,* trans. James and Alix Strachey (London: The Hogarth Press and the Institute of Psycho-Analysis, 1953–1974), vol. 21, p. 109.

39. The Foucauldian emphasis on the "incitement to discourse" functions by forgetting this other critical command.

40. *Unité d'Habitation* is a semicommunal apartment complex designed by Le Corbusier; *Seidlungen* are workers' housing complexes.

41. I rely for this comparison of Kant and Freud on Lacan's "Kant with Sade," trans. James Swenson, *October,* no. 51 (Winter 1989). Emile Benveniste's distinction between *histoire* and *discours* underlies Lacan's urgings that the discursive nature of the moral imperative must not be overlooked. For the film-theoretical implications of this distinction: "If the traditional film tends to suppress all the marks of the subject of the enunciation, this is in order that the viewer may have the impression of being that subject himself, . . . a pure capacity for seeing," see Christian Metz, *The Imagainary Signifier* (Bloomington: Indiana University Press, 1982). In "Sur le pouvoir politique et les mécanismes idéologiques" (*Ornicar?,* no. 34 [1985]), Slavoj Žižik uses Lacan's distinction for a definition of ideology.

42. Frances Ferguson, "The Nuclear Sublime," *Diacritics* (Summer 1984), pp. 4–10; despite my disagreements with it here, this is an exceptionally fine article.

43. Derived from the term *extimité,* used by Jacques-Alain Miller to describe the internal but nonintimate relation between the subject and its repressed desire.

44. Ferguson, "The Nuclear Sublime," pp. 8, 9.

45. Walter Benjamin, "A Short History of Photography," *Screen* 13, no. 1 (1972), p. 20.

46. Ibid., p. 25.

47. Jacques Lacan, *The Ego in Freud's Theory and in the Technique of Psychoanalysis,* ed. Jacques-Alain Miller, trans. Sylvana Tomaselli (New York: W. W. Norton, 1988), pp. 307–308.

48. Canguilhem, "What Is Psychology?" p. 46.

49. The fear and study of crowds developed alongside utilitarianism; for a good, general history of this period, see Robert A. Nye, *The Origins of Crowd Psychology: Gustave Le Bon and the Crisis of Mass Democracy in the Third Republic* (London and Beverly Hills: Sage Publications, 1975).

50. In "Woman as Symptom" (in *Sexuality in the Field of Vision* [London: Verso, 1986]) Jacqueline Rose analyzes the way the institution of cinema closes itself off by including the woman in this same way.

51. Two of the most compelling witnesses are Frantz Fanon ("Algeria Unveiled," in *A Dying Colonialism* [New York: Grove Press, 1967]) and Fatima Mernissi (*Beyond the Veil* [Bloomington: Indiana University Press, 1987]).

52. Clérambault, "Passion érotique des étoffes chez la femme" (1908), partially reprinted in Papetti et al., *La passion des étoffes*, p. 34.

53. Jacques Lacan, *The Four Fundamental Concepts of Psycho-Analysis* ed. Jacques-Alain Miller, trans. Alan Sheridan (London: The Hogarth Press and the Institute of Psycho-Analysis, 1977), p. 185.

54. Jean Clavreul, "The Perverse Couple," in *Returning to Freud*, p. 224.

55. Sigmund Freud, "Fetishism," in *SE*, vol. 21, p. 154.

56. Sigmund Freud, "An Outline of Psycho-Analysis," in *SE*, vol. 23, p. 203.

57. Renard, *Le Docteur*, p. 63.

58. Freud, "Fetishism," p. 156.

59. Clavreul, "The Perverse Couple," p. 226.

60. Renard, *Le Docteur*, p. 64.

Chapter 5

1. Jean-Jacques Rousseau, *Emile, or On Education,* ed. Allan Bloom (New York: Basic Books, 1979), p. 46.

2. Mary Wollstonecraft, *Thoughts on the Education of Daughters with Reflections on Female Conduct in the more important Duties of Life* (Clifton, NJ: Augustus M. Kelley Publ., 1972), p. 3.

3. As Sigmund Freud says ("The Uncanny," in *The Standard Edition of the Complete Psychological Works of Sigmund Freud,* trans. James and Alix Strachey [London: The Hogarth Press and the Institute of Psycho-Analysis, 1953–1974], vol. 17, p. 219), the uncanny is accompanied by "a special core of feeling." The specialness of this feeling of anxiety is made conceptually explicit by Lacan.

4. The pun on *presentiment* is made by Lacan in his unpublished seminar on anxiety (1962–1963).

5. The discussion of this dream appears in Jacques Lacan, *The Ego in Freud's Theory and in the Technique of Psychoanalysis, 1954–1955,* ed. Jacques-Alain Miller (New York and London: W. W. Norton, 1988) pp. 146–171. Erik Erikson's analysis of the same dream is found in "The Dream Specimen of Psychoanalysis," *Journal of the American Psychoanalytic Association* 2 (1954), pp. 5–56.

6. Lacan claims in his anxiety seminar (July 3, 1963) that "Oedipus did not have an Oedipus complex; his sin was that he wanted to know."

7. Among the ten commandments you will not find one that tells you that you must not sleep with your mother, and yet these commandments have no other aim than to hold you at a distance from the incestuous relation with your mother; they are as a whole the positivization of this interdiction—this is the point made by Lacan in *The Ethics of Psychoanalysis,* ed. Jacques-Alain Miller, trans. Dennis Porter (New York: W. W. Norton, 1992), p. 68.

8. Kant also notes that a nonpathological, that is, a *negative* satisfaction often accompanies one's adherence to the law.

9. Jacques Lacan, *Television/A Challenge to the Psychoanalytic Establishment,* ed. Joan Copjec, trans. Denis Hollier, Rosalind Krauss, and Annette Michelson (New York: W. W. Norton, 1990), p. 3.

10. On the *"coincidentia oppositorum"* of the contradictory definitions of the real, see Slavoj Žižek, *The Sublime Object of Ideology* (London and New York: Verso,

1989), pp. 169–173. Also see Jacques-Alain Miller, "Suture (elements of the logic of the signifier)," *Screen* 18, no. 4 (Winter 1977–1978), pp. 24–34, for its influential explication of this logic of negation.

11. Lacan, in *The Ethics of Psychoanalysis,* p. 70, is quoting the words of a poet friend.

12. Lacan, *The Ego in Freud's Theory,* p. 153.

13. Rousseau, *Emile,* pp. 43–44.

14. Wollstonecraft, *Thoughts on the Education of Daughters,* pp. 3 and 5.

15. Lacan's passing remarks on vampirism as an anxiety profiling the "drying up of the breast" are found in his seminar on anxiety (May 15, 1963).

16. Although it usually specifies the neck as the bodily zone from which the vampire drains its victim, Gothic fiction retains the traces of the true target of attack both in the mode of the threat, sucking, and in the sex of the victim, female. Most visual images of vampirism center on the female breast.

17. Jacques-Alain Miller, in his unpublished seminar on "Extimité" (1985–1986), developed the term *extimité,* which appears only a few times in Lacan, into a central theoretical concept.

18. The work on the "female Gothic" is extensive; I would like to acknowledge especially Mary Ann Doane's analysis of *Rebecca* (Doane, *The Desire to Desire* [Bloomington: Indiana University Press, 1987], pp. 123–175) and Claire Kahane's "Gothic Mirrors and Feminine Identity," *The Centennial Review* 24, no. 1 (1980), pp. 43–64.

19. The Freudian definition of consciousness as that which arises *instead of* a memory trace, and thus as a protective shield against trauma, is often understood *sociologically,* even by Freud himself. That is, consciousness, "immediately abutting as it does on the external world" (Freud, "Beyond the Pleasure Principle," *SE,* vol. 18, p. 26), is seen as a shield against shocks produced by this external world. The dream of Irma's injection allows us to see consciousness, rather, as a shield against the unconscious real.

20. See Freud ("Negation," *SE,* vol. 18, p. 238): "Judging is the intellectual action which decides the choice of motor action, which puts an end to . . . postponement."

21. The distinction between negation and the negativism of psychotics is made by Jean Hyppolite in his commentary on Freud's *Verneinung,* published in Jacques

Lacan, *Freud's Papers on Technique, 1953–1954,* ed. Jacques-Alain Miller, trans. John Forrester (New York and London: W. W. Norton, 1988), pp. 289–297.

22. This last sentence is a paraphrase of Lacan's description of the function of suffering in Sade; Lacan, *The Ethics of Psychoanalysis,* p. 261.

23. On the false choice between a vertical and a horizontal conception of rights, see Luc Ferry, *Rights—The New Quarrel between the Ancients and the Moderns* (Chicago: University of Chicago Press, 1990).

24. In her article on "The Nuclear Sublime," *Diacritics* (Summer 1984), pp. 4–10, Frances Ferguson speaks of the modern proliferation of rights as producing this experience of "consciousness impinging on consciousness." I am arguing that this misperception is not the inevitable consequence of the expansion of the domain of rights but depends further on the reduction of rights to demands. See Joan Copjec, "The Subject Defined by Suffrage," *Lacanian ink* 7 (Spring/Summer 1993) for more on the relation between *desire* and rights.

Chapter 6

1. Jacques Lacan, "Seminar on 'The Purloined Letter,'" trans. Jeffrey Mehlman, in *Yale French Studies,* no. 48 (1973), which is a partial translation of the essay published in *Ecrits;* an earlier version of Lacan's argument appears in *The Seminar of Jacques Lacan. Book II: The Ego in Freud's Theory and in the Technique of Psychoanalysis,* ed. Jacques-Alain Miller, trans. Sylvana Tomaselli (New York: Norton, 1988).

2. "Intersubjective" is not to be taken here in the psychological sense; it does not refer to a relation between subjects who can identify with either the position or thinking of each other.

3. Roland Barthes, "The realistic effect," *Film Reader* 3 (1978), trans. Gerald Mead from "L'effet de réel," *Communications* 11 (1968), pp. 84–89.

4. See Ernest Mandel, *Delightful Murder: A Social History of the Crime Story* (London: Pluto Press, 1984).

5. Richard Alewyn, "The Origin of the Detective Novel," in *The Poetics of Murder,* ed. Glenn Moste and William W. Stowe (New York: Harcourt, Brace, Jovanovich, 1983), p. 65. Whenever the link between detective fiction and democracy is made, it is usually attributed to the establishment of laws of evidence. See, for example, Howard Haycraft, *Murder for Pleasure* (New York: Appleton-Century, 1942), pp. 312–318.

6. I here acknowledge my debt to the brilliant work of Claude Lefort, who has theorized modern democracy not simply as a form of government but more radically as a "mutation of the symbolic order." The following chapter will describe more fully what this mutation entailed and how it is beginning to be replaced by a second mutation.

7. Alexis de Tocqueville, *Democracy in America,* part 2 (New York: Knopf, 1945), pp. 3–7. In his unpublished seminar *"Extimité,"* (1985–1986), Jacques-Alain Miller also stresses the relation between Cartesianism and democracy as he simultaneously sketches out their affiliation with psychoanalysis. Miller's discussion is much more extended and theorized than de Tocqueville's.

8. In describing her father, Dora used the phrase *"ein vermögender Mann* [a man of means]," behind which Freud detected the phrase *"ein unvermögender Mann* [a man without means, unable, impotent]." In proffering her description, Dora was declaring her demand for a master; in reinterpreting her description, Freud was indicating the sort of master the hysteric prefers.

9. Lefort uses this paradox to make a different point, which is that universal suffrage prevents the notion of "the people" from materializing, since numbers are inimical to substance. They desubstantify the very image of "the people." Lefort, *Democracy and Political Theory* (Minneapolis: University of Minnesota Press, 1988), pp. 18–19.

10. de Tocqueville, *Democracy in America,* p. 319.

11. The distinction between the primal and the ideal or Oedipal father on which this part of my discussion is based is drawn by Michel Silvestre in "Le père, sa fonction dans la psychanalyse," *Ornicar?,* no. 34 (July–Sept. 1985), pp. 14–40. Silvestre, of course, is elaborating Lacan's original distinction made in the chapter "Oedipe et Moïse et le père de la horde" of *L'envers de la psychanalyse* (Paris: Seuil, 1991), pp. 117–135.

12. George Bush's speech writer, for those who have already forgotten her.

13. Lefort, *Democracy and Political Theory,* p. 27. I have developed the logic of this difference between the two kinds of "no one" in a slightly different way in my essay "The Subject Defined by Suffrage," *Lacanian ink* 7 (Spring/Summer 1993), pp. 47–58.

14. Michel Foucault, *Discipline and Punish* (New York: Vintage, 1979), p. 202.

15. Sigmund Freud, *The Standard Edition of the Complete Psychological Works of Sigmund Freud,* trans. James and Alix Strachey (London: The Hogarth Press and the Institute of Psycho-Analysis, 1955–1974), vol. 13, p. 74.

Chapter 7

1. Marjorie Nicolson, "The Professor and the Detective" (1929), in *The Art of the Mystery Story,* ed. Howard Haycraft (New York: Simon and Schuster, 1946), p. 126.

2. Ian Hacking, "Biopower and the Avalanche of Printed Numbers," *Humanities in Society* 5, nos. 3–4 (Summer/Fall 1982), p. 281.

3. Hacking's work does not acknowledge this effect of statistics; it is Claude Lefort's remarks on numbers in *Democracy and Political Theory* (Minneapolis: University of Minnesota Press, 1988), pp. 18–19, that directed my attention to this important effect.

4. Ian Hacking, "How Should We Do the History of Statistics?" *I&C,* no. 8 (Spring 1982), p. 25.

5. For a concise statement of this thesis, see François Ewald, "Norms, Discipline, and the Law," *Representations 30* (Spring 1990), pp. 138–161.

6. Ian Hacking, "Nineteenth-Century Cracks in the Concept of Determinism," *The Journal of the History of Ideas* (July 1983), p. 469.

7. D. A. Miller, *The Novel and the Police* (Berkeley: University of California Press, 1988).

8. The phrase is Hacking's; see his "Making Up People" in *Reconstructing Individualism* (Stanford: Stanford University Press, 1986), pp. 222–236. Especially interesting for this discussion of *Double Indemnity* is the following passage: "Every fact about the suicide becomes fascinating. The statisticians compose forms to be completed by doctors and police, recording everything from the time of death to the objects found in the pockets of the corpse. The various ways of killing oneself are abruptly characterized and become symbols of national character. The French favor carbon monoxide and drowning; the English hang or shoot themselves."

9. Hacking, "Biopower and the Avalanche of Printed Numbers," p. 292.

10. Miller, *The Novel and the Police,* p. 162.

11. François Truffault, *Hitchcock* (New York: Simon and Schuster, 1983), p. 257.

12. Jacques Lacan, *The Seminar of Jacques Lacan. Book II: The Ego in Freud's Theory and in the Technique of Psychoanalysis, 1954–55,* ed. Jacques-Alain Miller, trans. Sylvana Tomaselli (New York: W. W. Norton, 1988), pp. 32–33.

13. Jacques Lacan, "Seminar on 'The Purloined Letter,'" *Yale French Studies,* no. 48 (1972), p. 54.

14. Jacques-Alain Miller, "Suture (Elements of the Logic of the Signifier)," *Screen* 18, no. 4 (Winter 1977/78), p. 27.

15. Helmut Heissenbüttel, "The Rules of the Game of the Crime Novel," in *The Poetics of Murder,* ed. Glenn Moste and William W. Stowe (New York: Harcourt, Brace, and Jovanovich, 1983), p. 88.

16. It is interesting to compare Roman Jakobson's description of the differential relation. As Jakobson demonstrates, the relation between /pa/ and /ma/ is not to be understood as a simple opposition, but as *two sets of oppositions,* between /pa/, which is itself an opposition, pure self-opposition or diacriticality, and the opposition between /pa/ and /ma/. In other words, /pa/ appears twice in these sets of oppositions, as the only element of the first opposition and as one of the elements of the second; although the second appearance retroactively effaces the first. Joel Fineman, in "The Structure of Allegorical Desire," *October,* no. 12 (Spring 1980), p. 59, summarizes Jakobson's argument thus: "/pa/ loses its original status as mark of pure diacriticality when it is promoted to the level of the significant signifier within the system as a whole. This new significant /pa/ is utterly unrelated to the first simply diacritical /pa/ that it replaces. . . . And it is precisely this occultation of the original /pa/, now structurally unspeakable because revalued as something else entirely, that allows the system to function as a structure in the first place." In other words, the articulation of /pa/ and /ma/ can only take place by rendering visible a certain empty place, a certain structural impossibility, which is not purely excluded from the system. A diagram of Jakobson's description would look like this:

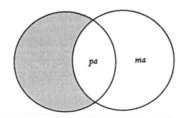

The shaded area represents the empty place, the structural excess produced by the articulation of the two signifiers; in short, the logic of suture is discernible in Jakobson as well as in Frege.

17. Dashiell Hammett, "Bodies Piled Up," collected in *Black Mask Boys: Masters in the Hard-Boiled School of Detective Fiction,* ed. William Nolan (New York: William Morrow, 1985), p. 84.

18. Jacques-Alain Miller's unpublished 1987–88 seminar, "Ce qui fait insigne," provides the most complete analysis to date of Lacan's distinction between desire and drive.

19. Jacques Lacan, *Television/A Challenge to the Psychoanalytic Establishment,* ed. Joan Copjec, trans. Denis Hollier, Rosalind Krauss, and Annette Michelson (New York: W. W. Norton, 1990), p. 74. The filmed interview is more explicit on this point than is the published text.

20. Pascal Bonitzer, "The Silences of the Voice," in *Narrative, Apparatus, Ideology,* ed. Philip Rosen (New York: Columbia University Press, 1986), p. 323.

21. Ibid., pp. 328, 329.

22. Roland Barthes, "The Grain of the Voice," *Image/Music/Text,* trans. Stephen Heath (New York: Hill and Wang, 1977), p. 182.

23. Bonitzer, "The Silences of the Voice," p. 328.

24. Ibid., p. 329.

25. Barthes, "The Grain of the Voice," p. 182.

26. Ibid., p. 188.

27. Jacques Lacan, *The Four Fundamental Concepts of Psycho-Analysis, Seminar XI,* ed. Jacques-Alain Miller, trans. Alan Sheridan (London: The Hogarth Press and the Institute of Psycho-Analysis, 1977), p. 195.

28. The introduction of the notion of two different *levels* in noir's defining characteristics—one primary and the other secondary, a reaction against the first— also helps to clarify some of the confusion that surrounds the theory of noir. The earlier presence of noirlike lighting techniques does not invalidate the belief in the specific, discrete phenomenon of noir, since their earlier use was descriptive and not "restorative," as they are in noir; that is, chiaroscuro lighting functions differently in noir than it did previously. Additionally, the absence of chiaroscuro lighting and deep focus cannot automatically disqualify a film from inclusion in the noir catalogue, since this list of films must obviously include those that demonstrate little or no defense against the drive as well as those that build an elaborate defense.

29. Christine Gledhill, *"Klute:* A Contemporary Film Noir," in *Women in Film Noir,* ed. E. Ann Kaplan (London: BFI, 1978), p. 17.

30. Slavoj Žižek, *Looking Awry* (Cambridge, MA: The MIT Press, 1991), pp. 60–61.

Chapter 8

1. Immanuel Kant, *Critique of Pure Reason,* trans. J. M. D. Meiklejohn (Buffalo, NY: Prometheus, 1990), p. 231; hereafter page references to this work will be given in the text.

2. Judith Butler, *Gender Trouble: Feminism and the Subversion of Identity* (New York and London: Routledge, 1990); page references to this work will be given in the text.

3. Sigmund Freud, "Femininity," *The Standard Edition of the Complete Psychological Works of Sigmund Freud,* trans. James and Alix Strachey (London: Hogarth Press and the Institute of Psycho-Analysis, 1964), p. 114.

4. Quoted by Jacqueline Rose in "Introduction II," in *Feminine Sexuality: Jacques Lacan and the école* freudienne, ed. Juliet Mitchell and Jacqueline Rose (New York and London: W. W. Norton, 1982), p. 47; the quotation is from Lacan's unpublished Seminar XXI.

5. Samuel Weber, "Closure and Exclusion," *Diacritics* 10, no. 2 (Summer 1980), p. 37.

6. For a further explanation of this psychoanalytic defense of ignorance, see chapter 4 of this book, "The Sartorial Superego."

7. Etienne Balibar, "Citizen Subject," in *Who Comes After the Subject?* ed. Eduardo Cadava, Peter Connor, and Jean-Luc Nancy (New York and London: Routledge, 1991), p. 49.

8. Freud, "On the History of the Psycho-Analytic Movement" (1914), *SE,* vol. 14, p. 62.

9. This statement need not be taken as dismissive of deconstruction, which would not itself claim that anything other than a signifier is "deconstructible," or negatable. As a matter of fact, it is only because the other of the signifier does not budge, cannot be negated, that deconstruction is possible in the first place.

10. Jacques Lacan, *Encore* (Paris, Seuil, 1975), p. 15.

11. Jacques Lacan, *Television/A Challenge to the Psychoanalytic Establishment,* ed. Joan Copjec, trans. Denis Hollier, Rosalind Krauss, and Annette Michelson (New York: W. W. Norton, 1990), p. 3.

12. Lacan, *Encore,* pp. 53–54.

13. Ibid., p. 73. This table also appears on page 149 of the translation of this session of the seminar that is included in Mitchell and Rose, *Feminine Sexuality.*

14. Lacan, *Encore,* p. 94.

15. Ibid.: "It is not on the side of extension that we must take the not-all."

16. For an excellent discussion of the relation of Kant's notion of indefinite judgment to the conflict of the first two antinomies, see Monique David-Ménard, *La folie dans la raison pure,* (Paris: Vrin, 1990), pp. 33 n.

17. Jacques-Alain Miller develops this Lacanian distinction between inconsistency and incompleteness in relation to sexual difference in his unpublished seminar "Extimité" (1985–86).

18. Borrowing from Fredric Jameson, Slavoj Žižek adapts the notion of the "vanishing mediator" for a Lacanian explanation of this disappearance of cause from the field of its effects; see Zizek, *For They Know Not What They Do* (London and New York: Verso, 1991), pp. 182–197.

19. Thomas Weiskel, in his notable book *The Romantic Sublime* (Baltimore: Johns Hopkins University Press, 1972), concludes the exact opposite; according to his explanation, the mathematical sublime is associated with "too little meaning," while the dynamical sublime is characterized by an excess of the signified, or "too much meaning."

20. Sigmund Freud, "Negation" (1925), *SE,* vol. 19, p. 236.

21. Ibid, pp. 237–38.

22. Ibid, p. 238.

23. Jean-François Lyotard, in his *Leçons sur l'analytique du sublime* (Paris: Galilee, 1991), argues convincingly that there are not two sublimes, but two modes of considering the sublime.

24. Immanuel Kant, *The Critique of Judgement,* trans. James Creed Meredith (Oxford: Clarendon Press, 1988), p. 109.

25. Lacan, *Encore,* p. 13.

Index